BRINGING MULLIGAN HOME

Herman Walter Mulligan and Steve Maharidge,
Guadalcanal, 1944. Photographer unknown

BRINGING MULLIGAN HOME

THE OTHER SIDE OF THE GOOD WAR

DALE MAHARIDGE

PUBLICAFFAIRS
New York

Published in the United States by PublicAffairs™,
a Member of the Perseus Books Group

PublicAffairs books are available at special discounts for bulk purchases in the U.S. by
corporations, institutions, and other organizations. For more information, please
contact the Special Markets Department at the Perseus Books Group, 2300 Chestnut
Street, Suite 200, Philadelphia, PA 19103, call (800) 810-4145, ext. 5000,
or e-mail special.markets@perseusbooks.com.

Book Design by Cynthia Young

Library of Congress Cataloging-in-Publication Data

Maharidge, Dale.
    Bringing Mulligan home : the other side of the good war / Dale Maharidge. —
First edition.
        pages cm
    Includes bibliographical references.
    ISBN 978-1-58648-999-1 (hardcover : alk. paper) —
    ISBN 978-1-61039-002-6 (e-book)   1. Maharidge, Steve, 1925–2000.
2. World War, 1939–1945—Campaigns—Japan—Okinawa Island.   3. World War,
1939–1945—Veterans—United States—Biography.   4. World War, 1939–1945—
Psychological aspects.   5. United States. Marine Corps. Marine Regiment, 22nd.
Battalion, 3rd.   6. Veterans—Mental health—United States.   7. Fathers and
sons—United States—Biography.   I. Title.
    D767.95.O45M35 2013
    940.54'252294092—dc23
    [B]
                                                    2012039518

10 9 8 7 6 5 4 3 2 1

In memory of Joan and Steve, my parents.

*To the men of L Company, 3rd Battalion, 22nd Marines,
Sixth Marine Division. Among some of those I came to know,*

Arthur Bishop
Karl Brothers
Danny Cernoch
J. R. Collin
Bill Fenton
Fenton Grahnert
Frank Haigler
Edward Hoffman
Joe Lanciotti
Malcolm Lear
Jim Laughridge
Charles Lepant
Hank Markovich
George Niland
Frank Palmasani
George Popovich
Tom Price
Joe Rosplock

*And to the civilians on Okinawa who wanted no part of war
and others in Imperial Japan who felt the same way.*

A bar of steel—it is only smoke at the heart of it, smoke and the blood of a man . . . smoke and blood is the mix of steel.

—CARL SANDBURG

There are no heroes. You just survive.

—SERGEANT STEVE MAHARIDGE, USMC

The battle for Okinawa in World War II began on April 1, 1945. In the ensuing eighty-two days, an estimated 150,000 civilians would die along with some 110,000 Japanese and 12,520 American soldiers. The Americans called it Operation Iceberg. The Japanese called it *tetsu no bofu*, the violent wind of steel.

CONTENTS

INTRODUCTION

Dale—

To me it was a state of confusion and FEAR with shouted hysterical commands, screaming, shells exploding, darkness and flame from flares and fire. I was there and I never saw the enemy but knew he was out there somewhere. Trying to kill us. I did not know what day it was, how high Sugar Loaf was, the caliber of artillery, the battle plan—which I knew was insane even as a PFC—regardless of what the asshole generals on both sides believed they knew from military school.

I fired at this dark hill that was scorched and smoking without having a target in my sights. I was a fucking sharpshooter who shot at rocks.

Dale—I hope you are still writing that same book that you talked about—"something that has never been done before." Remember?

When your father and I, and the other kids walked, crawled and stumbled down from Sugar Loaf with wounded minds that probably never healed we did not know whether the cause was artillery blast or mortar shells. We were reduced to the point of insanity from the general horror and fear of Fucking war . . . Slobbering, crying, shaking, vomiting, pissing and shitting your pants, screaming, mumbling, trembling, swearing, FEAR FEAR FEAR FUCKING FEAR— combat fatigue my ass.

Fuck the deadlines and publisher's demands, write a book that Steve and the rest those wounded guys now gone would be proud of.

Joe

—e-mail from Joe Lanciotti, eighty-six years old, February 6, 2012

Something was wrong in our house. My father had a depth of rage. The majority of the time he was a great dad. Then something would snap, and he temporarily became the worst. He was consumed by an anger that seemed at the edge of violence, but he always pulled back, except for one day in 1960, when he struck my mother. There was blood on the black and white wool wall-to-wall carpet at the base of the stairs. The domestic battle continued behind the closed bathroom door as our mother bandaged herself to stop the bleeding of her temple. The image of that ugly splotch coagulating on the carpet remained in my nightmares for years. Decades later Mom told me that she issued an ultimatum—she'd walk if that ever again happened.

Dad never again hit her. Yet the rage remained. It was never really targeted at us. It seemed to be focused on some unseen entity.

When I study my baby pictures, taken by my father with an Argus C3 camera, I smile in every frame. As a toddler, I grin ear to ear bundled up and wearing a wool cap while playing next to my sister in our side yard on an Ohio winter day. I was clearly a happy kid. In later pictures—age eight, nine, ten—however, I'm frowning, intense. My father's rage had become my own.

Dad seldom talked about the war. I learned pieces about it beginning when I neared puberty. Dad disclosed things when he and I were alone, usually in his basement shop, where he had a side business grinding industrial cutting tools. I knew instinctively never to ask questions. I just listened. I never broke this unspoken rule.

The war was always present in the form of a picture of my father and another man that Dad had set, at adult-eye level, atop the gas meter next to the machine where he most often worked. It clearly meant a lot to him. Dad once mentioned that it was taken on Guadalcanal. Except for one other time, he said nothing else about it. I became obsessed with the image. The picture came to represent everything that I didn't know about my father and the war, his rage that sometimes caused him to scream, and it was a great gnawing mystery as I grew up.

When my father died in 2000, the picture remained an enigma. That's when I began a quest to locate men who were with Dad in

L Company, "Love Company" in the military jargon of the era. Love Company, part of the 3rd Battalion, 22nd Marines, Sixth Marine Division, fought in the Pacific Theater during World War II.

Over the course of twelve years I spent ceaseless hours making hundreds of phone calls; I sent out hundreds of letters. Many men had common names—you can't begin to comprehend how many Robert Harrisons and A. Robertsons that I telephoned, all false leads. And there were those with complex names who appeared to have simply vanished. (A startling number died between 1946 and 1950, and though the database that I used to find their records didn't give causes of death, I'd learn that many drank themselves into early graves.) I got hold of sobbing widows, children who were more troubled than I was by their late fathers' war experience.

A majority of the men were dead by the time I finished—over two-thirds by a rough count, though I'll never know for certain.

I conversed with twenty-nine guys from Love Company and got to know half of them really well. What's remarkable is that most of these men, nearing the end, were talking. Many had spent their lives like my father, shunning any discussion of the war. These were in some cases essentially deathbed confessions. I discovered a World War II story that had been impossible to get for over a half a century. The silent generation was finally speaking in its octogenarian years.

I initially focused my quest on learning about the man in the picture with my father. That man represented something that happened to Dad, and I needed to know what it was.

I found six guys who were present when the man died. One Love Company veteran told me I was the first person in sixty-five years whom he'd talked to about the incident—he'd carried Herman Walter Mulligan's body that day. Despite this, Mulligan's body was, oddly, listed as not recovered. I fixated on finding his remains. For US Marines, there is *semper fidelis*, commonly shortened to "semper fi." It means always faithful or loyal—never leave a buddy behind. But I can't say that I was personally motivated by semper fi. I was never a soldier. I never heard my father utter those words. Yet he lived them by keeping Mulligan's memory alive his entire life. So in essence, for my father, I was abiding by semper fi as I sought to bring Mulligan "home," by at least putting a name on his grave. That would, I felt, put some of Dad's demons to rest.

My search, however, broadened as I came to know the men of Love Company. Mulligan was like a ghost I grew up with; to this day, after a dozen years of research, he remains something of a ghost. This book does not end with a surprise discovery of Mulligan's remains nor is it about his life and times. The picture that I was obsessed with as a boy turned out to be the vehicle that propelled me on a journey to learning something much larger and equally fitting to honor the memory of Mulligan: an understanding of that war. In addition, through this quest I finally came to truly know my father.

The years spent researching this book were at times traumatic. For a period in the middle, when my mother fell ill with cancer, I gave up. Frankly, a lot of it is a horrific story. I would have slept better many nights had I left it alone.

But I was pulled back. I needed to write this book because World War II followed a lot of men back to the United States. Ignored in many "good war" narratives is what really happened overseas—and most important, what occurred after the men came home. Many families lived with the returnee's demons and physical afflictions. A lot of us grew up dealing with collateral damage from that war—our fathers.

This is not a "trash your father" memoir, if it is a memoir. (I loved my father. At his core he was a good man. I also love the guys from Love Company, except for one—why will become clear later.) This is a reported book, told from a personal perspective, about the outfall of war. After unearthing what my father went through, I'm amazed that he wasn't more damaged. He grew less crazy tempered as he aged, and near the end I saw perhaps the man that might have existed before he set off for the Pacific.

As I was writing this book, a new generation of US soldiers was returning home after brutal tours of duty in Iraq and Afghanistan, many with the trauma of wounds both physical and mental. Some of those soldiers, especially those wounded by roadside bombs and suffering blast concussion, will have the same issues that my father struggled with. Their children will wonder why their mothers or fathers have rage or are depressed; those kids will face the puzzlement that I had as a boy. Joe Lanciotti and the other guys from Love Company know the answer. But they will be long gone. After my multiyear mission to learn from them, my goal is to put the past in touch with the future.

I hope this book helps those kids learn about their parents and war and also bring home to them an understanding of what happens once the bullets and bombs stop flying—wars never end for the participants and their families.

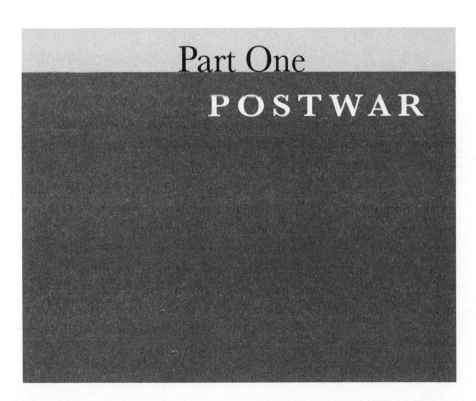

Part One

POSTWAR

Winter Night, 1965

The bed upon which I lie is on the second floor of a split-level house at the crest of the final hill of the Allegheny Plateau in Ohio, where the rolling eastern land of North America ceases and is disgorged on the flatness of the Great Plains. Our house takes the brunt of storms. Wind masses against the panes, and icy snow strikes the glass: *click-click, click-click.* There's a squeak, like that of a rusty hinge, from the American elm in our front yard, with its crossed limbs that rub on windy nights such as this. And there is the Cincinnati Number 2 grinding machine, a two-ton hulk of iron in the basement two floors below, its motor straining as the sandstone wheel rams into a steel tool, which means sparks are showering over Daddy's shoulders like the trail of a Roman candle, the machine sounding a steadily deepening *hawwwww!* Moments later, the heating duct delivers a burst of steel smoke.

Clicking, squeaking, *hawwwwwing!* These sounds—and the occasional screams of Daddy. Something is always going wrong. There's the clang of a big wrench hurled against a machine.

JeeeesusfuckinggggggChristGoddamnnnnnnShitMotherFuuuuuck!

Daddy is doing the very same work as he does by day at Cleveland Twist Drill, the nation's premier manufacturer of industrial cutting tools—drills, end mills, slab mills, all made from specially hardened steel. The most common, end mills, are like a drill that cuts down as well as sideways; they have anywhere from two to eight flutes, and they range from an eighth of an inch to two inches in diameter. They sink dies in softer steel used to stamp out car fenders and myriad other modern items. They cut metal and plastic parts. Daddy grinds their edges and bottoms to razor keenness. His nighttime side business is to re-sharpen this dulled tooling that can be used many times over by "job shops," companies that machine steel all over the Cleveland area.

From my father's labors, steel dust mists through the house. No matter how hard Mom cleans, a finger run along any upstairs surface shows gray. Steel dust is embedded in the cracks beyond the reach of mother's diligent scrubbing. It is in our marrow.

Our village of North Royalton, with its slogan, "High on a Friendly Hill" and spread across twenty-one square miles, has just over five thousand residents. Joan and Steve Maharidge were pioneering white-flight suburbanites, having left the South Side of Cleveland. They built this house the year I was born, 1956, with their own hands, on the site of an apple orchard and truck farm.

There is one traffic light north of our front door. Just beyond is a red-brick city hall and a town square patterned after those in New England. On the southeast corner is the sole tavern, Harry and Berny's, which the town fathers longed to close down. Then Berny placed a sign in the window, "Come in and get high on a friendly hill." This caused further outrage; it was the sole seditious act ever to occur in North Royalton in all of my youth. Up the street is Dr. Sandargas, a Victorian man in a Victorian office filled with dusty glasswares, who makes house calls—he came when I had scarlet fever. There's a hardware store whose owner, Gene, dispenses limitless free advice. A right turn at the light: Ukrainian Savings and Loan, a Slavic cooperative that lent our family $11,000 to build the house; Lawson's, a milk store; Mr. Eleck's musical instrument shop; Lenny, the barber; the Western Auto; the Eagle Market; the Searles and Bassett Funeral Home; and that is about it.

This is some of which can be told about our village, but what interests me are its vast blocks of woods. They exist behind our backyard, where the land gives way to a ravine with a cold brook slicing through Devonian shale rock on its way to the flatlands. The woods, owned by someone unknown, are my refuge when our house erupts. A trifle can set it off, such as one of us kids accidentally spilling a glass of water at the dinner table; Daddy will lose it, start screaming, setting off a chain of events; Mom will start screaming back at him because she, in her own way, is as tough as he; us kids yelling. There is no understanding this anger. It simply exists.

I fall asleep to the sound of the Cincinnati Number 2 motor winding down.

From two thousand rotations per minute, to hundreds, an incremental cessation of wheels and pulleys and brushes and copper windings. The odor of molten plastic bubbling in a chicken cooker, as Daddy dips freshly sharpened tools to protect the edges for transport. His hands are spat-marked from boiling plastic, and steel dirt blackens his cuticles, impossible to wash away. His hands are slashed from wounds in various stages of healing, inflicted by the razor-sharp tools and the wheels that sometime explode in the middle of a *hawwwww!*, spraying sandstone shrapnel, punching holes in the ceiling, tearing flesh.

I sometimes imagined him as I had often seen him, sitting on a stool near the quieted machine, staring at a picture from the war. A lanky man has an arm around Daddy. The man wears a .45 caliber sidearm and a crook-brimmed railroad cap. Daddy and the man are smiling.

Click-click—

Quiet now, save for the wind and the mournful note of the elm. Night terrors—

Awake.

Daddy's snow shovel scrapes driveway gravel like a spoon against a burned pot bottom. The clock says 5 a.m. I rise to my knees and peer out the window. Daddy is hunched, dark against the whiteness. The snow races horizontal against the light atop a utility pole. The car idles, steam emerging from the mouth of the open garage. The car will wait another half hour of digging. My father, knee deep in a drift, slings leaden slush thrown by the village-operated street plows at the road.

Snow compressed beneath the tires sounds like mouse chatter as the car carries my father away, down white roads to a cavernous plant that swallows his daylight hours, a realm of sparks and dust where he grinds steel on machines like those in the basement. Becoming an adult means going to a job in the dark and cold, coming home in the dark and cold. Growing up means sparks and unquenchable anger. Growing up means going to war.

Starkweather

The home at 798 Starkweather Avenue on Cleveland's South Side was one story and narrow, its length barely fitting on the small lot, which had a brief front yard of bare mineral earth. It consisted of five tiny rooms—three bedrooms, a living room, a dining/kitchen area—for most of my father's youth. A fourth bedroom and kitchen were later added.

Dimitro Maharidge and his wife, Anastasia, "Esther," raised eight children in the house. Their second-to-last biological child, born in 1925, was Steve.

Through the 1930s the bathroom was a backyard outhouse. The home was heated by a pot-belly stove. The family bathed in a zinc wash tub set on the kitchen/dining floor using water heated on the stove. Sometimes they were provided charity coal. Other times they used old railroad ties that Dimitro got for free from his job on the Baltimore and Ohio. A chore for the boys was to cut the ties into logs with a two-man crosscut saw and then split the short pieces. Dimitro worked two, maybe three days per week during the Depression; that and church-donated food kept them from starving.

Illustration by Steve Maharidge

The house was just up the street from St. Theodosius, the Russian Orthodox church with its thirteen onion domes sheathed in copper weathered to a green patina. It was perched on the edge of the Cuyahoga Valley and overlooked the mills. (Years later it was used for the wedding scene in Michael Cimino's film, *The Deer Hunter*.) It was visible from everywhere in the valley bottom, a black-iron world of blast furnaces, rolling operations, coal-coking batteries, Rockefeller's oil refineries, steel bridges. The onion globes towered above all the Starkweather houses.

Dimitro and Esther journeyed separately to Cleveland from the old country. Dimitro first worked in a coal mine in Pennsylvania. He was lured to Ohio by John Maharidge, a cousin who was instrumental in forming the Russian community on Cleveland's South Side after he arrived in 1895. He held a meeting in his home to plan what became St. Theodosius. It was constructed in 1911 and 1912, funded in part by Nicholas II, the last tsar; its design was based on a famous church in Moscow. Financing came from immigrants who bought lots from the church. They built houses and opened a Russian school.

View from the front yard of 798 Starkweather Avenue.
Photograph by Steve Maharidge

Dimitro went to this school and landed a job on the River Terminal Railway Company, later the B & O, in the car repair shop. The railroads were busy hauling coal for the coking batteries that supplied the industrialists' new steel mills filled with Slavic workers.

The Russians came to America for opportunity, but fate left many poor. These immigrants clung to old suspicions. There was disdain for Jews, in particular the "paper-rex" man, who came once weekly on a mule-drawn cart through the neighborhood collecting paper and rags to sell for scrap. As he shouted for paper and rags, it sounded like, "Paper-rex! Paper-rex!" The Russians muttered, "That kike has a Cadillac parked down the street! He only looks poor to make money off us!" It mattered not that no one ever saw the Cadillac. It had to be true. The Jew who ran the corner market was also viewed with no less hostility.

But the bitterness was different from what would have been directed at one of their own running the store—in that case, no one would have spent a single soiled penny there. In the old country they tell the parable about two men, one in the United States, the other in Russia, who both find a bottle on the side of the road, and upon rubbing it, a genie appears. The startled American is told he can have anything he wishes. "Well," says the American, "my neighbor has a boat and summer cabin on the lake and a much bigger house than me, so can I also have these things?" With a snap of the fingers, the genie grants the man his wish. When the genie appears before the Russian and offers a wish, the Russian's eyes brighten. "My neighbor has three cows and I have two. Can you kill one of my neighbor's cows?"

This attitude was transplanted to the South Side Russians.

Esther was old country and not just because she didn't learn to speak very much English.

She was tired from so many children, and by the time Steve came along, he wasn't paid much attention. Steve could barely communicate with his mother because of the language barrier. There was much tension in the house with so many people living in close quarters.

Esther spent a lot of time drinking at Hotz's, a bar at the far end of Starkweather Avenue. Dimitro drank beer with salt in it at Tymoc's Bar and sometimes ended up with prostitutes on West 25th Street. Yet each Sunday the couple worshipped at St. Theodosius, standing throughout the eternal services in the pewless chamber. As a cantor chanted, Father Jason Kappanadze, standing behind one dozen icons of saints rising over the altar, emerged in a flowing golden robe, illuminated by the light of 158 burning candles. The old ones stood for services in the house of copper and white brick of the same kind used to contain the heat of the blast furnaces.

For the children, their wants were satisfied on street corners. They stood ten deep, throwing dice, bartering guns, planning carnal actions. If it was warm enough (and often when it was cold), Steve slept out under the Clark Avenue Bridge next to the Jones and Laughlin Steel Mill or on the beach at Edgewater Park. Steve hung out with guys whose nicknames were Goon, Nose, Numbers, Pants, Shorty, Shutty, Yontek.

A different group of Russians lived a few blocks and a world away: singers from the Carpathian Mountains, members of the order

Esther. Photograph by Steve Maharidge

Lemkovina, clustering not around a church but Lemko Hall, a tavern. They were "Bolshies." The St. Theodosius Russians uttered this word with contempt. It wasn't that the Starkweather Russians were ardent Tsarists; they simply had no interest in politics or any matters that went beyond life on their street or in their jobs down in the steel valley.

This was the world as it existed for Steve Maharidge when Pearl Harbor was attacked. He'd dropped out of high school after his freshman year in 1941. The last job he'd held was as a stock clerk at Cort Shoe Company. That ended in January 1942. He was unemployed on his eighteenth birthday in May 1943. A draft notice arrived shortly after. He ignored it. A second notice arrived. He ignored it. His sister Mary said police came looking for him. After the third notice he went down to the selective service office on September 7, 1943. They wanted to put him in the US Navy. He chose to enlist in the US Marine Corps. He later cited the reason: he didn't want to wear bell-bottom pants. It wasn't clear if he was joking.

He was sent to Camp Pendleton, the US Marine Corps training base in California.

From the perspective of those living at 798 Starkweather Avenue, a different man came home in early 1946—quiet and dark, often intoxicated. Steve pretty much remained drunk for the next four years.

His "homecoming" was not exactly a warm one. The bitter Russian peasant mentality emerged one day not long after Steve came back from the war. An old woman saw him on the street. She screamed, "Why'd you come back and not———! The good ones died over there!" She spat at his feet.

Around this time his brother Bill, "Washy," had been hitting their sister Helen in the head as he always had before the war, only now Steve tackled him. He pulled a knife and put it to Washy's throat, the tip pricking flesh. Steve screamed that he'd "fucking kill" him if he ever struck Helen again.

Steve fought a lot after the war. He fought for any reason and most times none. Anyone who looked at him risked his fists. He ran a gambling operation and partook in at least one minor crime, the heist of

Steve Maharidge after boot camp, 1943.
Picture that the Maharidges displayed
during the war

commercial truck parts. In pictures from these years his eyes revealed a wild creature indifferent to consequence, empty as one imagines a person on the edge of homicide or suicide—or they displayed brooding intensity.

Who knows what the mind behind those eyes could or would do?

Uncle Washy never again struck my aunt after that day in 1946.

Steve, circa 1950.
Photograph by Joan Maharidge

Grinding

It was as though two men resided in the body of Steve Maharidge. There was the dark, raging beast. Then there was the guy who existed a majority of the time, who desired to be a great father.

Dad never fished before we came along, and I suspect he took up a rod and reel as a way to be a father. We went on summer fishing vacations to Canada. I'm not sure that angling was the best route to connecting with my older sister, Dawn, born in 1952, but she seemed to enjoy the trips. He often took me and my younger brother, Darryl, born in 1961, to a local pond. In the mid-1960s the three of us went on a "guys only" camping trip downstate. It was near the end of summer. The meadows of goldenrod were thick with bees and swallowtails. Dad landed a few bass.

The final evening on that trip my brother and I played with a toy yellow Caterpillar bulldozer at the lake edge, making pretend roads amid ragweed that we imagined to be pine trees. Later, around the campfire, Dad said, "Be your own boss. You got money, you eat the best beef. You got money, you do what you want, when you want. You got money, you walk into the bank, they treat you with respect. Don't do what I do."

I vividly remember the words because they were repeated often in my youth.

"Get that piece of paper"—a college degree—he said. "You don't want to eat dirt. The guys in the white shirts, they work the front office. Those guys, they don't know shit about how the place works. But they got that paper. With that paper, you don't get dirty."

Dad talked about the basement business and his dream of being his own boss. The company was named D & D Tool Salvage, but he never acknowledged if he'd used our initials with the notion that someday my brother and I would run it. He talked about how "they don't understand how important it is to be your own boss." The "they" actually was a very singular person, our mother, who took a dim view of what went on in the basement.

Dad noticed a tick in my neck. He burned it out with an unfiltered Lucky Strike. There was the odor of bass mixed with wood smoke, as profound to me as madeleines to Proust. I remember the splash of the Milky Way in the heavens and the burning ember of a Lucky Strike against the night and how hard my Dad was trying at this enormous thing, to be a father to us kids.

In this period Dad was on second shift. Those fall days just before heading off to work, he often sat on the porch when I came home from school. Every week or two he brought out the palm-sized black USMC compass that he'd carried through the war and would secretly set up co-ordinates and hide clues at stations around the yard. He started me off with a compass direction to the first station, where there was a new reading that I followed to a few more stations, ultimately leading to a small allowance. It was never explicitly stated, but I suspect that he thought I would someday require this knowledge when I was sent off to fight a war in a place we'd never before heard about.

Vietnam was heating up. There were scenes of the war on our black-and-white television, body counts of guerrillas. I knew about gorillas that dwell in jungles, but this word was new.

I'd do something to trigger Dad's rage, and he sometimes yelled that I'd be in for it in basic training. There had been a guy in boot camp at Camp Pendleton who didn't properly wash his underwear—the drill sergeant made that man chew the shit stains out.

"You'll see!" he'd bellow. I would someday have to chew shit stains from my underwear. "They'll teach you!" Mom always intervened, screaming at Dad to leave me alone. Mom was no pushover, no abused spouse—she constantly fought back and waged verbal combat with Dad. She was not a passive recipient of his eruptions. It's hard to tell if his rage generated or amplified her anger—and, for that matter, if Dad's issues spilled over to influence my own. But years later, in memory, it seemed like all rage in our house emanated from Dad's outbursts.

Though Dad was an enigma, Mom was the bedrock of my existence. She read to me when I was small. One spring she bought a plant and we put it in a flower bed. I watched it grow, bloom, and the first strawberry ripen. Mom took me out one day, and with great ceremony she had me harvest it. Every afternoon I climbed a stool at the end of the kitchen counter, watched her cook dinner, and we talked. When I got older and stayed up longer, I'd sit on the floor of the bathroom while Mom got ready for bed and smoked two or three Viceroy cigarettes. We also talked then. I could discuss anything with her.

There was no mystery with my mother. But my father . . .

An ancient apple tree from the truck farm remained in our front yard. The limbs were heavy with unripe apples late one summer. Dad picked some and mimicked how he handled grenades in the war. He held each green, rock-hard apple and counted a certain number of seconds, then threw them in phenomenal arcs across Ridge Road, into the woods on the other side, where I imagined Japanese soldiers were hiding. He suddenly doubled over from pain. It was his back problem, he said, from Guam. Not long after, he went in for surgery. That's when he talked about the piece of Japanese steel from a mortar round that couldn't be removed because it was so close to his spine.

Another day Dad talked about a "corpsman," pronounced "core-man." I understood that this was like a doctor. "He cut open the stomachs of the Japs to see what they were eating," Dad said. The corpsman studied the contents in his bare hands. My father smiled weirdly as he told this story. It made me uncomfortable. Why was Dad smiling? Decades later I discovered that the emotional result of fantastical violence is nothing at all like how the movies show it. That daytime smile in my father, common, I would later find, in people exposed to violence, came from some survival mechanism. Most of us only scream when we awaken from the nightmares.

I didn't know any of this at the age of ten or twelve. I'd remain confused for a long time.

Mother was Catholic and devout. Dad didn't believe in any religion. Thus, I went to St. Albert the Great, a Roman Catholic school, starting in 1962. The nuns immediately sensed something was wrong with me. They were always striking my backside, boxing my ears, hollering at me, often sending me to Sister Mark, the principal. "You have a bad attitude" was repeated numerous times in those eight long years at the school. This mantra defined my young life. The nuns, including Sister Ruth Mary, said I was disturbed. Mom was defensive and insisted that there was nothing wrong with me. She was in denial about what was going on in our house.

I too had a depth of rage. It wasn't directed at others. In the early grades it manifested itself in brooding isolation. In games of Red Rover I was the last kid to be called over. I usually ate lunch—often a bologna sandwich on white bread, a slice of box cake in wax paper; if early in the school year, there were tiny pear-shaped, red and yellow tomatoes from our garden—seated alone on a curb in the parking lot.

I didn't get into fights like Steve D., Chris V., Mike R., John D., boys who often duked it out. Only once did I hit anyone, when Donald Likowski spat on the back of my new coat. I spun around and slugged him in the stomach. Don was the wrong kid to hit. The nun who admonished me confided that Don suffered from cystic fibrosis and that he'd probably be dead by his twenties. (He made it to forty-two; he later went by the name Dameon and created dark fantasy paintings.)

In seventh and eighth grades Don and I talked a lot during our homeroom period as we spun, on a plastic portable phonograph, new releases by the Doors, Jimi Hendrix, and Led Zeppelin. Don was prematurely wise—he understood something about me. Perhaps it was because we were both outcasts. We never grew truly close; Don wouldn't allow that. One of the few kids who went to his house reported that Don's bedroom walls were painted black.

The winters of 1968 and 1969 found us boys talking about Vietnam. Don wouldn't have to go of course, but the rest of us faced that war. Some boys were certain they'd go. Others said they'd escape to Canada. I was simply scared—all I knew about war was based on how Dad was. The war reached into the school in the winter of 1968 when a woman's screaming sobs filtered to our second-floor classroom; we all froze. We learned that a fourth-grade lay teacher had just been told that her fiancée had been killed. World War II was not yet commonly termed the "Good War," but it was already clear to us kids that Vietnam was different and certainly not a good war.

Before sixth grade we boys outbragged each other about what our fathers had done in World War II. As Vietnam loomed, that kind of talk ceased those last two years at St. Albert the Great.

By eighth grade I was trying to come out of my shell. I volunteered for the Christmas play. Given my reputation, I agreed to be a Scrooge-like grouch. It was the first demonstrable thing I did to deal with my anger, and it began a lifelong process. I was thirteen.

Sister Ruth Mary took me aside and asked if I really wanted to play a grouch. I insisted that I did. During rehearsals I said my "bah, humbugs!" and had a lot of fun. Don played piano, and after one silly Christmas song, he played a moody piece; his ability was stunning for a person of his—or any—age. There were mostly girls in the play. We stood around the piano misty eyed. By then, we all knew Don would die before the rest of us, though as it turned out Barbara Cornhoff would go before him, her car careening off a road in the Colorado Rockies in 1978. She was twenty-two.

Dad got a job grinding at the Aluminum Company of America. He was on day shift. It was a ritual that when he arrived home at four-thirty in the afternoon, he'd flop on the living room floor with a couch pillow and nap for exactly thirty minutes. He had the ability to fall asleep at will. Steel dust fell from his hair, staining the pillow with a black halo—it couldn't be washed out. Mother often had to purchase fresh pillows for the couch. Promptly at five o'clock our family ate dinner. At five-twenty Dad went to the basement and began working on one of the seven machines.

I'd go down and watch. We talked as he worked.

"Get that piece of paper," he often said as orange sparks flew.

Dad viewed a college degree as a scam on par with the gambling racket he'd run on the South Side. He wanted me to be in on playing what he saw as that game because it would ensure that I had a comfortable life. Dad saw the world through the eyes of a working-class immigrant's son. The topic of immigrants in America came up a few times in conversations, about how hard they have it trying to make their way in a new country. "Their children don't have it much easier," he said. The only certainty by which he abided is that when you played in the big boy's system or dealt with the government in any manner, you'd get screwed. He wasn't one of those "patriotic" veterans—he was openly disgusted with guys who wore their uniforms to parades. He wanted to forget and couldn't understand how anyone didn't feel the same.

Dad was the consummate outsider. He never voted in any election. When I grew older I admonished him for this. "You were in the war!" I'd say, adding that he'd fought for that kind of right. He'd usually just swipe his hand at the air in dismissal. Or he'd say, "Horseshit." It wasn't that Dad despised the government; he pretended it didn't exist. It was as if he didn't live in the nation called the United States of America.

Dad was smarter than all this sounds. Even though he dropped out of high school and sometimes spoke in double negative sentences, his written English was grammatically flawless. And he figured complicated math to grind special tools. He simply didn't have the vocabulary from his experience in life to say anything more than, "Get that piece of paper." But who knew? No one in his family had ever walked through a university's doors. My sister would be the first to do so. If we didn't follow suit, my brother and I might inherit D & D Tool Salvage. Darryl, however, wasn't interested in grinding. But by the age of thirteen, I wanted to learn. One Saturday Dad called me to the basement.

Dad went to the Covel and chucked a half-inch end mill in the Harig Air-Flo fixture, a device with a long polished steel tube "floating" through a sleeve with air pressurized by a compressor whose pistons roared. Dad showed how to move, using his left hand on the tube, the fluted tool toward a steel finger set one-sixteenth of an inch beneath the grinding wheel that spun at fifteen hundred rotations per minute, while simultaneously using his right hand to turn a crank that raised the machine's bed so that the flute would touch the wheel to create a fine spark as it moved along the finger. One has to have the proper pitch on the cutting edge: two-thousandths of an inch drop on the "primary" cut. Too much or too little, and it would not function.

I sat upon a stool to reach the fixture. I raised the machine's bed too much, and the tool gnashed into the grinding wheel, shooting out a burst of sparks.

"Try again. You'll get it."

It was a rare moment of patience from Dad. I concentrated, did it right the second time, sending out a smooth stream of sparks. I was now creating the dust that I'd been breathing most of my life.

As I did a second and then a third tool, I gained confidence. As I ground steel that day, I was looked upon by the eyes of the two men in the Guadalcanal picture on the gas meter.

When Dad had orders from Ingersoll-Rand or La-Z-Boy, the furniture company, his two biggest clients, I'd go down after dinner and work with him—me on the Covel grinding side-cutting flutes, Dad on the LeBlonde a few feet away finishing the bottoms on those end mills. I averaged forty tools per hour. Dad paid me ten cents each. Four bucks an hour was a lot of money—the federal minimum wage was a buck-twenty-five. I also cleaned the machines. Each time, I dusted the picture on the gas meter. But I never asked about it.

One night as we were grinding away, Dad began talking about a night during the Battle of Guam, how men were dead all around him, including an unusually tall six-foot Japanese soldier he'd just shot and stacked on top of an American body, creating a wall of dead flesh to shield him from bullets and shrapnel as the Japanese came at them; how during a lull in the battle the marines around him whimpered, crying in fear, calling out for their mothers.

"Fuck you!" he shouted as the machine *hawwwwwed*. He spun a tool in the fixture and slammed it into the wheel, over and over, sparks spraying in an orange arc in my direction. The acrid smell of burned steel filled the room. "You don't have NO fucking mother! She's not here! Shut the fuck up! SHUT THE FUCK UP! SHUT THE FUCK UP! Your mother isn't going to help you *NOWWWW*!"

I realized that he wasn't screaming at or to me. It was what he'd shouted to the sobbing marines around him that night, when he was nineteen. I glanced at the other man in the picture from Guadalcanal. Did that smiling man become one of the bodies Dad stacked around him?

I kept grinding flutes as if I'd heard nothing. I knew better than to ask.

There was a black steamer trunk with faded brass hinges in the attic, filled with things my father brought back from the war. Other war items were in the basement—a Japanese samurai sword, a bolt-action Japanese rifle. But what that trunk contained was different: battle maps from Okinawa, US Marine code books, three Japanese flags, including a silk one signed with a bunch of American names. Most mysterious were the documents, books, and papers in Japanese.

It wasn't easy to reach that chest. The crawl space to the attic was in the ceiling of the closet in my sister's bedroom. I'd learned of the trunk when my mother pushed me up through the opening when I was seven or eight so that I could hand down empty boxes that Mom had pitched up there all year to use at Christmas for wrapping presents. In the dim light I'd lifted the lid and saw the trove. I couldn't linger then. But I never forgot that trunk.

A few years later, when I was tall enough and the coast was clear, I would bring a stool from the dining bar in the kitchen, push aside my sister's clothes, and pull myself up through the opening. The opportunity

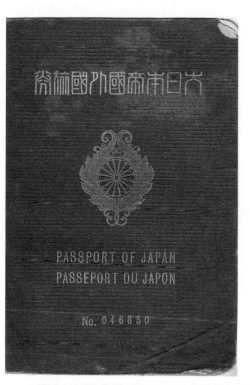

came infrequently, usually in the summer when my mom was on an errand, Dad was at work, and my sister was off with friends.

One object stood out—the passport of a Japanese man.

Surely it belonged to someone my father had killed.

There was some English in the passport. The man was from Okinawa. Did the rifle and sword in the basement belong to this man?

There was a wallet. It was made in Lima, Peru. Clearly the wallet belonged to the same man because the passport showed in English that he'd visited a brother in Peru.

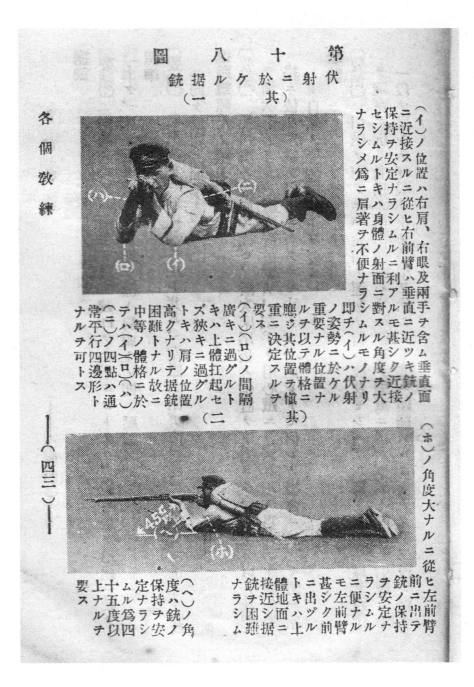

In addition, there was a training manual.

第十七圖
膝射ニ於ケル据銃
（其・一）

各個教練

成ルベク垂直ニ近カラシムルテ
要スルモ過度ニ之テ要求スルト
キハ肩著テ不可能ナラシム

概ネ肩ノ高サ

右股射面ニ對シ略ミ直角ナラシメ肩ノ方向ヲ毎回變セザラシム

（其・二）

頭垂直

—（四二）—

上體ヲ垂直ニシ且ツ左前臂ヲ成ルベク垂直ナラシベク脚ノ長短ニ依リ適宜ノ臂及脚ノ角度ヲ開閉ス此角度チ開閉ス

肘ノ突出部ト相接セザル如クス上體ヲ成ルベク垂直ニ保持シ得ルク如ク臂ノ長短

タル儘照準ヲ爲シ得ルニ依リ左手ノ位置チ前後ス

This was written inside a flap:

Was it someone's name? And there was a business card:

電話二・三七二三 **THE SECOND PING KANG LEE** 朝邱
　　　HIGH CLASS WHORES HOUSE 陽縣

　　　　　　　　　　　　　　　　　路路

　　　No. 26 Kiu Hsien RD.　　　十二

　　　No. 14 Chao Yiang RD.　　四六

　　　　　TEL 2-3723　　　　　　號號

　　　　　TSINGTAO

Aged twelve, I was especially interested in this item. Did my dad have sex with prostitutes?

I studied the face of the man in the passport. I wondered who he was, how my father had killed him.

After my father would go into one of his rages, in the aftermath I would fantasize that someday, when I got older, we could travel to the war places together and he could explain what happened. And then, perhaps, I'd know what hurt him.

I looked up the islands of Guam and Okinawa in an atlas at the library. Those specks amid the blue of the Pacific Ocean on the map were very far away from North Royalton, Ohio.

As I ground steel with my father into my teens, fragmented war stories continued to emerge. He talked about some of the guys he had known back then. One stood out because I heard about him so much: Kennedy.

"He had class," my father said. "He was from New York City. Park Avenue. Money."

Dad wanted money, and he saw Kennedy as the epitome of success. My father was a walking cliché of someone who wanted to attain the "American Dream."

Yet there was another side to the story of Kennedy. One evening for some reason unknown to me, Dad told me about how they were guarding some place on Okinawa. Kennedy and at least one other guy "went up a hill and raped a woman" in a "compound."

Dad was clearly bothered by this, and yet in the next breath he'd talk about Kennedy having class and money. He didn't like what Kennedy did. But he liked what Kennedy represented: social position. Dad viewed money as a path to respect.

Another night a few years later, while we were grinding, Dad said the military police were after Kennedy and that he was told he had to get off the island if he wanted to avoid being busted for the rape. "So he shot himself in the leg," my father said. The other guy involved also shot himself in leg.

"A lot of guys were shooting themselves in the legs," he said of others who simply wanted to get out of combat.

Dad smiled the same way he did when he told the story about the corpsman who cut open the stomachs.

The best year for D & D Tool Salvage was 1969. That year, Dad made some $18,000, nearly half from the basement shop. That was a fantastic income in those days. Our parents bought a new truck camper and we went on two vacations—to Canada and to Florida. We camped on the beach in St. Augustine, swam in the ocean, fished, saw Apollo 11 blast off from Cape Canaveral on July 16, 1969, on its way to the first moon landing. Dad never once lost it in anger. We all got along. It was an idyllic trip.

In 1970 I moved on to ninth grade at the public high school. After work one day Dad was at a service station owned by Andy Shymske, one of his South Side buddies. A car careened toward the gas pumps: Andy grabbed Dad and yanked him. It wasn't enough to keep Dad from being clipped by the fender, but Andy surely saved his life. Dad would have been crushed against a pump. The driver was drunk out of his mind.

Dad spent weeks in the hospital and was off work for months. Mom got charity food from church. With that, our garden, and a slim amount of money borrowed from my mother's impoverished parents who lived next door, we got by. It was years before heightened awareness about drunk driving; the driver had no insurance. That man put his house in someone else's name. Dad never got a cent out of the drunken fool.

Dad lost his job and the big D & D Tool Salvage accounts because of the accident. I didn't know how to grind the bottoms of end mills, a more difficult process than what I did to the flutes. I was angry with myself for not having learned. I'd failed my father, though he never once even remotely blamed me. Still, it ate at me. (After moving to California a decade later I still had nightmares of standing helpless at the LeBlonde machine.)

One constant customer was Star Metal Products. Bill Roble managed that shop and was loyal to Dad—we didn't lose that account. One evening each week I went with Dad to Bill's house in Parma Heights to deliver tooling, after Dad got off work from his new day job that paid just $4.50 per hour, half of what he made before he was injured. Bill was a good guy.

Dad was on pain medication after the drunk struck him. It made him a whole lot mellower and openly emotional in ways I'd never experienced. One night when we were grinding together on a Star Metal order, Dad stopped and looked over at the picture. For the first time he suddenly began talking about the mysterious man.

"They blamed me!" he said. "I came in that night with his .45. They said I killed him! But I didn't kill him! It wasn't my fault!" Dad went on—I forget a lot of what else he said, but it wasn't much more detailed than this. He kept muttering that it wasn't his fault. As usual, I just listened.

Then Dad went off his meds. His anger returned. He never discussed the picture again.

But he often returned to the subject of Kennedy. From those discussions you'd think the words "Park Avenue" were French for making it in America. I knew Park Avenue was ritzy. Maybe it was from the television show *Green Acres*, when Zsa Zsa Gabor sang, "Darling, I love you, but give me Park Avenue!" in the opening score. Or it came from what I read in the newspapers.

Money and power (and thus politics and business) interested me from a young age, perhaps as a result of my father's obsession with having neither.

I was quite aware of what was happening in American culture. I absorbed the first *Whole Earth Catalog* when it came out in the late 1960s. At the age of thirteen, in 1970, I led a "boycott the bus" walk to school for the first Earth Day to protest fossil-fuel pollution. A week and a half later four students were killed by National Guard troops at Kent State University, twenty miles from our house. That fall one of my English teachers, freshly graduated from that school, told us how he'd been standing next to Sandy Scheuer, who was not even protesting that day, when a fatal bullet sprayed her blood all over him. Something was very wrong about how affluence and being a global power had affected us as a country.

I was critically aware of the value of money. When my mother took me grocery shopping, I watched how much she spent and what she bought. She fed our family for twenty-five dollars a week in the mid-1960s. I observed her paying bills. I knew everything about our family's finances. This puzzled my mother. I was loathe to spend money I made from grinding with my father. "You have a Depression mentality," my mother told me many times.

Yet my father's intense desire for acquiring money was troubling. Of course I had the luxury of this point of view—I was born at a time in America when the white children of blue-collar workers could, with relative ease, leap forward in class in a way that was not possible before or after. I understood how Steve Maharidge grew up in that tiny Starkweather house with nine other people in abject poverty and how he was then sent to the front lines. He had a lot thrown at him before the age of twenty-one. All available evidence had shown my father that without money, you'd be screwed. He saw that by having money, you were insulated from a lot of the bad things in life.

The quest for money was just one reason for Dad's stunning work ethic. By nature, he was driven. After his injury he wanted to make the business thrive again. He doubled down and bought more machines.

My parents' home was on land zoned for commercial use. Dad had masons construct a brick shop in our backyard. My father and I put on the roof ourselves. Having the business in the basement was a code violation, and my father feared being busted. Now legal, Dad put a small sign in the front yard for D & D Tool Co., the "salvage" removed from the name. In 1973 the company grossed only $3,443.52. He had a long way to go to come back.

Dad was hired as a US Postal worker. He aced the test. Plus, he was given an additional ten points for the war wound. It's the only time I saw that he got any tangible advantage for being a veteran, aside from a disability check. It began as $11.50 per month in 1946; by the 1960s it was some $30; by 1998, $98. The paperwork said the disability was for a "right forearm injury." His arm was fine. It didn't mention the piece of Japanese steel next to his spine or blast concussion. The government had fought his claim, and my father had to appeal.

It seemed the military didn't want to acknowledge my father's real injuries.

When I graduated from high school in 1974 I enrolled in Cleveland State University and remained living at home. Dad was delivering mail by day and couldn't do much to promote the business. I had free days, so I became a sales representative for D & D Tool Co. Dad and I took a gray-green metal file-card box, cut a piece of foam to size, bored holes in it, and inserted samples of end mills to show the quality of our work.

I had to look the part. Dad drove me to a downtown shop that sold $19 suits. The day would come, Dad hoped, when we could both get custom suits made. That is what having money meant: "You wear the best clothes." We chose a purple polyester suit off the rack, with a darker purple tie, wide in the style popular in the 1970s. I'm thankful no pictures exist of me in that outfit.

I was eighteen but looked fifteen. I was quite shy. The suit, I believed, would give me confidence. I drove the family's hand-me-down Buick Skylark to make cold calls at tool-and-die shops. I felt primal terror as I went from shop to shop asking to see the person in charge of the tool crib. "Some kid wants to see you," was commonly said. A surprising number of guys met with me. Slowly, I became more confident. I offered an introductory deal of sixty cents for end mills smaller than a half-inch in diameter. (We made our money on special orders.) The kicker: I promised same-day service on those rush orders. Our competitors weren't this nimble.

Tool-and-die shops always needed fast turnarounds. The calls began coming in. We'd jam out those orders. Many times we'd never again hear from those companies. But we started getting all the business from others. By 1975 I'd brought in about $20,000 in annual accounts. In 1976 my father quit the Postal Service. Accounts continued rolling in. In 1978 the business grossed $54,094.83.

I grew close to some clients. One of those early cold calls was to Heron Industries. An older gentlemen came out—Mr. Heron, the owner. Each time I delivered tooling, Mr. Heron and I had long talks. I learned that connecting with people was as important as the work we did. When he was full time, Dad started making these rounds. By nature he was insecure; his upbringing in that small house on Starkweather Avenue was not one that bred confident children. But more and more, he gained a sense of assuredness.

I was now about as close to my father as I'd ever been. Yet the war and its impact on him remained a mystery. He talked about it as infrequently as he did before. In the new building Dad stationed the picture from Guadalcanal near the Cincinnati Number Two. Later Dad built a small office so that visitors had a place to wait. The Guadalcanal picture went on that office wall, near a breasty pinup calendar that the Latch Company, a supplier, sent us each year.

I was in and out of college during this period. By then I wanted to be a writer. Yet earning a living by the written word seemed impossible. Perhaps I would indeed take over the business. My uncertainty changed one day in 1977.

I'd driven across the Harvard Avenue Bridge to drop off tools for our biggest client, ALCOA, where Dad once worked. The plant was on the east side of the Cuyahoga Valley, near the J & L Steel works, across and upriver from the onion domes of St. Theodosius. I signed in at the security gate and went to a building that contained a three-story stamping press where the tool crib was located.

The milling cutters were in heavy wooden crates that required two trips. As the crib man signed off on the bill of lading, I heard the big stamping press winding up. Curious, I turned away from the exit, going deeper into the building. I went along a plywood wall that had been erected to conceal the press: my father said ALCOA was doing top-secret work on military jet parts. One was supposed to have security clearance to go behind the partition. I cut through an opening.

The press, operated by a man in a booth so lofty that he rode an elevator to reach it, had risen nearly to its apogee. The machine created a minor earthquake each time it struck, and it could be heard all over the valley.

The press was in a cavernous building. The upper reaches were composed of hundreds of foot-square glass panes blackened by decades of grime; most disallowed light. Here and there glass had broken out. One shattered pane was situated so that a beam of sunlight penetrated to shine on the press. The air was misty from dust and burned coolant. The shaft of light illuminated the machine as if it was a painting of the Resurrection.

The press dropped.

There was a gust of machine-created wind and a thunderclap from the mashing of metal that echoed, I imagined, across the steel valley to Starkweather Avenue where my Russian grandparents had lived their sad lives. I staggered backward, choking from the billowing dust. My ears hurt. I thought of a line from a *Pink Floyd* song: "Welcome my son, welcome to the machine." It seemed impossible to escape. I was born into metal and sparks and anger; I would die after a life of metal and sparks and anger.

Not long after, I drove my motorcycle to the *Cleveland Plain Dealer*, entered the newsroom, and announced to a section editor that I wanted to write for him. I'd come with an idea: doing that was no more crazy than making cold calls at tool-and-die shops in a purple polyester suit. "I'll look at it on spec, kid," editor Bob Roach told me. When I delivered the piece, Bob ran it on the cover the following week. He began regularly publishing me. I was soon writing dozens of stories for the newspaper.

My biggest champion, after my mother, was my father. He didn't want me eating steel dust the rest of my life. My parents tolerated me living at home rent-free for the next few years. I continued grinding with my father amid working on stories as I built my portfolio.

In this period of the late 1970s my father poured money into his ultimate dream for becoming rich: a "one chuck" grinding fixture. He melded two fixtures that already existed on the market into one unit. This fixture would grind both the bottoms and sides of end mills. He figured a lot of tool-and-die shops would buy it to reduce resharpening costs.

My father had faith that a copious amount of money would heal all that had happened to him.

Art, a client who ran a one-man shop, was a genius with a Bridgeport milling machine. Dad made patterns that he had poured at a foundry. Art machined these castings. Art could bore a hole within an accuracy of one-tenth the thickness of a human hair. When you put a sleeve into one of Art's borings, you could hear the rushing of air. Art was extremely fair. He charged Dad a very basic rate. Still, that money added up. The real cost was the patent attorney. Between 1975 and 1979 Dad spent about $60,000 on developing the fixture, something like $200,000 or more in today's dollars.

On January 16, 1979, my father was awarded US Patent 4,134,235 for the "One Chuck Grinding Apparatus for End Milling Cutters and the Like."

United States Patent [19]

Maharidge

[11] **4,134,235**

[45] **Jan. 16, 1979**

[54] **ONE CHUCK GRINDING APPARATUS FOR END MILLING CUTTERS AND THE LIKE**

[76] Inventor: **Steve Maharidge,** 14410 Ridge Rd., North Royalton, Ohio 44133

[21] Appl. No.: **798,245**

[22] Filed: **May 18, 1877**

[51] Int. Cl.² **B24B 3/04**
[52] U.S. Cl. .... **51/92 ND; 51/225**
[58] Field of Search .... 51/92 R, 92 ND, 224, 51/225, 231, 218 R, 218 A

[56] **References Cited**

U.S. PATENT DOCUMENTS

2,332,510	10/1943	Franzen	51/225
2,401,874	6/1946	Kilbride	51/225 X
2,690,037	9/1954	Meyer	51/225
3,365,843	1/1968	Robinson	51/225
3,624,718	11/1971	Ribich	51/225
3,680,263	8/1972	Johnson	51/225
3,722,148	3/1973	Grahn	51/225

Primary Examiner—Nicholas P. Godici
Attorney, Agent, or Firm—Alfred D. Lobo

[57] **ABSTRACT**

Apparatus for manually sharpening the bottom, radially divergent, flute ends or cutting edges of an end milling cutter (hereinafter referred to as an "end mill") which apparatus includes a stationary, beveled disc-type or plain grinding wheel mounted for rotation about a horizontal axis (or y-axis), so as to present the face of the wheel to an operator, and a tool-holding fixture having a base member mounted on the worktable of a conventional tool grinder. The worktable of the grinder is capable of movement along three axes, namely a longitudinal axis (or x-axis), a horizontal axis (or y-axis) toward and away from the circular face of the disc, and a vertical axis (or z-axis), by manual manipulation of individual table-adjusting wheels. The fixture includes a workhead mounted on a carriage which in turn is translatably mounted for linear to and fro motion, on a base member with bearing means. The workhead is mounted on the carriage for pivotable movement about a longitudinal axis (x-axis). An end mill holder comprising a bushing or collet is rotatably disposed in the workhead so that the end mill may be rotated about the end mill's longitudinal (vertical) axis. The end mill is held in a vertical plane, and index plate means are preferably provided for indexing each cutting tooth or edge of an end mill along the y-axis before it is sharpened. Once the end mill is locked into the holder, or "chucked," the end mill may be dished and gashed, and primary and secondary clearances of the flute ends may be provided, all without removing the end mill, hence the "one chuck" designation.

3 Claims, 10 Drawing Figures

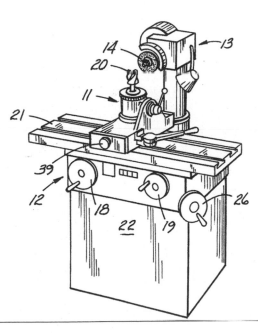

Dad dreamed of multiple offers. But just one company in Buffalo was interested. "You're going to be rich," one of the owners told my parents over a dinner. My mother was skeptical. "Don't talk to me like I'm stupid," my mother said to the man when she recounted that meeting.

The Buffalo company never made a solid offer. Those guys drifted away.

In 1980 it was time for me to take the next step. The *Cleveland Plain Dealer*, despite my prolific record, wasn't going to hire me. I decided to drive to California to find a newspaper job.

Days before leaving, I went to our Catholic grade school's ten-year reunion. Sister Ruth Mary was there—we had a lovely peace-making conversation. At twenty-three, I was now old enough to understand that the nuns weren't my problem. I was dealing with my anger issue, and I knew that it was something that I'd have to work on my entire life.

I put my hometown in the rearview. I literally stared at the mirror in my Datsun pickup as I drove down that hill that is the final crest of the Alleghenies, into the west and my uncertain future.

After three months of living out of the truck I was hired at the *Sacramento Bee*. I returned to Cleveland about twice a year. Dad's business was grossing between $60,000 and $85,000 annually, decent money in those years. But he was tired of the dust and hard work.

In 1985 my parents sold the business and house. They had visited me in California and liked Sacramento. They bought a house in the suburb of Carmichael.

I wondered about how much easier their life would have been had my father put that $60,000 spent on the patent into an investment property. My mother had fantasized about living in an oceanfront condo, which would have cost about that amount in St. Augustine, Florida. If they had bought one and rented it while remaining in Ohio, one of those condos would have appreciated eight- or tenfold; they would have had a serious chunk of money for retirement. My father didn't understand that to make that much money with the fixture, he would have needed to have sold a few thousand—an impossibility given the limited industrial market. Yet managing real estate was too scary for my parents.

Steve in his shop, 1983

I guess my father was a quintessential American. Mark Twain also wanted to be wealthy, and he invested in a typesetter and other dubious things that were duds.

Patent number 4,134,235 expired in 1996. I don't recall my father being aware of its cessation. As far as I know, the "One-Chuck Grinding Apparatus" was never commercially produced after it entered the public domain.

Counting Grapefruit

Dad arrived in Carmichael in 1985 with several of his patented fixtures, two machines, and other equipment. He rented space on California Avenue a few miles from Paxton Court, a cul-de-sac where my parents bought a house. He called his new business Paxton Industrial Tools. He was fifty-nine.

Dad didn't realize there were few tool-and-die shops in Sacramento. Still, he could have advertised in the trade magazines and shipped orders. But his heart wasn't in it. For one year he went to Paxton Industrial Tools and sat. The Guadalcanal picture hung on a wall. When he gave up the lease, the picture came home and was put above the garage workbench, affixed to the far-right door of a cabinet. Dad spent a lot of time puttering. He bought a small table saw. He liked making planters and hanging baskets.

Not long after arriving in California, my sister (who was living with my parents as she established herself) told me that she came into the kitchen one morning. Dad looked up. She told me that he muttered, "I wasted my life."

Dad grew obsessed with the yard and its six citrus trees. He kept a logbook and precisely counted how many grapefruit and tangelos came off each tree. He'd spend days following the movements of ants. By the mid-1990s we didn't have much to talk about. I'd listen about the ants or focus conversation on the past. I tried to find projects we could share: I helped him dig trenches to build planters, or we repaired rotting wooden fences.

In the late 1990s my sister, then married, arranged a camping excursion to Bodega Bay, north of San Francisco. We caught stone crabs. As I brought one in, Dad reached with a net and the car keys spilled out of his windbreaker pocket, vanishing in the foaming, ten-foot deep water. I tensed. Had this occurred when I was a boy, Dad would have gone off in a fury, ruining any chance that he'd be able to enjoy himself the rest of the day.

Instead, he said, "Well, your mother has a spare set of keys."

The new mellowness came with a cost. Dad grew increasingly forgetful; he'd lose track of conversation. Alzheimer's didn't run in his family.

I saw my parents a lot in California. I relished each visit. Before dinner we drank highballs of Wild Turkey and ginger ale.

In June 1998 Dad sent a letter to St. Louis asking for his US Marine records kept by the National Personnel Records Center. One evening as we drank highballs, he produced the lengthy file. "You won't be able to get these after I'm gone," he said. I muttered something about how he shouldn't talk that way. I retained the reticence of childhood—the war was something never to probe. I realized years later that Dad was reaching out. It was his way of saying that it was okay to ask questions, probably even about that mysterious picture I stared at any time I went into the garage workroom.

But the habit of not asking was too deeply ingrained.

In 2000 I got an assignment to cover the presidential election. I flew out of Sacramento. It was early June. Dad drove me to the airport. He seemed very tired. We said goodbye the usual way—abruptly and without emotion. I flew to Washington, DC, then drove to Tennessee and on to Texas. In Austin I called Mom. She announced that my father had terminal cancer. The doctor didn't know where it started, but it was now in his liver. Mom put him on the phone. Dad insisted that I not rush back. He said the doctor told him that he had a few months to live. "Finish what you're doing," Dad said.

Dad was reflective in that phone call. "I should have been dead a long time ago. I should have died in the war. A lot of times." He added that he also should have died when the house on Starkweather Avenue caught fire and he suffered smoke inhalation or when he was hit by the drunk driver. Then he laughed, almost a giggle, as if he were surprised that he'd made it to seventy-five.

I continued working. My sister phoned days later when I was in Tennessee. She told me to get home—fast. Dad was going down in flames. I raced back. My mother bitterly blamed the doctor for not saying time was that short. Knowing my father, I'm sure the doctor told him. He was reverting to being a US Marine, the kind who didn't cry out for his mother when facing death. He was going out in his own way.

I arrived on June 26. Dad looked hideous. He could no longer wear dentures, so his mouth was sunken, and his skin was yellow. It was a stunning decline from when I'd last seen him three weeks earlier. The next few days were a blur of sleeplessness. I took notes.

June 27, 1:15 p.m.

Dad could barely sit up. "I wish this was over with." He sat at the edge of the bed. Then his eyes closed. "I didn't want it to happen like this." He wanted to go fast, like his mother. Bam. Heart attack—dead. "I guess I was a bad boy."

"No, you weren't," I said.

He lay down. Dad was in and out of consciousness. He mumbled stories. "I'm ready to leave this place," he said. He was not religious, and I wondered what he meant. I thought of the time when we were grinding steel together and he suddenly started talking about hell for no apparent reason. "Maybe this is it—we're living in it now," he said. Then he went back to grinding. Now, years later on his deathbed, he talked about a Japanese soldier he killed. He was walking through a field and the man came out of some brush; he turned and they faced each other. "It was him or me." I believed that this was the only man Dad killed in broad daylight, looking the man right in the eye.

I convinced myself it was the man in the passport.

June 28, 9 a.m.

I sat at the kitchen table with Mom. "He talked a lot about the war and his childhood and all the things he never did," she said of the days before I showed up. "He said, 'We weren't stupid. But we kept being beaten down.'"

I mentioned that when the time came, I'd use my pull to get an obituary in the Cleveland Plain Dealer. *She snapped, "I don't want his parents mentioned in it!" She was bitter. "That woman ruined my life," she said of Esther, Dad's mother. She guessed that Esther would scream when he dropped things. "That's why he went into orbit every time you kids spilled something." She allowed that Dimitro, Dad's father, was nice. She liked him.*

June 28, 7:30 p.m.

I was in the room many times through the day, but Dad was always sleeping. Now he was awake. "Did you find the gun yet?"

"No."

He meant the Colt .45 semi-automatic pistol he bought from Tony Thomas, one of his South Side buddies. I was there that day he paid Tony twenty-five bucks for the piece that was surely hot. Dad bought the pistol mostly for me. We'd been deer hunting together, and I was into those kinds of things then. It resembled the weapon on the hip of the man in the war picture. It was now stashed in a box in the cedar chest in Mom's bedroom.

His gaze was weak, yet his exhausted eyes, gray in the center and yellow from jaundice in the whites, bore on me. It was the most lucid he'd been in a dozen hours. I did something most unusual for our family and with him in particular: I told him exactly what I felt.

"I just want to say that I appreciate everything you did. You were a great father. You busted your ass."

"If it wasn't for your mother, you would have turned out—" his eyes closed. There was a long pause. His eyes snapped back open.

"Lousy," he whispered.

"No," I said. "You were a great father. You took us fishing, to Wilshire Lake all those times, and all those other times we went camping. All those vacations."

He shrugged.

"You taught me a lot with the business."

He sputtered, "I just wish I could be around longer to see—"

I filled in the ensuing silence.

"Damn, you'll never get to use my toilet," I said, referring to my having put a septic system in an off-the-grid house I was building. I'd used an outhouse for five years.

Dad smiled. His sense of humor remained. His eyes closed.

"I'll see you later," I said.

He never regained consciousness.

June 30, 9:10 a.m.

Father died about 8:30 a.m. No one was in the room. Mom said he was still breathing sometime after 8. I got to the house just now.

I thought of all that was not asked, not said. My emotions surely weren't any different from millions of others who've had a parent die. Thanking my father was too little, too late. I was in a state those final days. I wanted more. I consoled myself that no matter how long Dad had lived, we'd never really have talked the way I desired.

I imagine that we all tell ourselves such things.

The Quest Begins—And Ceases

Two days after the Neptune Society took Dad's body out on a gurney, I went into his bedroom. It smelled of bilious death. The room was remarkably sparse. Dad had slept alone since my parents had moved to California, and yet after fifteen years there were few personal possessions. Among them was a drawer with a box of war ephemera, including the Purple Heart he was awarded after nearly dying in the Battle of Guam.

There were two other pictures of the man in the Guadalcanal image and there were words written on the reverse.

Dad had given me a name. Both pictures had been written on at different times—in fountain pen back in the war era, ball point much later. Did he do this for me as a clue? I'd like to convince myself of this, but if it was true, he might have also written what happened—even a few words.

It's often difficult to pinpoint when an obsession begins. As a man obsessed with many subjects over the years, I can't exactly date the births of passion for most things. But I know this for certain: July 2,

Mulligan

HERMAN MULLIGAN

Lt. W. Mulligan
South Carolina

GUADALCANAL
LIVING QUARTERS
IN REAR

1944

2000, marks the day that began my most personal obsession. I had to discover all that could be learned about my father and the war. I focused at first on Herman Walter Mulligan. I wanted to know who he was, how he died, and why my father was compelled to keep his picture in sight for the previous fifty-five years. The unsettled issues with my father were impossible to deal with, but the search was something I could do in an emotional situation that was otherwise beyond control.

I had a lot of strange energy in the aftermath of my father's death. I felt untethered. I know this is not uncommon. I've always immersed myself in work to avoid bad emotional periods.

I had two starting points. A quick Internet search and a phone call to Washington, DC, revealed that to learn more about Mulligan, I had to file a Freedom of Information Act Request with the Department of the Army, US Total Army Personnel Command. The other was the silk Japanese flag in Dad's drawer that guys from his unit signed.

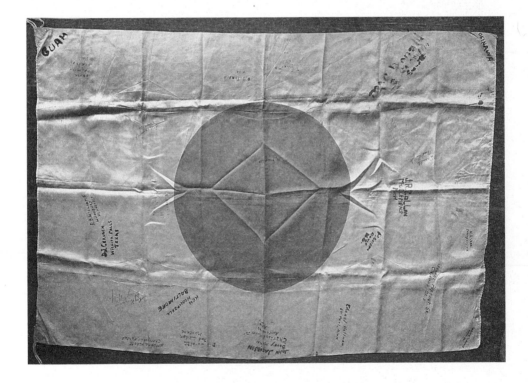

The response to my FOIA came in two stages. The first part, the USMC Casualty Report, arrived within days.

I was confused by "body not recovered." And what did "Blast Conc Atmos***" mean? It appeared that Mulligan was close to something that blew up.

```
USMC CASUALTY REPORT        DATE  8.Jun45    CARD Yes  CAS. NO: 050460
NAME ★                                RANK        CLASS        IDENT. NO.
MULLIGAN, Herman Walter, Jr.          PFC         USMCR        496478
ORGANIZATION                          TYPE OF CASUALTY   AREA        DATE OF CASUALTY
CoL-3Bn-22Mar-6MarDiv-FMF             KIA         Pac          30May45
DATE APPT./ENLIST   PLACE OF APPT./ENLIST   DATE. ACTIVE DUTY   PRIORSER. MISC. STA.  MARITAL  RACE
19Nov42   Savannah, Ga.                                    NO            S
DATE OF BIRTH   PLACE OF BIRTH            LEGAL RESIDENCE
30Jun23   Williamston, S.C.             Greenville, S.C.
NEXT OF KIN                          RELATION   ADDRESS OF KIN
Mr. Robert G. Owens(Grandfather)     Guar       4 Donwood Ave.,
Mr. Herman Walter Mulligan, Sr.,     Fath       West Greenville, S.C.
Address: Rte.#2, Box#154, Laurens, S.C.
BENEFICIARY (Name and Address)  DBO: Mr. Robert G. Owens (Guar)
                                Same as above.
PLACE OF CASUALTY      NATURE OF WOUND              PRESENT STATUS
Okinawa, Ryukyu Is.    Blast Conc Atmos***          *BODY NOT RECOVER
REMARKS (Additional Information  Disposition of Remains )

DATE AND SOURCE OF REPORT  RAD#012205 NCR#30180 fr 6thMarDiv to   CHECKER
SecNav-TAB REP#46-REC'D CASDIV 5Jun45.
NAME                                  RANK        CLASS        IDENT. NO.
MULLIGAN, Herman Walter, Jr.          PFC         USMCR        496478

S/R rec'd 29Aug45.(adr)
***Form F Card fr 3rdBn, 22nd Mars, 6thMarDiv 11Oct45.(td)
Re   of Cas fr Div Sup  Re                F'F  to C Rep'    S
                    Bo                WIA           )
Cert of Death fr BuMed & Surg, Navy Dept. Wash. D.C.
rec'd 8May46, states Disposition of remains unknown.(mf)
*Determined non-recoverable by Field Board 22Dec49 (mls)
```

I turned to the flag. I couldn't locate a lot of the guys. Then I found a phone number in a town north of Minneapolis for this name:

I got an answering machine. I verbally stumbled—I was nervous making the first call, and I wasn't sure I had the correct Edward Hoffman. Someone suddenly picked up.

"—I just walked in. Who is this?"

"Dale Maharidge, I—"

"Oh, Steve! Are you any relation to him?"

I broke the news of my father's death.

"I was five-nine and so was your dad. I looked up to your father, like a father figure," Hoffman said. He told me how he came into the unit as a replacement at the age of seventeen in the middle of the Battle of Okinawa, just days before Mulligan was killed. He didn't know Mulligan. He didn't meet my dad at that point. "He was hit," Hoffman said. "He came back to the outfit at the end."

Hoffman had gotten to know my father on Guam when they were stationed there in July and later when they were sent to Tsingtao, China.

"He was a cool cat, is what they say now," Hoffman said of my father. The last time they had met was when Hoffman was passing through Cleveland in 1955, the year before I was born, and they had a beer in a bar. Hoffman said my dad was working as a movie projectionist on the side.

We talked for perhaps an hour. Hoffman was friendly. It felt unreal to be talking with someone who had served with my father. It was the start of a phone friendship—I would call Hoffman numerous times in the coming years. Hoffman said during that first call that he'd send me a directory from the Sixth Marine Division Association as well as copies of the muster rolls, the official records of everyone who had been in the company, compiled by months, on Okinawa.

While I waited for them in the mail, I found a phone number for a second name from the flag:

George Popovich, Sr,
Cleveland, Ohio.

A woman answered. I asked for George Popovich.

"Which one?"

"The one who was in World War II."

"Who is this? What do you want him for?!" The woman was terse. I blurted that I was the son of a man who was in the Pacific with Popovich. The woman cut in, in a much kinder voice, "He can't remember what he had for breakfast. He's losing his mind. But he remembers the past real well. I'll put him on."

"Oh, I wish I coulda seen Steve one more time," Popovich began. "I'm eighty years old. I know what I want to say, but it's pretty hard to concentrate." He paused. Then he talked fast. "Did your father tell you about the Jap counterattack that night on Guam? On the Orote Peninsula? They broke through our lines. I just lay in my foxhole. They jumped right over me."

He said that in the morning my father lay wounded in his foxhole. Two guys in foxholes on either side of Dad were dead, probably killed by the same mortar round.

"That was the night Gabby [Fenton Grahnert] was in a hole with [Bill] Corbitt. Gabby's B.A.R. [Browning automatic rifle] jammed. He took it apart, got it working again. A grenade rolled into his hole. It blew, but it didn't hit him.

"On Okinawa, when we landed that first day on the island, we had no casualties. Then we got hit by Japanese mortar fire. I jumped into a hole, a bomb crater. [Bernard] Blair jumped in next to me. All of a sudden, sand blasts my face, I couldn't see. I rubbed my eyes. When I opened them, there was a shell that landed right between my legs. It was a dud. Blair said, 'I'm digging in with you from now on. You've got luck!' We went up north. Gabby butchered a pig."

My dad had told me about chasing down pigs on the northern part of the island and killing them with hammers. There are only two pictures of my father that exist from Okinawa.

"Harrison, he got hit coming off a hill. He raised his hand, said 'I'm going.'

"We had a problem with a guy, some hanky panky with some Okinawa woman. Kennedy. Did your Dad tell you about Kennedy? Him 'n [another guy], they raped a woman. Up north, at communication hill. We were dug in there. They took advantage of a woman. A marine from our unit told the battalion. They were looking for Kennedy, 'til he shot himself to get off the island. He was facing rape charges."

Okinawa, 1945:
Angus Robertson and Maharidge butchering a pig

Okinawa: Robert Harrison and Maharidge

Popovich went on about the litany of men who were shot or blown to fragments by Japanese shells. (He grew emotional about one man in particular, Wilbur R. Reddick, killed May 11, 1945, as the unit approached Sugar Loaf Hill, the grimmest part of the Okinawa battle.) "Reddick got hit. A shell hit a tree, exploded, and a piece of shrapnel opened up his chest. I gave him a cigarette. Then he died." In the coming days about three thousand Americans and three thousand Japanese would die or be wounded on that hill. "On Sugar Loaf Hill . . . we started to crack up.

"Did he [Steve] tell you about the Japanese cave, the time we went in and ate their food? Ate tangerines, shrimp in cans. We drank their beer. And we drank their sake. We got real drunk.

"I lived a couple of tents away from Steve, on Guadalcanal. We made our own booze, in a Lyster bag, with sugar and raisins. Your dad stole the raisins. And one time your dad and I, we stole some whiskey from the army, from the officers.

"Your dad ended up in the brig," he said. "He was drinking, got into an argument with some guy. He wanted to kill him. He was a fighter. I was the sergeant of the guard that night. That time we put your father in the brig, he went and got the rifle. He would have killed the guy. We put him in the brig to stop him from doing that. I took him a loaf of bread, put food inside for him. As small as he was, he wouldn't take no shit from no one. You had to know how to handle him. He was an awful good squad leader. You could depend on him. He was second squad, Harrison was third."

At that point in my quest I was interested in two main things: details about my father and the fate of Mulligan. I interjected and asked about him.

"Mulligan." Popovich paused. "He was a Jewish fella. He went on patrol one time, got hit. He went off the island. Then he came back."

"What happened? How did he get killed?"

Popovich told me he was in the hospital when that happened and that he didn't know; I later learned that Mulligan was wounded that first time on April 10, 1945.

When I bid George Popovich goodbye, I didn't understand the pieces of his story. I had not yet learned enough to know what questions to ask him. Popovich died not long after we talked, and there was no going back to him to fill in blanks. More than any other guy I would find, he knew more intimate details about my father than anyone. I was rattled. I was learning about my father's war, but trying to figure out the story was like watching shadows on a cave wall.

The material from Ed Hoffman arrived by mail. Some men from L Company were members of the Sixth Marine Division Association—the group covered a wide range of companies, and most members had nothing to do with my father's unit. The association list gave me a few leads. The majority of guys weren't members because, like my father, they wanted to forget the war. What helped most were the US Marine muster rolls Hoffman sent me. They contained the names of over four hundred guys who were cycled through Love Company during the Battle of Okinawa. (The unit suffered over a 100 percent casualty rate from injury and death; new guys kept coming in as replacements.) I began the laborious multiyear process of tracking them down.

When guys did not specifically remember my father, all my questions focused on Mulligan at that early point in my search. I finally learned something more specific from Bill Fenton, who lived in Kansas, about how Mulligan died.

"I wound up in the hospital just before that happened," he said, from injuries on Sugar Loaf Hill. "I heard what happened from others. Everyone was sealing caves. One of them had a big ammo dump inside. They didn't know it. Herman threw in a grenade. The whole hill blew up. Herman ducked, a great big rock fell on him. All I remember, all I can tell you, is his mother was Jewish, his father Irish."

Obsessed as I was, it was slow work. I was struggling with Dad's death, and each call took a toll. It wasn't until March 8, 2001, that I had the emotional energy to telephone Fenton Grahnert. He quipped about the oddity of Bill Fenton having his first name as a last name.

"I always told Bill we're second cousins twice removed."

I liked Grahnert right off. I found that these guys were a lot like my father—except willing to talk about the war. Even so, I only learned a fraction of what Grahnert knew that first phone conversation.

Grahnert didn't remember my father by name, nor did he recall the names of many other guys. Yet apart from the names, his memory was sharp. I asked about Mulligan.

"I don't remember him."

I told details of what little I knew—

"I forgot his name! That was him! He was a bleeder!"

"What do you mean?!"

"A hemophiliac. He told me on Guadalcanal, 'Don't you tell no-body! I don't want anyone thinking I'm a coward.' He was Jewish. Good lookin' fella. He threw a grenade into a cave, a tomb, the damn thing was full of explosives."

Okinawan custom is to bury the dead in elaborate concrete tombs dug into most every hill. They are especially plentiful on the southern part of the island. There are two kinds of tombs, the "turtleback" variety that evokes a womb, and the square cottage-style kind.

Illustration from Nansei Shoto,
US War Department, 1945

"The whole hillside blew out at him," Grahnert continued. Like the others I found, he also was in the hospital at the time, but he had heard what happened. "He got hit in the face with a rock. It was the first hill outside of Naha. He'd been wounded, was out of the company."

George Niland, living in Massachusetts, came into the company in the middle of the Okinawa Battle as a replacement. George told me he went back to Okinawa in 1995 for the fiftieth anniversary of the war ending. "I couldn't believe what I saw. It's all developed—big main roads, high buildings."

Niland went on bitterly about Captain Frank Haigler, who took over after Captain John P. Lanigan was wounded. He said Haigler was focused on collecting souvenirs and shipping them home. "Haigler was not my favorite officer."

I found my way to Haigler, who lived in Southern California on a two-acre horse property in Fullerton, only Haigler didn't have horses— he had military vehicles of all types. Some time before I called he told me he sold a WWII Japanese tank and a US Sherman tank. I asked if he knew my father.

"I remember him because he was a sergeant," Haigler said. But the gulf between the enlisted men and officers meant that Haigler didn't recall much more. I was going to be in Southern California, and he agreed to meet.

When I showed up in Fullerton, Haigler, a retired obstetrician who was tall and fit at seventy-nine, was gracious. We descended to his basement. It was a museum to the war. There were hundreds of items: rifles, swords, flags, maps, and a helmet with a bullet hole in it, small where it

went in the front and large where it exited. Bloodstains were visible on the interior liner.

It belonged to Second Lieutenant James R. Bussard, who was killed June 12, 1945, just two weeks after he joined the company as a replacement. This happened when Love Company had captured Hill 53, which was the Japanese Naval

Headquarters where Admiral Minoru Ota and his staff committed suicide in a maze of tunnels. A Japanese sniper shot him when the marines were "near the crest."

"When Jim was hit I immediately ran to his side," Frank had written on a piece of paper, dated June 12, 1995, next to the helmet. "I felt he had a chance to survive. He was immediately evacuated to our battalion aid station and thence on to regimental aid where I learned later he died. At the time he was hit I saved his helmet and later one of my men gave me the helmet of the Jap soldier who was probably the sniper. I saved both along with several personal items, intending to give them all to his parents when I returned after the war. I realized later such a gesture would not be appropriate and I never mentioned to his family I had his helmet."

Nearby was the Japanese soldier's helmet, possibly from the man who killed Bussard:

What was of most interest to me was a file that Haigler said was filled with correspondence spanning many years to family members of dozens of men killed on Okinawa. He said he wrote to Bussard's parents and sisters—and to Robert G. Owens, Herman Walter Mulligan's grandfather. I stammered, asked if he had those letters.

"Of course," Haigler said.

This is the first letter Haigler wrote to Owens on July 24, 1945:

Dear Mr. Owens,

I know that whatever I may say at this time will be of little consolation to you, but there is so much I want you to know about Herman and what he meant to those of us, the officers and men he served with. Throughout the Okinawan campaign, he was one of my finest and most dependable men. Due to casualties early in April Herman was made an acting Fire Team Leader, and his experience, good nature and leadership were continually a source of inspiration to the men underneath him.

Herman was severely wounded on May 30th while my company was engaged in mopping up pockets of enemy resistance located in caves on Nob Hill on the outskirts of Naha. On one particular instance, Herman threw a grenade into a cave filled with Japanese ammunition and was severely wounded in the resultant explosion. He was immediately rushed to our first aid station where our battalion surgeon administered to his wound. However, because of the nature of his injury Herman died shortly afterward very peacefully, having suffered very little. I might add that earlier in the campaign he was injured on the Northern end of Okinawa, but volunteered to return to his outfit, showing a courageous spirit and devotion to duty.

On the 1st of June Herman was buried at our division cemetery on Okinawa near Yontan Airfield. He was buried with military honors with our chaplain administering the final religious rights. I wish so much that you could have been there and seen where our boys lie—it is truly a beautiful and peaceful scene. Each grave is neatly outlined with white tile with a neat white cross at the head.

In the center of the cemetery is a beautiful little stone chapel which faces westward overlooking the East China Sea. Palm plants are growing at the ends of each row of crosses and in time grass will be sown over the entire area.

I could not ask for a finer example of a real marine than Pfc. Mulligan, and where he now is I know that he is happy and content, and we who are left behind will always hold him in our hearts. We must console ourselves with the thought that we must all die someday but how few of us are able to die for something—and Herman died for his country and a lasting peace on earth.

Owens replied,

```
9-30-45
                 Dear sir,
i am writing you about
my ward P.F.C. Herman Walter
mulligan jr. i Have Got
a letter saying That they
Have no Record where
He was Buried an i
would like very mutch
For you to let me Know
just How He was Killed
an where He was Hit at
an if He was Buried are
not You say in your
Letter That He was Buried
```

```
The First of June an i would
like to Know For sure
Hoping To Hear From you
soon
        Your Truly
        Robert. H. Owens
        4 Donwood ave
        West Greenville, S.C
```

On November 19, 1945, Haigler wrote to the quartermaster corps, which handled the remains of fallen soldiers, asking for an investigation. That same day, he wrote Owens, saying in part,

I am unable to account for the fact that at the time you inquired, there was no record of Pfc. Mulligan's burial. I naturally assumed that he was buried in our division cemetery and thus wrote you as I did. One reason which may explain it is this: at the time Herman was killed the 6th Marine Division together with the 1st Marine Division on the left flank were in the attack to break the Japanese Naha-Shuri Line on Okinawa. Due to bad weather and the shortage of roads the route of evacuation for wounded and killed casualties to rear area hospitals and the two marine division cemeteries was the same. In several instances marines of the 1st Division were buried by mistake in the 6th Division cemetery, and vice-versa. I believe that at the time we left Okinawa in July several of these errors were being corrected. Also, there is another good possibility, and that is that in some way the identification tags were lost [and] Pfc. Mulligan was buried temporarily as "Unknown" until the reports came back from Washington identifying his body by fingerprints which are taken in all cases prior to burial to lessen any possible error that might be made regarding identification. I feel certain that one of these errors has been made in Herman's case and I shall do all in my power to help you, Mr. Owens. I have written to Island Command, Okinawa in this regard and requested them to make a thorough check of both the 1st and 6th Marine Division cemeteries, and their records, to help clear up this matter. So, in this regard, you will either hear directly from them or I shall write you the results of this check should they not do so.

On December 28, 1945, Haigler got a terse reply from the quarter-master corps. "There is a possibility that the deceased may have been evacuated to another base before internment . . . he may be carried as 'unknown.'" It added that "tooth charts and fingerprints are being made at present."

Owens then wrote,

> Greenville S.C.
> march 16, 1949
>
> Dear Frank,
>
> Just a few lines to ask if you could get me any information concerning P.F.C. Herman mulligan, I received a telegram stating that he had been killed on Okinawa may 30, 1945. I received a letter from his captain say he had been buried in the sixth division grave yard. Then when I wrote for his body they knew nothing concerning his burial. If you know anything concerning him would you please write to me and let me know. I take it that you knew him by the Christmas card which you sent me, I suppose he told you about me I am his grandfather and I am blind, and sure would appreate any information you could give me.
>
>   thank you
>
> mr R. G. Owens
> 4 Donwood ave.
> Greenville
>   South Carolina
>
> P.S.
>
> Please let me know as soon as possible so I will know what to do.

Haigler responded on March 21, 1949. He urged that Owens keep on the officials to continue trying to solve the case. It was the last letter in the file.

My head reeled—even though there were no answers as to what happened to Mulligan's remains, what Haigler possessed went far beyond my wildest expectations. Haigler and I talked a lot that day, but the most interesting conversations were to come years after this first meeting.

When I later got the complete file on Mulligan's case from my Freedom of Information Act request, the long file concluded with this disposition:

DEPARTMENT OF THE ARMY
OFFICE OF THE QUARTERMASTER GENERAL
WASHINGTON 25, D. C.

IN REPLY REFER TO
QMGMN 293

DEC 22 1949

MEMORANDUM FOR: Commandant, U. S. Marine Corps
Washington 25, D. C.

SUBJECT: Non-Recoverable Remains of
MULLIGAN, Herman W. Jr. Pfc 496 478 USMCR

    1. The remains of the subject named decedent have been declared non-recoverable by Special Boards convened in the field and in the Office of The Quartermaster General.

    2. A complete record of the findings is on file in the Office of The Quartermaster General under 293 File of subject decedent.

W. E. MARSDEN
Lt. (jg) M3C, UON
Navy Liaison Officer
Memorial Division

Copies furnished:
  BuMed(Death Records)
  293 File

It seems that no one really tried to find Mulligan's remains.

My father repeatedly said, "I fucked up, but they made me sergeant anyway." He never specified how or what he goofed up. I speculated that perhaps my father, in a desperate attempt to stop the bleeding, had ripped the dog tags from Mulligan's neck. Or that, as squad leader, he ordered Mulligan to throw the grenade into the tomb. Or both.

It's possible that Mulligan's body was buried as an unknown in the division cemetery on the island; remains were later transferred to the National Memorial Cemetery of the Pacific, commonly known as the Punchbowl, on the island of Oahu in Hawaii. I needed to find his relatives to get DNA. I wanted to bring Mulligan home, or at least put a name on his stone. I made numerous phone calls to the Mulligans and Owens listed in the Greensville, South Carolina, area—all dead ends.

Amid this, my mother was diagnosed with a chordoma, a rare cancer of the spinal cord. She went in for a surgery. It arrested but didn't stop this aggressive affliction.

In 2002 when Mom was well enough to travel, it was time to deal with Dad's ashes. Throughout his life he talked about how he could be buried at Arlington National Cemetery because of the Purple Heart. And he said it would cost nothing—Dad always loved a bargain. I felt a hole in the earth at Arlington was the least the government could do. My sister and I made the arrangements.

Our family converged on Arlington that early fall day. I hadn't told my siblings or our mother much about Mulligan. I placed the picture of Dad and Mulligan on the box of ashes.

Photograph by Michael S. Williamson

I briefly told about what I'd learned. The soldiers who were present listened, rapt. I asked if we could bury the picture with my father. Dad got his twenty-one shots. The blasts were jarring. Then the flag that had covered the remains was presented to my mother, Joan; my brother, Darryl, is seated next to her.

Photograph by Michael S. Williamson

Mom grew sicker. Something about burying Dad sapped the energy for my search. Mostly, I needed to help my mother. When I told friends I was stopping, they were incredulous. Some urged me to write about what I'd learned. I had no interest. It wasn't about a story—it was all too personal.

I told myself that at least I'd discovered a whole lot more than I had known the day my father died. This was something. But I was burned out—it was all too depressing. I was done.

Reimmersion

In early 2008, when I had a month free of teaching duties, I spent that time with my mother in California. In a reversal from when I sat on a stool in the kitchen as a boy, Mom now watched me cook. One afternoon I came in from the backyard, where I was repairing a fence blown down by a storm, to make lunch. Mom, visibly troubled, was at the kitchen table.

"I wonder what my life would have been like if I'd never met your father," she announced. After Dad died in 2000 he came up commonly in conversation. As the years wore on, Mom talked about him less frequently.

Mom went on to describe how in 1949 she was walking a few blocks from her parents rented flat on West 11th Street on Cleveland's South Side. She was sixteen.

She passed 798 Starkweather Avenue, where Dad had lived drunk since coming home from Tsingtao, China, in January 1946. He was in the front yard. Mom described how he followed her for blocks, hitting on her. She spurned him. Somehow, he got her address. He kept after her in the coming weeks. It was a frontal assault of a romantic sort. Joan Kopfstein and Steve Maharidge were married on November 4, 1950.

As I placed sandwiches, soup, and chips on the table, Mom speculated about all that she might have done had she not met Steve: finishing haircutting school or even going to college. Mom bitterly launched into how my father was great the year they dated, but after they were married and she became pregnant with my sister, his raging fits emerged. "He kept that from me," she said as she gazed at the far wall.

Joan Maharidge, age 17.
Photograph by Steve Maharidge

There was an uncomfortably long pause.

"Ah, why bother thinking about it? You can't change the past."

It was the last time she ever talked about Dad with me. In the remaining year and few months of her life she never again uttered a word about him. After lunch I went to the garage workroom to get metal brackets to finish repairing the fence. I stared at the picture of my father and Herman Walter Mulligan, which still hung on the far-right cabinet door.

I was troubled by my mother's words.

When Dad was living his last days, in a turnaround, any time he started getting angry, he would quickly stop himself. "I don't want to do that to you," he said to us. Then he calmed. He faced death with, well—words fail me. I'm not sure they exist to describe what I mean. Heroism? Dignity? Grace? These overstate as well as understate. Looking back, if the mind has any control over these matters, he was choosing the fast way out. He let go. Perhaps this was because he had a lot of training for death. He had watched Mulligan die. He watched a lot of other men take final breaths. Perhaps he knew what he was doing.

Mom died in an opposite manner. She hung on and on. The home hospice nurse told me that in her nearly twenty years on the job she'd never seen anyone keep going in Mom's situation. One day, the nurse said the signs showed that Mom was beginning the death process and that it would be a matter of days; weeks later Mom remained alive. Mom didn't want to acknowledge death. She talked about getting better and vacuuming the house. It was a slow and horrible end.

In the aftermath of her death I did a lot of thinking about my parents' marriage. In contrast to Mom, my father expressed his love to the very end. Five days before he died, he walked to the kitchen under his own power with great difficulty. Mom was smoking a cigarette. She went through almost three packs per day; Dad had quit in the early 1980s. He'd smoked Lucky Strikes since the war—they were given free to soldiers. One day he decided to stop, and he never smoked again. No nicotine patches or gum. It was the tough marine in him. Now he studied the cigarette in Mom's hand. He had difficulty talking because his body was wasting away; unable to wear dentures, his mouth was all gums. He wanted her to quit so she could remain healthy after he was gone. "I want you to promise," he implored. "This is a deathbed wish."

"I can't," Mom said.

She smoked until the day she died.

Many relationships have an inequality of need, and I realized years later that my father required her in his life more than she had to have him in hers. She was his anchor after the war. In meeting her, he pulled out of his four-year drunken spiral. They had us kids. Dad tried to wrap himself in the cloak of normalcy as he fought the raging demons of brain injury from blast concussion and dark memories of the war; Mom (and we kids, to a degree) were a shield against submitting to those specters.

But Mom paid a high price for being that shield.

The only thing I knew for certain after Mom died is that I had to reimmerse myself in finding out what happened to my father on Guam and Okinawa. It was now more than just about locating Mulligan's remains. I would continue to pursue that, of course. But I would vastly expand my search. I needed to know everything I could about my father's role in that war. I realized that the war impacted my parents' marriage, my mother's life, how we kids grew up in their house—my life to this day.

Part Two

PLACES AND HISTORY

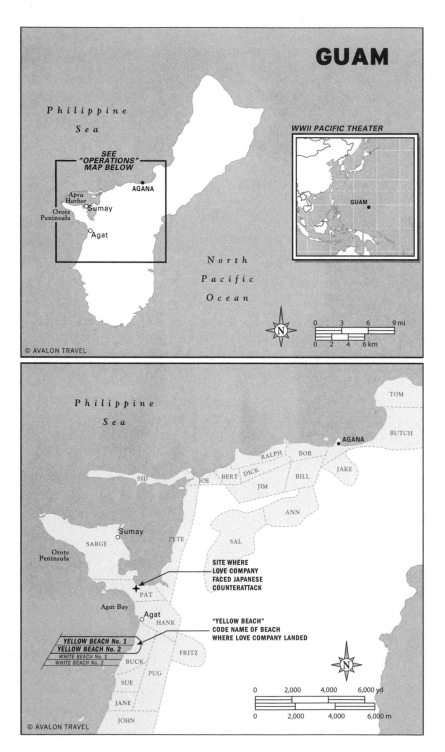

The men from L Company, 3rd Battalion, 22nd Marines were involved with two major battles—the retaking of Guam in 1944 and the Battle of Okinawa in 1945.

Guam

Two days after the attack on Pearl Harbor, on December 9, 1941, five thousand Japanese troops landed on Guam. This 210-square-mile island had been an American possession since being seized in 1898 following the Spanish-American War.

Senator Albert Beveridge, justifying the expansion into Asia and summing up America's imperialistic goals, said, "the trade of the world must and shall be ours. . . . This is the divine mission of America, and it holds for us the profit, all the glory, all the happiness possible to man." The Philippines was also taken: in response to a rebellion against American foreign rule that followed, US soldiers massacred Filipino citizens, executed prisoners, burned villages, used water torture, and tens of thousands died.

Republican Senator George Boutwell, an opponent of the war with Spain, had correctly predicted that Japan and the United States would someday end up at war because of American imperialism in the Pacific. The 1940s' war boiled down to one imperial power, in the wrong for occupying and killing other peoples, attacking another that was in the wrong for occupying and killing other peoples. Victimized were civilians—the Manchurians in China, the Chamorro on Guam, the nonviolent residents of Okinawa, and many others—not to mention all the millions of young men in Japan and America who had no interest in war.

The Japanese overwhelmed the 153 US marines based on the Orote Peninsula. At that early stage of the war the Imperial Japanese Army took prisoners; later, as things grew more desperate, they did not. Some 400 American POWs, both military and civilian, were put on a ship to Japan. Six American radiomen hid in the jungle. Five were captured and beheaded. The sole survivor was George R. Tweed, who was aided by the Artero family, indigenous Chamorro. The Arteros hid Tweed in a cave for nearly three years until the Americans came back.

The Japanese were cruel to the Chamorro. Pedro Artero, whose father sheltered Tweed, described to journalist Alice Brennan that each time he passed a Japanese-occupied building or a soldier, he had to bow and say *arigato gozaimus*, "thank you very much." If they were not obsequious, the Chamorro risked being beaten, cut with swords or bayonets. Once, Artero was forced to witness the beheading of a small boy. If he didn't watch, he was told he would be next. Some 340 Chamorro were killed, and many others were wounded during the Japanese occupation.

My father's part as a soldier in this collision of empires started on February 17, 1944, when he was in a few days of battle on the Enewetok atoll some seven hundred miles east of Guam. Love Company then went to Guadalcanal, below the equator in the South Pacific, which other marines had wrested away from the Japanese in 1942. "The Canal," as the island in the Solomon Islands was known to marines, was a staging area. In March 1944 the 22nd Marine Regiment joined the 4th Marine Regiment there to become the 1st Provisional Brigade.

The target was Guam, two thousand miles away, in the North Pacific, halfway between the Canal and the Japanese mainland.

The 1st Provisional Brigade was scheduled to land on Guam on June 15, 1944. But the American conquest of Saipan, just to the north, was more difficult than expected. The marines remained at sea for weeks.

The landing, code-named William Day, was reset for July 21. The navy had hammered the beaches with a stunning tonnage of artillery shells for ten days. Exactly at 6:30 a.m., Fenton Grahnert, Kennedy, Charles Lepant, my father, and others from Love Company scrambled down nets of the ship *San Francisco* into landing craft that raced them toward "Yellow Beach 1" on the western shore near the south end of the island. The boats had to cross five hundred yards of jagged coral reef—the widest of any yet encountered by the Americans. Boats were blown to bits by direct hits. Small arms fire raked others. Men drowned when they hit deep spots. Land mines awaited them on the beach.

Two hours after the landing of fifty-six thousand American soldiers that left hundreds of dead marines on the beaches, the 1st Provisional Brigade had moved one thousand feet inland. On the third day of battle Lieutenant Colonel Clair Shisler's 3rd Battalion—including Love Company—broke through Japanese strong points and advanced fast, right to the base of the Orote Peninsula.

The next morning the 3rd Battalion struggled forward. The Japanese were trapped on the peninsula; they hit the Americans hard through the day. There was no cover for the marines. The Japanese were in groves of coconut trees. At three that afternoon some Japanese troops tried to escape on barges, but they were turned back by American fighter planes and artillery, according to the *History of the Sixth Marine Division*, edited by Bevan G. Cass. "The exit by sea was emphatically slammed shut and now the Japs had only the choice of being annihilated on the peninsula or making a suicidal *banzai* charge. They chose the latter," the volume reported. The Japanese drank sake to get liquored up. The doomed soldiers were so near that the Americans could smell the booze in the air.

That night of July 24–25 was the worst of all of World War II for the men of my father's company, they told me. Love Company was dug in directly in front of some five hundred cornered Japanese. "Dug in" is a misnomer—hard coral rock lay just beneath the thin soil. It was difficult to make foxholes and when the Japanese tried to break through Love Company, the result was hand-to-hand combat. This is where my father screamed, "Shut the fuck up!" to marines crying for their mothers. The hard ground explained why he had stacked bodies around him for protection. My father said that before the attack he could see the Japanese just yards away, moving between the trunks of coconut trees.

"They were right there," my father said.

The first charge came at 10:30 p.m. When the soldiers shouted "*Banzai!*," which means "ten thousand years" in Japanese, they were invoking patriotism for the longevity of their nation and the emperor. The actual term for this suicidal combat is *kiri-komi*, "to cut into" and also "to attack." A second assault came at 11:55 p.m., a third at 1:30 a.m. Between midnight and 3 a.m. the US Navy fired twenty-six thousand shells that landed on the Japanese, according to the Marine Corps history book that quoted one marine who said, "Arms and legs flew like snowflakes."

During the third *kiri-komi*, the mortar shell blew up behind my father. He told me that some guys said it was a grenade, but he disputed that—he insisted it was a mortar round. "Despite every effort to evacuate the wounded, the job could not be completed until the following morning," the Marine Corps history book said. There were no attempts that night to do anything, the men of my father's company told me. It was sheer luck that my father didn't bleed to death before dawn.

There were 1,744 dead Americans and 5,308 wounded in the entire battle of Guam. In the initial combat 10,971 Japanese were killed. Over 6,000 holdouts hiding in the jungle were hunted down and slain in the weeks that followed. Some surrendered in the coming months, most later in 1945—the published numbers range from in the mid-400s to 1,200. The last known holdout was Corporal Shoichi Yokoi, who, on February 9, 1972, "surrendered to amazed Guamanians, some of whom hadn't even been born when he disappeared from civilization" nearly three decades earlier, wrote William Manchester in *Goodbye Darkness*.

It appears there were no prisoners taken in the battle and its imme-diate aftermath. The myth promulgated by the American military and accepted by many historians is that the Japanese fought to the death. It's true the *bushido* warrior code dictated this for a lot of them. But some Japanese had no interest in a code that told them to die—they surrendered. On Guam they were executed on orders from US officers. And few prisoners were taken on other islands.

"As early as April 1944," Japanese morale was in decline, wrote John W. Dower in *War Without Mercy: Race and Power in the Pacific War.* Dower cited a government report that the Japanese could be persuaded to surrender "if a serious effort were mounted to this end . . . but the low-ranking experts in Washington found it virtually impossible to convince commanders in the field of either the value of prisoners or the possibility of taking them in large numbers."

In other words, prisoners were being killed after surrendering; thus, remaining Japanese soldiers became more "fanatical," a justification by US war leaders for Americans having to fight all the way to Tokyo.

"The astonishing statistic that in the whole of the Pacific war, the largest number of Japanese POWs held by Americans at one time was a mere 5,424," according to historians Stephen E. Ambrose and Brian Loring Villa.

Okinawa

As soon as Steve Maharidge healed from his near-fatal wounds on Guam, he rejoined Love Company on Guadalcanal. The picture of him on the page following the map was taken sometime in 1944 in the jun-gle near the unit's encampment. In no other picture from the war does he look this vulnerable. He knew all too well from what he went through on Guam that the next battle would hold more horror. Where would that battle be? No one in the lower ranks knew.

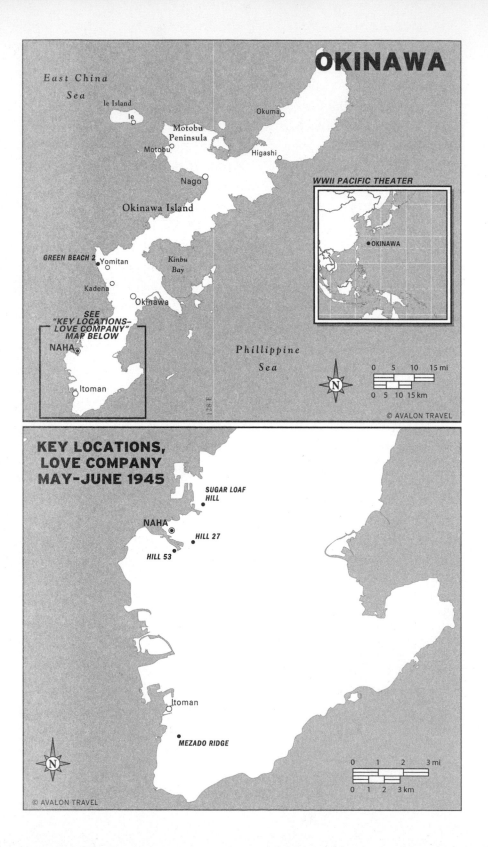

*Steve Maharidge, 1944, Guadalcanal,
near his unit's encampment*

The men trained, attacking mock villages. But many of them were engaged with equal energy in other activities such as making "raisin Jack," as the bootleg booze was called. My father said he drank a lot of raisin Jack and that he also spent time in the jungle with his B.A.R. He enjoyed opening up on full automatic at coconuts in the palm trees, watching them explode.

This is Steve Maharidge with his B.A.R., from an official group photo of Love Company's First Platoon on Guadalcanal, from Captain Frank Haigler's collection. The canvas sacks hanging over his shoulders were designed for B.A.R. ammunition.

The fate of Love Company and all the other marines on the Canal for the remainder of the war was being decided before they even left Guam; that meeting happened while the Guam operation was yet under way. But it was not a harmonious decision.

General Douglas MacArthur received a cryptic message that he was to attend a conference at Pearl Harbor. MacArthur wrote in his autobiography, *Reminiscences,* that he suspected it would be a meeting with President Franklin D. Roosevelt over war policy. It was the first and last time he was invited "to sit in on any of the big conferences."

The stakes were high. Because of intermilitary rivalry, the Pacific Theater was divided into two commands. Admiral Chester W. Nimitz was in charge of the Central Pacific, with the US Marines under his control. MacArthur, with the US Army, commanded the Southwest Pacific. Both Nimitz and MacArthur had moved their troops north toward Japan in 1943 and early 1944 via these two side-by-side routes.

But there was nothing similar about how Nimitz and MacArthur prosecuted the war.

Nimitz, through his theater commander Admiral Ernest J. King, went from island to island, employing beach landings like that on Guam, then fighting inch by inch to claim these specks of coral rock in the ocean. Major General Lemuel C. Shepherd, who was in charge of the Sixth Marine Division under Nimitz, called this approach the "corkscrew and blowtorch" method—marines threw grenades (the corkscrew) into each cave they came across and then incinerated (blowtorched) the Japanese inside with napalm flamethrowers. The Sixth Marine Division took virtually no prisoners, and the Japanese fought furiously.

MacArthur had a different approach. Why bother frontally assaulting every Japanese division he came across? He often said, "Hit 'em where they ain't."

MacArthur began at New Guinea, an island some 1,400 miles long. General Hisaichi Terauchi expected MacArthur to mimic Nimitz, "fighting for village after village," William Manchester wrote in *American Caesar: Douglas MacArthur, 1880–1964.* As a result, the Japanese moved their forces to the city of Wewak in the south. But MacArthur did the unexpected—in April 1944 he landed north of them up the coast in the city of Hollandia, today known as Jayapura, "a tremendous 400-mile leap . . . over two hundred miles behind the enemy supply depots," Manchester wrote. The Japanese in Wewak were cut off and rendered helpless.

MacArthur continued leapfrogging, gaining two thousand miles of ocean territory with fewer casualties than Nimitz. As MacArthur noted of the Borneo-Celebes area that was bypassed, "the Japanese Sixteenth, Nineteenth, and Thirty-Second Armies were helplessly cut off, and constituted no threat to an Allied drive toward Japan." In Rabaul alone, on the island of New Britain east of Papua New Guinea, one hundred thousand Japanese troops were orphaned.

This was the back story when MacArthur landed in Hawaii on July 26, 1944. MacArthur came with just a few minor aids. Nimitz had a large presence: top staff armed with maps and elaborate plans. Admiral King, who opposed MacArthur's methods of combat, had left just before his nemesis arrived. Nimitz "asked if I had been informed of the subject to be discussed, and if I had been asked to bring my important staff members. When I told him I had not, he seemed amazed and somewhat shocked."

Someone had sandbagged MacArthur, but the general didn't speculate other than to say that Nimitz was not the kind of guy to do such a thing. (Yet by all accounts Nimitz did not like MacArthur.) MacArthur wrote, "I began to realize I was to go it alone."

Nimitz argued for a continuation of the island-by-island advance on Japan. MacArthur wrote in *Reminiscences*,

I was in total disagreement with the proposed plan, not only on strategic but psychological grounds. Militarily, I felt that if I could secure the Philippines, it would enable us to clamp an air and naval blockade on the flow of all supplies from the south to Japan, and thus, by paralyzing her industries, force her to early capitulation. I argued against the naval concept of frontal assault against the strongly held island positions of Iwo Jima or Okinawa. In my argument, I stressed that our losses would be far too heavy to justify the benefits to be gained by seizing these outposts. They were not essential to the enemy's defeat, and by cutting them off from supplies, they could be easily reduced and their effectiveness completely neutralized with negligible loss to ourselves. They were not in themselves possessed of sufficient resources to act as main bases in our advance.

In the next day's meeting MacArthur wrote that he told Roosevelt, "The days of the frontal attack should be over. Modern infantry weapons are too deadly, and frontal assault is only for mediocre commanders. Good commanders do not turn in heavy losses."

MacArthur was ignored save for his being allowed to retake the Philippines. The Tenth Army and the marines, under the navy command of Nimitz, went forward with planning Operation Iceberg—the code name for the conquest of Okinawa, using the "corkscrew and blowtorch" method.

The prognosis didn't look good based on what happened on Iwo Jima in February and March 1945. Nimitz and other navy brass thought the eight-square-mile volcanic spit, where the Japanese were entrenched in caves, would be neutralized by the 21,926 navy shells that pounded the island on top of six weeks of aerial bombing. Manchester wrote in *Goodbye Darkness* that this "merely rearranged the volcanic ash overhead and gave the invaders dangerous illusions of easy pickings." Navy leaders believed that the island would be taken in a matter of days. After weeks of battle, there were 6,821 American dead and 21,000 Japanese corpses.

A similar defense awaited the Americans on Okinawa, one thousand miles southwest of Tokyo.

The island was a backwater ignored by the Japanese military. But after suffering crippling losses to the United States, the Imperial General Headquarters began arming the island in March 1944. The 32nd Army would defend it. High school boys were conscripted to build airfields and tunnels. The Japanese Naval Headquarters of Admiral Minoru Ota had more than fifteen hundred feet of tunnels on multiple levels. The island's many natural caves offered other defense; some of them were expanded.

The 32nd Army wouldn't waste manpower like the Japanese military had done on Guam. It would allow the Americans to land uncontested so they could be hit at the "Shuri Line," a system of fortified positions in the south, near Naha, the island's largest city.

American intelligence didn't see this. The Joint Intelligence Center, Pacific Ocean Areas, JICPOA, had an inexplicable transfer of experienced photo analysts out of the unit just before the Battle of Iwo Jima; they were weirdly replaced with greenhorns, Jeffrey M. Moore wrote in *Spies for Nimitz: Joint Military Intelligence in the Pacific War*. Nimitz had no idea that Iwo Jima had been transformed into a cave-infested defense system. In addition, the US Navy had also grown cocky about believing that it could take any island it wanted.

On Okinawa JICPOA predicted a beach defense, and so the Navy "wasted its massive preliminary bombardment on empty shores," Moore wrote.

The Japanese tricked the Americans by moving forces to the secret inland defensive caves. "JICPOA did not notice that the Japanese had changed the game plan in the bottom of the ninth, so to speak, and so the U.S. victory on Okinawa was costly," Moore wrote. He further stated,

> The fact the JICPOA lost all of its experienced photo analysts to an administrative rotation policy . . . during the Iwo Jima intelligence operation is preposterous. The fact that this same problem plagued the Okinawa operation borders on criminal negligence. Planners . . . knew the effects it had had on Iwo Jima, so why did they allow it to happen again? U.S. lives were at stake. The mission was at stake. Yet nothing was done to correct the problem. . . . In any event, whether because of a Navy administrative deficiency or JICPOA's inability to rectify it, this particular facet of Operation Iceberg represents an intelligence failure.

The objective for the 32nd Army wasn't victory. It would be to slow the Americans down before the Japanese soldiers were exterminated.

Without resupply, impossible because the Americans had destroyed so many Japanese ships, the 32nd Army was doomed. The view of the military leaders in mainland Japan was that each day Okinawa held out meant one more day of preparation for an invasion of the home islands.

The gentle Okinawans "had no chance to resist the hostilities into which Japan was pushing and dragging them," wrote George Feifer in *Tennozan: The Battle of Okinawa and the Atomic Bomb*. Initially, the commander of the 32nd Army was General Masao Watanabe, who arrived March 29, 1944. He told islanders that civilians would die along with soldiers. "An enemy landing here means just three things," he informed civic leaders, according to Feifer. "Death for you, death for me, death for all of us. Have you seen the tanks and anti-aircraft guns we've got on this rock pile? Just so much junk." Watanabe, who may have suffered a nervous breakdown, was relieved of duty after four months. Replacing him was General Mitsuru Ushijima.

By late 1944 American forces cut Okinawa off by sea from mainland Japan. On October 10, 1944, American fighter planes dropped six hundred tons of bombs along with thousands of rockets. They hit military targets but also used incendiary bombs on Naha, with its sixty-five thousand civilians. Because of strong winds, fires raged, and it's estimated that in that raid alone between 80 and 90 percent of Naha was left in ashes. Some believe that at least one thousand civilians were killed, but no one really knows for sure.

Operation Iceberg began on the morning of April 1, 1945, when 1,457 Allied ships appeared on the horizon in the East China Sea to deposit 182,112 US soldiers on Okinawa to battle some 110,000 troops of the Imperial Japanese Army.

An invading force in such a situation "needs at least a three-to-one ratio to successfully defeat an entrenched defender," Moore wrote in *Spies for Nimitz*. "During the Pacific War, U.S. Navy expeditionary forces preferred a four-to-one ratio. In today's U.S. Marine Corps, operations personnel prefer a six-to-one advantage for amphibious assaults."

It wasn't even two-to-one on Okinawa. JICPOA had predicted there were seventy-five thousand Japanese soldiers.

"If the intelligence picture had been more accurate, planners might have proposed landing ground forces to the rear or flanks of Japanese lines," Moore wrote. "They might even have fortified the northern half of the island and waited for the Japanese to attack. Certainly, they would have used more troops."

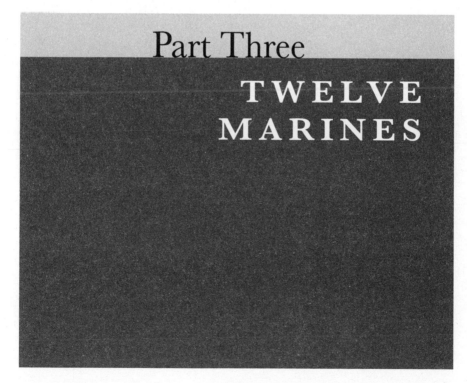

Part Three

TWELVE MARINES

Charles Lepant, in uniform

Charles Lepant in 2011

"Marines, You Die!": Lepant

As the *San Francisco* steamed toward Guam for the July 21, 1944, landing, Charles Lepant listened to Lieutenant Colonel Clair Shisler brief L Company.

"He had a big map, a topographical map, down in the mess hall," Lepant recalled six decades later. "I remember to this day, the last thing he said was, 'Don't be taken prisoner. And I don't want any prisoners.' Those were his exact words."

Lepant, eighteen, was from Ross Township, just north of Pittsburgh. He joined the Marines before finishing high school. His oldest brother, Fred, was in the Army Air Corps. Another brother, Ken, was in the Navy on the battleship *Nevada*. Lepant chose the Marines to be different.

"I thought it was a glorious thing, and I think it was a mistake for me. I didn't even know what the Marine Corps was then."

He trained at Parris Island, South Carolina. When sent to the Pacific, he was an ammunition man on a five-person team that operated a .30 caliber air-cooled machine gun. His buddy, S. J. Carpenter, convinced a sergeant to transfer Lepant into the mortar company because guys on the machine guns were the first the enemy targeted. And mortarmen were normally behind riflemen, theoretically a safer position. But that wouldn't help him on Guam, where he'd hit the beach and be right up front with the riflemen. And he was destined to be struck by bullets from a Nambu machine gun on Okinawa's Motobu Peninsula. His rear end was literally shot off, the exit wound on his thigh looking as if a fistful of muscle was scooped out—he showed me the cavity of missing flesh.

Yet Lepant said the night of July 25, 1944, on Guam was far more terrifying.

"Guam, to me, it was the worst, honest. It still affects me. It's hard to think that your dad was in that. Whatever he said, it's true," Lepant told me. "That was the most horrible night, that night of the counterattack."

I visited Lepant in Pittsburgh three times. We talked at least six hours on each occasion. He always went on about that night in cinematic detail. Sometimes he trembled. He didn't always use complete sentences; often with the worst stuff, he simply stopped mid-story. I always left drained.

Over and over Lepant not only spoke about the noise; he imitated it: the sound of the sixteen-inch shells, five feet long and heavy as Volkswagen Beetles hurtling overhead; explosion after explosion; bullets whizzing past; at night, the "*POW!*" of illumination flares going off followed by a "*PAHHHHHHHHH!*" as they glowed, falling like dripping molten wax.

When Love Company's members clambered down nets strung from the *San Francisco,* they were in the first wave to hit the beach at the town of Agat in landing boats with the ramps that came down in front. "The bombardment from the ships was going over, we were going right under them," Lepant said. "They were—

"*Boom-boom-boom-boom-boom-boom-boom-boom-boom.* There's so much noise. It's *boom-boom-boom*—

"You can hear the sixteens one after another. Them landings is what, oh, that's what affected you—

"Them landings. I hear them artilleries. That haunts me. The planes were coming over and strafing. I thought they were shooting at us. But it was the casings falling down on us. As we were approaching the beach, over on my right, the Japanese hit a landing craft. When we landed, there was a rise right at the beach that we all went up against. We laid there waiting. Nobody would move. We had a Sergeant [Johnny C.] Jones. Sergeant Jones, a few minutes later, said, 'Let's go!' Everybody got up and moved in over the top. You didn't get time to think on the landing. You just reacted. We were brainwashed from boot camp. That's why you had close order drill. 'Right-left-rear-huh-hee-huh. You didn't hesitate. And when someone told you 'go,' you went.

"I went about from here maybe to the door or a little bit farther," he said of the fifteen feet to the kitchen door in his daughter's house where we met. "I was running and something caught my eye. A sparkle. Here, a guy got hit, and he had a ring on and the sunshine glowed off his ring as I ran by. He was dead. And Sergeant Jones—I slowed down for a minute—he said, 'Move!' I'll never forget to this day that ring shining in the sun. I don't know who he was.

"Moving up to the peninsula, you was so tired. I mean, you didn't hardly sleep. Foxholes? You know what would happen? We'd dig a hole. They'd say, 'We're moving up thirty yards.' You'd do that three times. The guy behind would say, 'I've got a good hole here.' So you got to the point that you jeopardized your own self by not digging deep and piling stuff up in front because they would say a few minutes later, 'Move up thirty.' We got to the point, 'Why dig a hole?'"

A few days later they moved into position at the base of the Orote Peninsula, some thirty yards in front of a grove of coconut trees. To the right was a mangrove swamp. In front amid the trees were the hundreds of trapped Japanese soldiers. Lepant and Carpenter dug into the hard, shallow soil, beneath which was coral rock. Even if they wanted to, there was no making a good foxhole.

"They couldn't get out," Lepant said of the Japanese. "They started at about ten o'clock at night, screaming, the Japanese. You'd be laying there real quiet and you'd hear—I try to mimic it:

"MARINES, YOU DIE!"

Lepant shouted in a high and eerie falsetto. It reminded me of the evening my father screamed at the men around him crying for their mothers: it seemed that Lepant was channeling the exact pitch. "That's the only thing they knew in English. There was gibber jabber and other screaming."

Marines dug V-shaped foxholes that kept the men apart except for the bottom so that they could tap each other's feet; one might live if a grenade landed in the other's hole. Carpenter was next to him, in the dark.

"Now, Guam wasn't cold, but he said to me, 'Are you cold?'

"I said, 'No. But I'm scared.'"

Though there were three waves of attack, in Lepant's recounting it all seemed like one constant assault. A half hour after the screaming started came the first one.

"You could hear the Japanese tanks, *GGNNNrrrrrr!* You know, the treads making the noise."

The Japanese stormed the marines. Lepant said the Japanese ran within two or three feet on either side of his foxhole.

"That close. But in something like that, you didn't show your hole. Unless they were coming right in at you, you didn't shoot."

He said of two Japanese soldiers, "I probably could've tripped them," by simply reaching out. "Then a few minutes later you heard a lot of gunfire right behind, *bang-bang-bang-bang-bang,*" he said of marines shooting the Japanese as they stumbled into foxholes to the rear.

"They were trying to break out. But they didn't. Did your dad ever tell you about the flares?"

Lepant and Carpenter were more or less helped by the illumination flares fired from navy ships. The light allowed them to see, and it also temporarily blinded the Japanese. But if they weren't careful, it also blinded them. He and Carpenter took turns opening and closing their eyes.

A flare would go, "*POW!*" Lepant said. "It made that weird sound, with stuff dripping off. And Carpenter would say, 'Your turn.' Or I'd say, 'My turn.' You both didn't want to have your eyes open because they were so bright. I'd keep my eyes closed, and he'd look to see if he could see anything moving when they were burning. As soon as they went out, you'd be blind. You couldn't see. You were vulnerable."

The enemy would freeze in the light. The man who left his eyes open would talk about landmarks such as tree stumps. Was that stump there before? Or was it a crouching Japanese soldier?

"You didn't know if it was a Jap, or you'd say, 'Oh, that was there.'"

In one of the attack waves a marine was hit in a foxhole behind and about five feet to the right of Lepant.

"His leg was blown off. The thing that haunts me today is he kept saying, 'I don't want to die.' Hearing that all night long. Nobody could get to him."

They'd been ordered to remain flat. Anything standing was considered Japanese. Marine machine gunners to the left and right created a crossfire. "Thank goodness for all the machine guns. They'd go *pow-pow-pow-pow* and you'd see the tracers going just above the ground level. Some of the Japanese were cut in half almost when they hit that."

In a quiet period Lepant heard rustling in the thick sword grass in front of his foxhole.

"Here was this Japanese, right there, crawling past. I lay with my carbine and I followed and followed him."

There was a knocking sound—the soldier was tapping a grenade against his helmet; that's how Japanese grenades were activated. Lepant braced for the grenade coming his way.

"We was always told: if the grenade comes in the hole, get out of the hole then get back in."

But the grenade never came. The explosion happened out front.

"He killed himself. All I heard after it went off was, '*Arghgggghh.*' After that it was over. It was quiet."

"**S**ergeant Jones come in the morning when it was safe. He said, 'What's this?'" Lepant said of the dead Japanese soldier in front. "I said, 'What?' He said, 'Here, take a look.'

"I got up and looked over the grass to where this Jap had crawled. I said, 'I didn't do it. He killed himself.'"

As for the marine with the missing leg, "He was still alive. In the morning a corpsman did get to him. He used a lot of sulfa. Below his knee got taken off."

Another soldier Lepant knew was wounded. "Rich Levine, they shot him in his privates. He lived, but he was killed on Okinawa." Richard C. Levine would die at Sugar Loaf Hill on May 16, 1945.

There were hundreds of bodies of Japanese dead and wounded scattered around and in front of Love Company.

"They were all over the place. And there's some nasty things too. The next morning, you know what they had to do? They—

"They shot every one of the Japs that was still alive. Actually shot them. That's what their orders was. Thank God I didn't get into it because I wasn't brought up that way. I saw some of them go over to them. I remember this one, this fella [Donald] Hanafee, he said, 'Look, this Jap is still alive.' He was wounded. He shot him again."

A few days later Lepant witnessed another prisoner who was captured.

"They brought him up to Colonel Shisler's tent. I wasn't far away. They said they found him where there was a dead marine with his privates laying on his chest. I don't think he did it, personally. And Colonel Shisler, I remember him saying to this day, 'What'd you bring him to me for? I don't want him.' He said, 'He's yours now. Take him. You go feed him and take care of him.'"

Lepant grew emotional as he told how other marines took the prisoner out to the road.

"They pushed him. He didn't want to go. They were trying to get him to run. It was an old dirt road, and they were all standing there. They were pushing him with their rifle butts, 'Go! Go!' Oh, he knew. He was begging and talking. They gave him a push and he finally went.

I guess five guys shot him. I couldn't watch as a human being. I did hear this *bang-bang-bang-bang*. They could've taken him prisoner, but they shot him. Still I think of it. He was somebody's father or husband. He wanted to live the same as I wanted to live."

However, some Japanese who "surrendered" were dangerous.

"I remember one day on Guam, we went in this building and they came out with a Japanese walking like this," Lepant said, holding up his forearms, but with his upper arms close to his body. "He had grenades under his armpits. After they shot him, the grenades, they went off.

"The flamethrowers was a horrible thing. They would shoot the flames, and you could hear them screaming inside, when the flames got inside the caves. You're bringing a lot of things back I remember."

Lepant would fight on Okinawa. Thirteen days after the landing—Friday the 13—Love Company was under heavy fire when a sergeant ordered him to run across a road to get mortar ammunition. The Japanese had the road sighted in from a Nambu machine gun nest. It was a death trap. Lepant knew it.

"At that time, you were disciplined to do that job and I didn't question it. I didn't say to the officer, 'Why?' You just did what you were told to do. Today, I would say, 'No, I'm staying down behind this wall.'"

He ran fast. But he couldn't run faster than bullets.

"I swore that a Jeep had hit me. I said, 'Gee!' I thought, 'You damn dumb driver.' I turned and there wasn't no Jeep there. It went through this leg, through the cheeks, and out the other cheek. I never seen blood coming out like that. It was just squirting in the air. A corpsman, I think his name was Valdez, he come running up and rolled me over on my back."

Lepant said he saw the dust in the road kicking up from bullets in a straight line toward them.

"And he went, 'Ughhhh.' The machine gun hit him. I thought, 'Oh my God.' Anybody was crossing that road was dead duck."

Lepant, in a letter home dated May 8, 1945, wrote,

*Somehow we put our arms around each other and crawled to a
ditch about 30 yards away where we were for the next 45 minutes.
One of the fellows from my company came by and put a dressing on
our wounds and sent for two stretchers. Doc was hit four times,
three in the leg and one in the side. I know that if he hadn't been
bending over me at that time they would have hit me.*

Both were evacuated. Valdez survived as well.

Lepant convalesced back on Guam for eight weeks. Then, unbelievably, he was ordered back into combat on June 20.

"The officer said, 'We got to send you back.' I went back up and joined my mortar section again. The lieutenant wanted to put me in as an ammunition man. And Carpenter said, 'No, he was a squad leader and that's what he's getting back.'

"I consider myself lucky. I wouldn't be here today if I hadn't gotten wounded when I did because the worst was still to come going south," he said of the battle at Sugar Loaf Hill and later at the very bottom of the island.

He was again wounded by a mortar fragment; he was treated by a corpsman in the field. Fortunately, it was the last few days of the battle.

Lepant and Love Company were sent to Tsingtao, China, in late 1945. A lot of guys went crazy drinking and having sex in the brothels. Buddies kept inviting him to join in, but he never went. He said the "women" were just fourteen-, fifteen-year-old girls.

"I was a young, innocent kid yet. I mean there was no sex in my life. I wasn't drinking because the way I was brought up." His mother was a very strict German. "My mother, as crude as she was, when I would go out on a date, she would say, 'Keep your pants zipped up.'"

In 1946, "When I came back, I almost cracked up. If I think into it deep enough, I can get tears come to my eyes thinking about it. Sometimes I think I was cheated in a way. I didn't even get to go to my high school graduation. I lost three good years of my life."

Lepant went into trade school to learn heavy equipment repair. He worked for Harrison Construction Company, building runways for the Pittsburgh International Airport. He also worked on the Pennsylvania Turnpike. On that job he met Vivian Clara Whited, a waitress at the Hotel Brunswick in Lancaster, Pennsylvania. He and Vivian married in 1951. She had two sons from a previous marriage. The couple had three children: Linda, born in 1952; Charlene, 1954; and Chuck, 1956.

In the 1950s Lepant also worked on building the Ohio Turnpike. Harrison Construction went bankrupt, and he lost his pension. He then went to the John F. Casey Construction Company. Among the jobs he did was the massive Kinzua Dam on the Allegheny River. But there were times when work was slow and he was on layoff—he remembers worrying about being able to make the $80 monthly mortgage. He never missed a payment. In those years, if he made $8,000 annually, it was a lot.

Vivian had mental health issues, probably early Alzheimer's, Charlene said. Vivian separated from Lepant and died at the age of sixty-six in 1989. In 2003 Lepant had open heart surgery.

"Right before he went in," Charlene said, "I remember him waking up and he was crying. He was going back and having flashbacks about the war."

Lepant said that right after he came home from the war he went to a fireworks display with a girlfriend; he ended up hiding beneath the bleachers.

"Fireworks—oh my goodness. I want to crawl into the ground," he said. "I have a hard time today with them, I'll be honest with you."

"It's worse when they're detonating at the end," Charlene said. "He has posttraumatic stress syndrome."

Fireworks make Lepant relive the flares from that night on Guam's Orote Peninsula, going *POW!* and then, "Dripping down and dripping down . . . and it'd come right by you—"

Lepant showed me a government documentary of the Guam landing. "If I put it on today, I start to shake," he'd told me earlier. The sound of explosions emanated from the television. It's possible that Lepant was both in the living room with me and on the screen: scenes showed soldiers moving through the jungle as a voiceover identified them as the

Lepant found this photo in Sumay

22nd Marines. But as with all the World War II footage, you can't really make out facial details. "I always wonder if one of those guys is me," Lepant said. Perhaps my father was also in the film. My gaze alternated between the screen and Lepant's eyes riveted on the set; he occasionally muttered, "Oh, my, oh, my."

On another visit we were as usual at the kitchen table of the home belonging to Charlene and her husband, Jeff Hildebrandt. Lepant brought out a picture that he found in a schoolhouse in the village of Sumay on Guam's Orote Peninsula, a few days after that horrible night of July 25, 1944.

"I said, 'Oh, gee.' I picked it up and stuck it in my backpack."

"That's the Japanese that were killed," he said of the 140 or so men in the picture. Because of proximity, it's extremely likely that some or all of these men were in the grove of coconut trees that night of the counterattack.

Their deaths bothered Lepant. He noted that most of those guys probably didn't want to be in the war any more than he did. Plus, he was guided by faith: Lepant was raised Lutheran, as were his children. But in college Charlene became a born-again Christian. "I came home and shared this with my sister and dad, and both of them received Christ not soon after," she said. Jeff also believes. She said that all three of them feel their connection with God is more personal than going to church and saying prayers and more complex than what the term "born-again Christian" conjures to many people.

Due to his faith and his nature, Lepant wanted somehow to get the picture back to Japan. He wished the families of the men could see it.

"After the war they asked if we had anything to turn over so it could be given back. I should have turned it over."

I noted that the photograph probably would have ended up destroyed or buried in an archive. I said that by publishing it, perhaps

*Close up images of some of the Japanses soldiers
in the photo Lepant found*

descendants would contact me—I promised to send digital copies to anyone in Japan who inquired.

Jeff and I flatbed-scanned the tack-sharp image. Then we zoomed in on the computer. It was the first time Lepant had seen the faces close up. Lepant gazed deeply as Jeff used the mouse to move from man to man. Some soldiers looked mean and brutal. Others looked innocent and/or scared.

"They're all dead. None of them made it," Lepant said, shaking his head. "They got to have had a lot of guts. I have no ill feeling to this day. It would be nice to talk to a Japanese soldier who was in it, to see what their feelings were, if it was just a job, or if it actually was hate. I can't say in the war that I had the feeling of hate. I mean, I just wasn't brought up that way. They were doing what their officers told them to do, and I was doing what my officers told me to do."

I recalled a time at D & D Tool when representatives of Nachi, a tool company in Japan whose end mills my father sold for a good markup, were coming to visit our shop. I asked my father if it bothered him doing business with the Japanese. He shrugged his shoulders and said essentially the same thing Lepant later told me—that the Japanese were just doing what they were told, that it was nothing personal to him. Because of anti-Japanese resentment just three decades after the war, Nachi did not stamp the company's name deep into the metal but instead used an ink-like compound; my father and I did what the company apparently hoped we would do: we used a buffing wheel to remove the name before selling them.

Still, looking at that picture of Lepant's, I thought about how one of those guys possibly fired the mortar round that wounded my father. Yet I didn't feel hate either as I studied the faces.

"Any war is a waste of human life," Lepant said. "Did anybody win? I don't know if anybody won or not."

As I prepared to leave that evening, Lepant and I were alone in the kitchen. I expressed how grateful I was that he shared what happened and how it was helping me understand my father.

"It helps me too," he said. He grew emotional. We hugged. "I appreciate getting it out and that somebody is listening."

Fenton Grahnert in uniform

Fenton Grahnert in 2010

Coming Back from the Dead: Grahnert

Fenton "Gabby" Grahnert was born on a homestead outside of Rapid City, South Dakota, in a shack. "You wouldn't put pigeons in it now," Grahnert said. The family barely eked out a living during the Great Depression. They drove to Oregon in a Ford pickup truck in May 1938. They lived in Portland. His older brother, James Dewey Grahnert,

South Dakota, 1930s:
This picture of Grahnert was taken not
long before the family moved west.

joined the US Marines in 1939. Fenton looked up to him. James was captured in the early days of the war on the island of Corregidor, in Manila Harbor, the place where General Douglas MacArthur famously said, "I shall return."

When he was drafted, Grahnert was asked if wanted to be in the Navy or Army. He chose the Marines, though the corps officially didn't take draftees. (They actually did but didn't want to admit it.) "Oh, a tough guy," the draft board guy said.

"'No, my brother is in the Marines. He was captured in the Philippines. He's a prisoner of war,'" Grahnert recalled saying.

"'Okay, you got to go convince that tough old sergeant over there,'" the guy told him. If that sergeant appeared tough, it probably was an act: Grahnert was taken.

Guam was Grahnert's first big battle. The landing craft he was on got hung up on a reef. "We just turned around in circles." Japanese shells were landing all around them.

"Everybody got the hell off. There we were with all of our gear. The first guy out, he disappeared, went down in the water." The second guy went under too. "I said, 'Shit, I'm not about to go there.' I was the third guy off, and I couldn't swim. Still can't. I could see rocks sticking out of the water. I walked around a bomb crater. So everybody started following me."

Two days later the company moved toward the Orote Peninsula. Navy ships fired illumination flares.

"It was god-damned near dark. You could see everything that was moving with the flares. I was pretty close behind this tank. Well, there was a hole in the ground, and I tiptoed up to peek in, and there was a Jap, wearing one of those little bill caps. He shut his eyes. Well, he knew that I saw him, and so he come out of there with a grenade to throw at me. I wheeled around with my B.A.R. I fired three shots. I hit him here, here, and here," he said, pointing to his chin, nose, then forehead. "I just fired from my hip; how I hit him, I don't know. He fell back down in the hole and the grenade went off, blew up between his legs. First live Jap I'd seen, and I shot him. Looked him right in the face. First man I ever killed. I was shook up as hell and then we moved out. I couldn't think straight because I killed a man."

Inexplicably, the tanks turned around and drove back to the distant rear, out of firing range. Love Company was left facing the nearly five hundred trapped Japanese soldiers in that coconut grove dozens of feet away without tank support.

"We started digging in and we got down about four inches and hit solid coral. So we moved ahead." In the new spot they were able to dig just a little bit deeper. He was with Bill Corbitt, one of the guys who signed my father's flag.

"We got this damn deep," he said, showing about six inches. "Solid coral. We piled dirt and rocks and shit around the edge and used sticks of wood we could find. We had less than a foot in our foxhole. That ain't very deep."

Grahnert realized that out of dozens of foxholes, theirs was like being at the tip of a spear, closest to the Japanese. "Instead of moving back, we were ahead of the rest of the guys." He had a length of wire that he strung between small trees so that any advancing Japanese soldiers would run into it before hitting their foxhole. Most men behind lay on their bellies, "turtle-like," facing the enemy. He chose to lay on his back with his feet to the front, peering over the low foxhole edge, the B.A.R. at the ready across his torso.

Thus the night began. He could see Japanese soldiers moving in the coconut grove by the light of the flares. Marines in foxholes behind him began snoring. He nodded off—barely.

"I woke up and I see these damn Japs are hitting the wire, turning and going to the left. And I have one hand grenade and a B.A.R. What the hell do you do? Shoot some guy down there? If I did, the guy in front would shoot me."

He figured he'd throw the grenade and that would alert the men around him that the Japanese were beginning to attack.

"The grenade would make more noise than I could. You see the movies where the guys pull the pin on the grenade with their teeth? Shit! I couldn't get the damn pin out! I was pulling like a son of a bitch. I fought it, finally got it out. So I laid there for a few seconds trying to figure out what the hell I wanted to do. It takes five to seven seconds for it to go off. By the time it snaps, makes that noise," he said of letting the grip go to arm it, "them Japs were going to start shooting. I held it in my hand for three or four seconds, then I threw it out in front of them. And then all hell broke loose. All the goddamn shooting—

"There's a Jap right out in front of me. He had an automatic rifle, the kind the Japs had, a Nambu, he was going to shoot me in the head. I raised up my B.A.R. and shot him in the face. I put ten to twelve rounds in his head and front part of his body. And he fell over, with his ass lying across the back of my foxhole. Our artillery opened up. They couldn't tell where we were at. They had air bursts hitting in the trees above us—in fact, within ten feet of us.

"The Japanese had grenades they had to hit on their helmets to arm them. You could hear the 'tap, tap, tap' out there. All of a sudden, here they come. You could practically see them. One of them hit me on the leg. I tried to find it in the foxhole. I had some palm fronds that I'd laid down to make it a little softer from the rocks, and I couldn't find it. So I jumped out of my foxhole."

The grenade went off as he was leaping out.

"Corbitt, he didn't get nothing. I got a whole side full of shrapnel."

He rolled back in, picked up the B.A.R., but it wouldn't shoot. It was jammed with dirt from the grenade blast. He disassembled the weapon. He washed it with his canteen water. Luckily, the first wave attack had ceased, and he got it to function.

The other two attack waves came.

"If I go to war again, to hell with a B.A.R., a rifle. Give me a 12-gauge shotgun!" he exclaimed.

At dawn "My head was lying on a dead Jap's foot. There was 495 of them dead. It stunk. The wind was blowing at us. The smell—of death, the wounded, the guts, the blood, the sake, and the blowed-up vegetation. And the powder smoke. There was thirteen of us still standing out of the whole platoon. There were ten foxholes in a row—everybody was dead, shot through the head. They were sound asleep, snoring and shit. Bullets through the helmet. We went out walking through the field, checking out there. One guy, I looked at him, he didn't look like the rest of them, so I fired through his head, and he was still alive. He was laying there waiting for us to go so he could run inland."

"Was there a policy of not taking prisoners?" I asked.

"No, not really. We wasn't told not to. They didn't surrender."

Suddenly, the Japanese opened up with artillery. Grahnert said it was drilled into him never to leave his foxhole. "There's a million-to-one chance that a shell is going to hit me. So I jumped into my foxhole. But all these guys were running, heading back. Something told me to run. So I grabbed up my rifle and ran. I went back after the shelling stopped. Somebody had jumped in my foxhole. A shell had hit, and it blew him all to hell. Part of his guts was on my pack. And his head was lying there with his helmet on. You couldn't recognize that blowed-up head," he said of the dead American.

"Then the tanks come up and they drove through the middle of the dead people. Right over them," he said of the Japanese. "They were just things, I guess."

Grahnert wasn't treated for his shrapnel wounds. He moved on with the remaining company toward the tip of the Orote Peninsula. As they went around the mangrove swamp, the unit stopped. A guy went into the mangroves to urinate. "He never come back. Nobody ever saw him again," he said. The unit met resistance near the old prewar Marine barracks. Grahnert jumped behind a log. But it wasn't a log—it was metal. Japanese bullets pinged it. He realized that he was behind a torpedo. He ran.

When the fighting was over, Love Company was near Sumay, an Orote Peninsula town on Apra Harbor.

"They brought this Jap prisoner in. They said they found a marine down there dead with his privates cut off and that they caught this Jap there and he surrendered. And then [Colonel Clair] Shisler said, 'Why that dirty son of a bitch . . . take this son of a dog and dispose of him.' They made the Jap run down the road and *bam!* They shot him in the back and just killed him deader than hell. Well, Shisler got demoted for that. They come to find out that the guy that was mutilated, he had been hit with a grenade and his privates was blowed away rather than cut away."

I asked where Mulligan was at this point in the battle.

"A story about Mulligan, that dumb asshole. He goes down the hill right where we was dug in, by Sumay. He found a Japanese uniform in a building. And he put the damn thing on and come walking back up through us guys, he had the cap on. We goddamn near shot him. He damned near got killed. He was being smart. He was having a ball. He was laughing. He was half-Jew, dark complexed, and he looked just like a goddamn Jap."

After twenty days of battle on Guam, Love Company and the 22nd Marines were shipped back to Guadalcanal. No one knew the next target, but they trained for it from late August into early 1945. In this period Mulligan told Grahnert that he was a hemophiliac.

"I said, 'Hell, I'm going to tell the doctor.'

"He said, 'No, goddamn you, you ain't gonna tell the doctor on me. I don't want anybody calling me a damn chickenshit. Getting out of the service because I'm a bleeder. To hell with it. Keep your damn mouth shut.'

"I said, 'You're going to die. You got insurance?'"

"He said, 'Hell no, my folks are rich. They don't need no damn money. I'll keep the money for myself.'"

Mulligan's father was not on the scene, his mother was dead, and his grandfather was clearly poor, so he was blowing smoke about his family's money.

For marines who wanted the insurance, it cost some ten dollars a month out of their fifty-dollar pay, Grahnert said. It would pay out $10,000 on death.

"It was hot. We all wore shorts. One old sergeant said, 'Boy, I'd like to take him to bed—he's got the prettiest legs,'" Grahnert said of Mulligan. "He was always a neat-looking guy. Your picture shows it. Your dad's pants looked wrinkled, Mulligan's didn't. His clothes always looked like they come from the god-damned cleaning shop."

On March 15, 1945, Love Company set sail on the *USS Sumter.* On March 21 the unit arrived in the protective waters of the Ulithi Atoll in the Caroline Islands, a major navy staging area that was so secret the

American public was largely unaware of its role in the war. They transferred to an LST ship simply named 951, and on March 25 they sailed toward Okinawa. One morning they were fed steak and eggs for breakfast. That meant a bad day lay ahead.

That day was April 1. Huge casualties were expected on that landing, which oddly was both Easter Sunday and April Fool's Day. But when Love Company went in on the landing zone code-named Green Beach 2, there was no resistance. Jokes were made about the Japanese playing an April Fool's prank. The Sixth Marine Division went up a hill and rapidly overran the Yontan Airfield. Love Company went across the island, came back to the landing side, then moved north. There were a significant number of enemy soldiers on the Motobu Peninsula. The company engaged them for a few days. Then the men moved north.

Love Company came to a broad bay with deep blue water and a beach with snow-white sand on the China Sea. The First Platoon was told to remain here. Miles of communication wire had been strung. There was a relay station where these wires came together and the signal was given a power boost. It was the platoon's job to guard this station in Okuma, though they called it Hichi, a village some two kilometers inland. Hichi may have been used as a reference point because Okuma had been flattened by US warships. It appeared there were no Japanese soldiers for miles around. The war was distant.

Captain Frank Haigler from Headquarters Company sent a few men to climb a conical hill rising south of the Okuma River estuary. From there the men reported that they could see the very northern tip of the island twelve and a half miles away.

Grahnert and a few guys wanted to eat fish, so they lobbed grenades, manufactured by the DuPont Corporation, into pools of the reef—they called the grenades "DuPont spinners." Most of the dead fish were carried away by the current: one hundred decomposing fish washed up a day later at the north end of the long crescent beach. But they were able to collect a few and fry them on a huge saw blade from a lumber mill, set over a campfire.

Grahnert was on guard duty one night at the relay station near the Okuma River. With him was a guy they called "Pop" because at forty-two, he was the oldest guy in the outfit. Also present was Kennedy.

"He had money to loan you," Grahnert said of Kennedy. "If you needed money, he had it. He was a smartass—you know the type."

They were dug in on a hill above a dam with a waterwheel and a grinder that removed the hulls from rice. It was a dark night. Kennedy had a .38 caliber pistol on his hip in addition to carrying his M-1 rifle. Pop had a B.A.R.

"A group of people walked up the road in front of us, along the estuary on the bay there," Grahnert said. "We had orders to shoot anything that moved—that didn't stop. Pop hollered, 'Halt!' They didn't stop. He hollered again. And they didn't stop. So he fired a burst at them and knocked them all down. A little baby started crying. So you knew this wasn't a Jap. It was a civilian.

"Pop wouldn't go down there. He was so upset. He was the nicest old man you ever saw. He had a wife and three or four kids at home. So I went down there. I was the first guy there. There were two little babies. One was strapped on the man's back and one was strapped on the woman's back. The man and woman were both dead. One baby had his hand blown off. The other one had a wound on her.

"I untied them off the mother and dad's back I was going to take them up to the corpsmen. I was married and had a baby. Had a girl, two years old—"

Kennedy materialized out of the dark.

"'Hell, we ain't gonna take these goddamn Japs up there,' Kennedy said," Grahnert recalled. In an allusion to the Japanese being an enemy for a generation to come, Kennedy added, "'They'll be killing our kids.'"

"I said, 'What are you going to do with them?'"

"He said, 'We'll shoot them.'"

"I said, 'Who in the hell is going to shoot these little babies?'"

"'Oh, by God, I will,'" Kennedy replied.

"I said, 'Well, by God, no you won't.'"

"He said, 'By God, I'll shoot you. You're not taking these Jap bastards up there.'

"And he pulled that little pistol and shot the babies. Shit. Shot them
in cold blood. One he had to shoot twice." Grahnert, telling this sixty-
five years later, paused as his eyes welled with tears. "He's a real bastard.
Cold-blooded murderer."

Softly, he said, "I couldn't do that."

"'If you say anything, I'll shoot you,'" he recalled Kennedy saying. "I
was scared. Shit, I figured he was going to shoot me. So I just shut my
mouth and didn't say nothing. And that's bothered me ever since."

A few days later Kennedy came to Grahnert and announced that he
and three to five other guys were going up a nearby hill to "screw this
gal," a teenage Okinawan girl who was living up there with her
mother.

"'Hell no,'" Grahnert replied in disgust. "'I ain't going up there!' I
wasn't going to do anything like that."

Among this group was Pio "Maggie" Magliaro, Kennedy, and another man.

"So these assholes went up there," Grahnert continued. "They were
gone a couple of hours. This Kennedy, he had that pistol. She grabbed
his pistol. She put it up to her head and pulled the trigger—wanted to
kill herself rather than be raped by them guys. He had it unloaded. She
bit the one guy in the arm. They put the mother in a hole in the
ground and covered her up so she couldn't do nothing to them. They
told me this."

The mother and girl went to the US 10th Army's Military Police.
The 10th had command of the ground operation under General Simon
Bolivar Buckner Jr.

"Here come the MPs. And there was the woman and all of our officers. They lined us all up. She went down the line and she pointed to
two of them. But she didn't recognize the other two of them. Magliaro,
he had a big beard and he had cut his beard off and cut his hair.

"Kennedy, she picked him out, and the other guy too. They said,
'We weren't doing nothing. We just sat there, we were guarding that relay station.' Our officer checked them, checked the woman, and said

there was no evidence of rape. The officer knew that they would hang if they were caught for rape. She was an Okinawan woman, a native. He didn't want to turn his own men in."

But it wasn't over. The 10th Army military police would continue to investigate. "Island command wouldn't take the officer's word for it," Grahnert said.

After the rape the company went south. It met heavy combat at Sugar Loaf Hill just north of Naha town.

"It started getting dark. That's when they started shelling the hill I was on. I could see the artillery shells hitting down the hill from me. The next one would be closer. They kept walking them up the hill, and the last one hit, she went off, and I looked out of my foxhole, and there was a hole five feet deep. I could spit in it from my foxhole. I was right on top of that hill, in what was left of a little tomb. You could feel the shells go over the hill. *Shooo! Shooo!* I could feel the wind from them going over my head, they were that close. They was hot. They just shelled the hell out of us. My foxhole, especially. So—I kind of went off the deep end a little bit, from being shelled. The next day they sent me to the hospital with combat fatigue, from the shelling that night."

Kennedy was on this hill as well that night of May 16. Yet the investigation into the rape by the 10th Army Island Command continued. Word was that the two men identified by the woman were going to be brought up on charges of rape. Apparently, she would have to once again identify them. Grahnert said Lieutenant Carl Massey went to Kennedy and the other one to warn them.

"Here come Lieutenant Massey," Grahnert said, "he said, 'You two guys have got to get the hell off the island, because the division is coming after your ass and is going to hang you for rape.' Rape is a hanging offense in the military."

Both Kennedy and the other man shot themselves in the leg, Grahnert said, so they could be sent off the island. The official muster rolls show both men wounded on May 18. In almost every other case the muster roll noted the nature of the injury. But with those two, there was no notation.

"He broke his damn leg," Grahnert said of Kennedy's accomplice. "Shot it all to hell. He missed. He was yelling and hollering and the corpsman run out there to help him. He [the corpsman] said, 'You damn fool, you got to do it right.'"

Man after man was falling, dead or wounded. By the time Love Company got to the southern tip of the island below the city of Naha, there were few original guys left who had landed on Okinawa back in April.

On June 13 Grahnert and Pio Magliaro were fighting together on Hill 53, the Japanese Naval Headquarters. They were under fire. Grahnert jumped behind a tree. "And a bullet went clear through the pine tree, right above my head." The bullets were coming from a cave.

"They got a bazooka and fired into that hole. A Jap came out of the cave and threw a grenade at us. The only hole we could find to jump into was a Jap outhouse, two logs you sat across, ankle deep with shit. Maggie [Magliaro] said, 'Oh god, what did we jump into?' That's where he got hit. The Jap snuck up behind him and shot him. It went through his arm, and cut his back in two. So I run down and grabbed him and pulled him down the road so they couldn't finish him off. That maybe killed him. I don't know because his spine was severed. I didn't like him at first because he was a big-mouthed Italian. I got to where I liked him.

"The day I got wounded, the sixteenth of June, there were only two of us left in the platoon that I knew. We had so many replacements. I didn't know any of them."

Grahnert was on the Mezado Ridge, Hill 69, the tallest hill around. He was near the top, shooting at Japanese soldiers down in a village. Nearby, he saw a guy he vaguely knew, named Alabam' who was in K Company, on Love Company's left flank.

"He was the only one there. K Company got the order to move out and around the hill, and he didn't get the word. I heard a bullet hit him, *whap!* And there he was laying on his back up there hollering, 'Hey, buddy, come and help me!' Good kid, younger than I was. So I ran up there. I yelled for the corpsman. He got shot in the back of the neck, and it paralyzed him. The corpsman put a bandage on it and he said, 'Well, you stay here with him, I'll go get a stretcher.'

"So I was sitting there, and the first thing I knew a bullet hit my pack and it almost knocked me down. I seen rags and shit flying out of my pack from where the bullet went through it. Then another bullet went through my pack. Two Japs stood behind a big square rock. I fired at them two, and they ducked down behind the rock. They threw a grenade at us. It landed by Alabam'. I ran to Alabam', pulled him away from the grenade, and laid there with him 'til it went off, and then I run back down to where I was at, waited for those guys to stand up to look and see if that grenade got either one of us.

"I was in kneeling position, had my rifle up, and I'm ready to pull the trigger. They stood up, and I pulled the trigger. And at that same time a [different] guy over there started shooting at me. The bullet went in near the left side of my nose and went out the side of my right ear. I fell over on the ground, on all fours, and I was wheezing. I couldn't breathe. The blood was flying out of me and I thought, 'Jesus Christ, I've got to do something because I'm going to die here. They're going to kill me for sure.' So I jumped up and grabbed my rifle and emptied it. And then I run up to Alabam' . . . I helped him to his feet. I couldn't have left him lying there."

Somehow, Grahnert lifted the wounded Alabam' and carried him.

"I said, 'Let's get the fuck out of here!' I run at least one hundred yards toward the rest of L Company."

Sergeant Bernard Blair saw him coming and ran to help.

"He chased me, tried to catch me, Sergeant Blair. He was just ready to grab me when he got hit in the back. I heard the bullet hit him with a *whack!*

"He said, 'Shit! I'm hit too!' And away he went. He ran off. I don't know where he went to. I run until I couldn't see. Everything turned black.

"The corpsman told me that if he'd have seen me lying up there on the hillside unconscious, 'I wouldn't have even took your pulse.' The whole side of my head was blowed off. They didn't have no stretchers. They found a couple of poles and wrapped a poncho around the poles and taped it. They put me in that makeshift stretcher and four, six guys started off across the rice paddies."

The men had to set Grahnert down a few times when they came under fire. They got him to a Sherman tank, which took him to a Jeep.

"The Jeep took me down the road. They landed a Piper Cub and put me on the airplane and flew me back. They got me out of the airplane, and they put me in an army ambulance, and I remember cussing them out, 'What in the hell are you putting me in a goddamn army ambulance for? Put me in a navy ambulance.' The driver said, 'You goddamn crazy marines. Damn near dead and bitching about what kind of an ambulance I'm going in.'

"In the hospital I asked the doctor, 'What in the fuck do you think you're doing?' He said, 'Well, I'm trying to make it quit hurting.'

"I said, 'Well you're doing a piss-poor job of it. It hurts like hell.' I'd like to see the doctor that operated on me. He did a wonderful job, who-in-the-hell-ever he was."

The bullet took some of Grahnert's teeth out. There was no brain damage. He would never again have feeling in much of his face. He spent much of his long recovery in a hospital back on Guam.

"I went to the theater there, and I saw old Blair, Sergeant Blair, sitting on a log, waiting for the show to start. And I say, 'Blair, hi! How you doing?'

"And he said, 'Get the hell away from me! You're dead! You can't be here! I told everybody you died. Got the whole damned side of your head blown off!'

"He wouldn't touch me. Wouldn't shake hands with me or nothing."

A biting memory of the war is the loss of his brother, James Dewey Grahnert. They had been inseparable growing up. After being captured, James and 345 other American prisoners were taken to Palawan

Island in the Philippines as forced labor to build an airfield. As it became clear that MacArthur's troops were closing in, on December 14, 1944, James and 149 other American POWs were told to go into underground, log-walled bunkers built for air raids. Japanese soldiers poured barrels of gasoline into them and set the Americans on fire. James died in the inferno.

The US military didn't tell the Grahnert family this until 1948.

Grahnert was married to Marjorie Arlene French Grahnert. Their daughter was Linda, and the couple had two sons, Jim and Wesley. On my third visit to Vancouver, Washington, to meet with Grahnert, Jim confided to me his amazement that his father worked in a slaughterhouse most of his life, in blood up to his ankles.

"I worked with him when I was sixteen," Jim said. "On hog day my job was to go into the pen of hogs, shackle them on the rear hooves, and this thing would haul them up in the air. And Dad would slit their throats and they'd bleed out—blood and gore."

To Jim, it seemed a grim reminder of what his father had been through in the war. That hard work took a toll, and Grahnert had to retire in 1974 on disability following a severe injury.

Grahnert loved taking his family on trips through the American West. They collected fossils and rocks. He also got into wood carving. He made walking sticks with snakes carved into their length, with their heads and beady eyes near the handles; a stubborn mule tethered to a rope. He also painted.

Over the course of three visits spanning two years along with many phone conversations, a curious thing happened: Grahnert's memory grew sharper. In ever-greater detail he told me about incidents confirmed by other guys in the company, including names. His stories matched theirs perfectly. I was surprised until I witnessed this happening with other guys; it seemed for a few, as they neared the ends of their lives, the movie that was the war played more vividly in their heads.

On my last visit Grahnert told me he'd started dreaming about the war all the time. This bothered me. I worried that my questions were causing trauma. I confided my concern to Jim, away from his father.

"Oh, it's good!" Jim assured me. He felt it was therapeutic that his father was talking. "It was all bottled up and hidden. And now it's kind of out."

Jim said his father only really started talking about the war some ten years earlier, about the time my own father died.

"So the stuff I've been hearing, you never heard it as a kid?" I asked.

"Oh, no, never. The detail is so much better now than I've ever heard. Since your first visit his memory has been stirred. He remembers these places, and that's why he's getting more flashbacks of it."

I mentioned that I believed the blast concussions that my father went through may have caused traumatic brain injury. I related some of my father's behavior when I was a child.

"Sharp noises bother my dad," said Jim. "Dropping something bothers Dad if he doesn't see it. Something startles him—he doesn't like it. I believe that's shell shock."

Jim and I went back inside the modest house.

"Do you remember Captain Haigler?" I asked Grahnert.

"Yeah. I don't like him. That son of a bitch. That rotten son of a bitch." And that was all he would say.

I asked about his lingering health problems. After spending a year in the hospital recovering, Grahnert had frequent nosebleeds. Those tapered off. But from the night of the counterattack on Guam, he was still peppered with shrapnel. He showed black marks on his arm. On one visit Jim found his father using a knife in an attempt to dig shrapnel out of his chest. Jim insisted his father see a doctor.

"The doctor took an X-ray and he comes back and says, 'Well, which one of these do you want me to take out?'" Jim recalled the doctor saying.

"He said, 'You have forty of them in there,'" Grahnert added. "I've got a whole face full of them. It looks like the tail of a comet in an X-ray."

Despite being shot in the face on Okinawa, Grahnert said, "That night on Guam was a hundred times worse. There was nothing worse than that outside of Sugar Loaf."

I asked if he was unlucky or lucky—unlucky that he got hit, or lucky that he lived.

He answered fast. "I've thought about that a lot of times. Lucky. Because I make more money now than if I never had got hurt. I'm better off financially. That was my free money. My compensation."

"But you earned it!" I insisted of the monthly US veteran disability check.

Then, in the only anger I saw him exhibit about his military service, Grahnert said, "A cop shoots someone down here in Portland, they get one hundred goddamn psychiatrists on that. Everyone that's even heard the gunshot go off, they give them people treatment. So here, they turned us—eight and a half, nine million people loose from the military after World War II. Just kicked your ass out in the street with not a goddamn penny of psychiatry help or nothing. You was on your own."

"Do you feel resentful?" I asked.

"I don't feel bitter."

"Do you still hate the Japanese?"

"Yep. Only good one's a dead one."

"That's a pretty succinct answer," I said.

"Doesn't eat Japanese food," said Jim.

"We've got a checker at the Fred Meyer I go to," Grahnert said. "A little Japanese kid. And I'd just soon as shoot the fucker in the head than look at him. I wouldn't go through his checkout stand for nothing. If he's the only checker there, I'd leave my groceries sit in the cart and go out. He's just a nineteen- or twenty-year-old kid, a Jap, and he looks just like those sons of bitches we shot over there."

"It's good for him to talk about it," Jim said in the presence of his father. "My mother never understood some of the anger he had."

"I come back a different person," Grahnert said. "I was just a goddamned nineteen-year-old kid that went into the service, and when I come back I was a damned seasoned old man, more or less."

Frank Palmasani in 2010

Lucky Strike: Palmasani

This is one of the twenty-two names on my father's captured Japanese silk flag.

There was a white pages listing for Frank Palmasani in Scranton, Pennsylvania. Repeated calls, however, failed. The phone just rang and rang. I sent a letter to the address, as I did in a few dozen similar cases. Only twice did I hear back. An e-mail arrived from Palmasani's daughter-in-law Rosanna saying that he was in a care facility. She gave me a phone number.

"There's a story behind that flag," Palmasani said when I called. He didn't give any hints.

It was a bleak winter day when I drove past gray shale bluffs into Scranton and found the facility. Palmasani was in his room watching a football game. He was gruff but friendly in his own way. He told me his memory was going—he keenly remembered some things, but recollections were often fragmented. He jumped from story to story. Yet some were astonishingly detailed.

"I was only sixteen when I went in," he said. "I went in December the eighth of '41. Got a fake birth certificate. I had a brother in the Navy and one in the Army, and I joined the Marines."

Palmasani was in the 1st Raider Battalion during the Battle of Guadalcanal, when the Marines were undersupplied and written off as a lost cause by Washington. Palmasani was the only man I talked with from Love Company who'd been in the war from the get-go. It was hard to follow all the many battles he was in, from the Marshalls to the Gilbert Islands. On one tiny island "there was about 600 Japs," Palmasani said. He was one of 240 marines. "Took two or three days. Killed every one of 'em. We used C2, you know what that is? High explosive. A little blob this much, I could blow half of this building up, if you do it right. That's how powerful it is."

He was in the 3rd Marine Division when he landed on Guam—he wasn't transferred into L Company until later. (He was in five different Marine units.) The 3rd landed in the northern mountainous part of Guam. "I got shellshocked there myself. Everything got screwed up on that invasion. We were left out in the water, up to here," he said, a hand high on his chest. He went on like this about Guam, and it was difficult to follow the story. Then he focused.

"I shouldn't say this," Palmasani said. He paused. "They had a lieutenant that surrendered there."

"This was a Japanese guy?" I asked.

"Yeah. He was a second lieutenant. He graduated from Stanford University in California. He could speak English better than me. I said, 'Who in the hell is this guy?' And he knew his Japanese. I didn't capture him. Somebody else did. The colonel wanted him in his office, where he was bivouacked. The colonel checked him out, talked to him. He said [to me], 'Take him to the stockade. Down by the aid station. They'll take care of it.' He said, 'Don't take up too much time, just drop him off at the stockade down there with the rest of them.'"

Frank added, "There was nothing there."

He meant there was no stockade. Palmasani marched his prisoner outside.

"The first thing he asked me for was a Lucky Strike cigarette. The only cigarettes we got was from the Seabees in the Navy, Wings cigarettes, four in a pack. I said, 'I got Wings. You want a Wing?' I pulled out the Wings, there was two cigarettes in it. I was going to give him one. He said, 'No, I want a Lucky Strike.'

"So I said, 'You want a Lucky Strike, huh? I'm gonna give you one.' And I stuck the bayonet right in his neck." Palmasani paused. "I killed him. Rolled him over in a hole. That was the end of him."

"You didn't get in trouble?"

"No. He was going to get it anyway, whether I did it or somebody else. What were we going to do with him?"

"Was it hard to do?" I asked.

"No," Palmasani replied, fast. "Nuh-uh. I never liked any of them alive."

"How do you feel about Japanese people today?"

"Same way."

"You didn't take any prisoners on Guam?"

"None. None at all."

Palmasani joined in with Love Company on Guadalcanal in August 1944. He remembered my father.

"He used to fight with the gloves on. I used to see them there in front of the tents. They'd put the gloves on and fight."

Then Palmasani suddenly jumped to a new topic. "I wanted the flamethrower for a long time when it first came out, but they wouldn't give it to me. I had to be trained." The United States invented napalm in 1942, and Palmasani got his wish that fall of 1944. His choice struck me as odd. The life expectancy of flamethrower men was about the same for those with heavy machine guns. The Japanese would target them first.

"And I carried my pack," he continued. "I carried a B.A.R. I carried a machete. I only weighed 147 pounds. The tank, it would stick up over your head. It weighed a lot when it was loaded."

Palmasani was ready to use the flamethrower when the unit arrived on Okinawa.

"When we landed on Okinawa, everybody felt good. Boy, we're on the land and nobody fired back at us."

When Love Company moved north to the base of the Motobu Peninsula, it was not the kind of combat for a flamethrower.

"The snipers were there. They were all over the place," Palmasani said. But they remained unseen to the company. I remember my father saying that when, in the forest, a guy would fall wounded or dead, they'd hear the shot but, my father said, "You couldn't tell where it was coming from." It wasn't like the movies, where they could pinpoint the source of the danger.

It was in the southern part of the island where Palmasani used the flamethrower.

"How much did I torch?" He couldn't quantify. It was a lot, from his description. He burned "pillboxes," the concrete defense structures with narrow horizontal slits at the top. Mostly he burned tombs and caves.

"You had to go right to the front. First, I threw the grenades in. I'd put the phosphorous and the shrapnel grenade in there, and then give it the napalm."

"Why the phosphorous grenade?"

"They went out of breath. It comes out white. And they choke. Then the shrapnel grenade. You shoot the flamethrower, the flames do this," he said, showing a rolling action with his hands. "It rolls. You think it's slow, but it's not, it's fast. Real fast. The flame would go in about twenty feet. The tank would last half an hour if you kept it open. You don't know how many's in there. And if they were in there, I'd get them. You burn them with the napalm, they won't go on. The Japs weren't afraid of nothing but the fire. Once you get burned, nobody can recognize you."

One of Captain Frank Haigler's photographs showed the effect of the napalm, which reaches 1,200 degrees Fahrenheit and would burn on the bodies for as long as twenty-four hours, reducing them to ash in the shape of a human. The Japanese soldier on the next page was napalmed by someone in Love Company. There weren't that many flamethrower men—it's possible Palmasani burned him.

Palmasani wasn't happy that the United States stopped napalm use after the 1960s. (It had a negative image after children were shown burned in Vietnam.)

"If they used them in Iraq and Afghanistan, it would be all over for those guys with the turbans and the gowns, those guys setting the land mines."

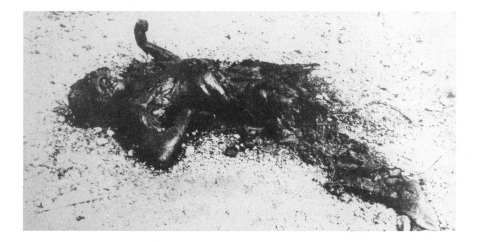

Palmasani told of the battle of Sugar Loaf Hill.

"It rained for fifteen days and fifteen nights. It must have rained fifteen or twenty inches. I don't know if your father told you this—the mud was this high," he said, showing a line on his upper thigh. "Tanks couldn't move. We couldn't navigate. And when we went to pull our feet out of the mud, we didn't have no shoes. They rotted. He ever tell you that?"

"No."

"You know where we got new shoes? From the poor guys that were dead. We had to take their shoes. They weren't picked up yet. They fit, we wore them. That's the truth.

"Their artillery, the 80-millimeter gun, was on the other side of the Sugar Loaf. They used to come out on the track, come out of the cave. They'd fire and go back in. Come out and fire again," he said of how the Japanese avoided having the guns destroyed by American firepower. "The machine guns were on this side. Five o'clock at night they would let you know they were there, 'cause they would shoot at you. They would counterattack every night. Couple of hours. Thirteen times we went up to that place," he said of the days of stalemate on Sugar Loaf. "And the thirteenth time we took it over to get into Naha."

Palmasani said that the flag my father had kept came from Sugar Loaf Hill. He recognized his signature when I showed him a picture of the flag. "That's my writing. This was the last couple of days of the Sugar Loaf." He had seen two enemy soldiers. "The Japs were maybe fifty, sixty feet away. You could see them from where we were. But they couldn't see us. The lieutenant said to me, 'Get the B.A.R.'"

Palmasani opened up on full automatic on the Japanese marines.

"I went in and rolled the first Jap over to make sure he was dead. I had my knife out. If he wasn't dead I was going to stab him. The second marine was where the flag was."

(Weeks later, when I went home and spread out the flag, I noticed for the first time that it was stained with blood.)

"We had a marker that we used. I don't know if your father ever told you this. We had a marker because our code changed maybe five times a day. And if you didn't get the right code right, boy you were in trouble. So I took my marker, I wrote my name on that flag. That won't come off."

I expressed amazement about writing on the flag amid the battle. He explained that he wanted to make sure the flag was claimed as his. Souvenirs were an obsession among many soldiers; it's why my father had that chest of Japanese items.

Part of me wondered about the veracity of Palmasani's story. Two things caused me to believe every word of it. First, evidence pointed to Palmasani writing his name under duress: he didn't put the "N" in Scranton, the town where he was born. He wouldn't make that mistake unless he was in a hurry. Second, as the story went on, his demeanor told me he'd been angry about the fate of that flag for many years.

Palmasani then stated, "That flag."

"Where was my dad in all this?"

"Well, here's what happened. By that time, the action started. So I had to leave my pack there—my grenades and everything but the B.A.R. and the flamethrower. So the next day I went back, but my pack was gone. That was the end of the flag. He must have went in my pack. He knew it was mine."

He was visibly agitated, and so I changed the subject. I asked Palmasani about prisoners on Okinawa.

"There was lots that surrendered. They'd come out of the catacombs and out of the caves. We didn't take any. We didn't have time for that. The lieutenant said, 'Kill them all as you come on them and keep going.' See as we were going, as we were making progress, [General] Buckner was putting pressure on everybody. 'Get over the island. Go through it. Every bit of it.' And it came down to our colonel [Clair Shisler]. And he gave the orders out to his company commanders."

None of these orders are written down, at least not that I've been able to discover. The closest General Lemuel C. Shepherd Jr., in charge of the Marines, ever came to addressing this appeared in a transcript of interviews with him in 1966 and 1967 for the Marine Corps Oral History Program. Shepherd said of prisoners, "Very few—we took very few prisoners, because they fought to the last."

Question: "Was it a 50–50 deal—50 percent you couldn't get prisoners and 50 percent they didn't want to take prisoners?"

"Perhaps." Shepherd went on to describe how "The Japs seldom gave up" and despite how records show that very few prisoners were taken, he said on Okinawa that "they came around to the idea that they'd save their own skins." He continued, "You've got to instill in your men the will to kill the enemy to the point—perhaps because they were heathens, so to speak—that killing a Jap was like killing a rattlesnake. I didn't always have that feeling in Europe, about some poor German family man, but I felt with a Jap—it was just like killing a rattlesnake."

The Japanese knew they'd be killed. That explains some of the "fanaticism" for them fighting to the death. Commanders made no provision for taking the prisoners to the rear.

"I don't think they were thinking the battle was going to last so long," Palmasani said. "Even [Admiral] Halsey thought it was going to be quicker."

The line blurred between who was a civilian and who was a soldier.

"They spoke good English, the Japanese women. They'd call out, 'Marine, marine, help me.' They'd tell you anything. Two or three o'clock in the morning. The lieutenant said, 'Shoot them.' And that's what we did. Then in the morning when it was light, they was strapped with grenades and dynamite was under their kimonos. Their kimonos went all the way down their legs. That was all the time. You got to kill them. It's either them or you. They carried enough explosives they could blow half of this building up."

I turned my questions to what happened the day Mulligan was killed. From other interviews and Captain Haigler's records I'd already pieced together some of Love Company's movements. I knew that as dawn's light broke on the overcast day of May 30, 1945, the men of L Company in the 3rd Battalion, 22nd Marines, crossed single file on a temporary plank footbridge set across a canal that connected the Kokuba and Asato Rivers in what was left of the city of Naha. Love Company's platoons—First, Second, Third, Mortar, Machine Gun—moved through the 1st and 2nd battalions of the 22nd Marines. They fanned out. They were part of the drive south now that the US military had broken through the Shuri Line after the fall of Sugar Loaf Hill.

Some went north of what the battle map called Hill 27, the others south. The men of Love Company called it Knob Hill. To the Japanese, it was Mount Jokagu. It wasn't much of a hill—just a mound, really, atop a gradually ascending slope. Yet, "enemy machine guns emplaced in burial tombs on Hill 27 in east Naha . . . checked the infantry," Roy E. Appleman wrote in *Okinawa: The Last Battle.* The plan was for elements of Love Company to double back and attack while others came at the hill from the north in a flanking action.

There was a shallow swale the men from the south used for cover as they moved forward. They had a clear view of a series of concrete tombs near the top, most of the "turtleback" variety, that were sheltering the Japanese machine gunners.

I offered a photocopy of the topographic battle map I scanned from Captain Haigler. Palmasani quickly traced the route with his finger, shown with arrows on the map. He said the first platoon of L Company headed south.

Palmasani said they then did a dog-leg turn, coming back on the hill.

"It was a long and very gradual slope leading to those tombs. There was a little knoll on top here. Understand? The ground went like this. It

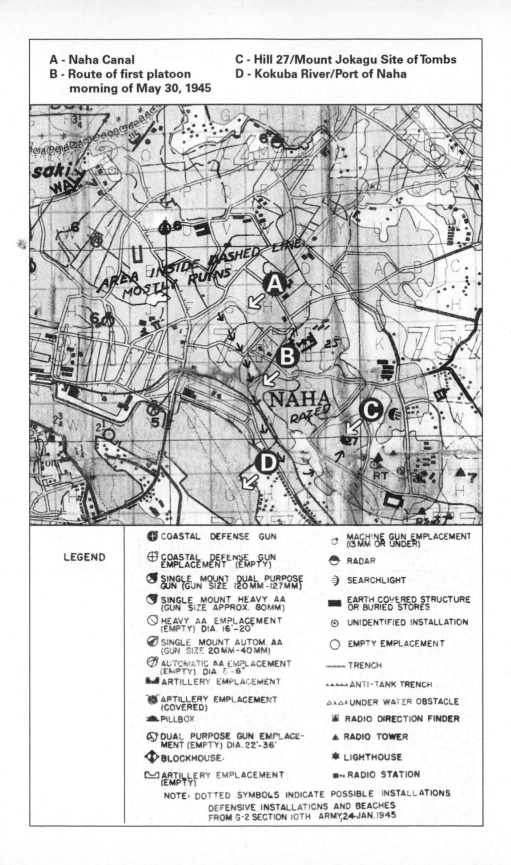

A - Naha Canal
B - Route of first platoon
   morning of May 30, 1945
C - Hill 27/Mount Jokagu Site of Tombs
D - Kokuba River/Port of Naha

LEGEND

⊕ COASTAL DEFENSE GUN

⊕ COASTAL DEFENSE GUN EMPLACEMENT (EMPTY)

⊗ SINGLE MOUNT DUAL PURPOSE GUN (GUN SIZE 120MM-127MM)

⊗ SINGLE MOUNT HEAVY AA (GUN SIZE APPROX. 80MM)

⊘ HEAVY AA EMPLACEMENT (EMPTY) DIA. 16'-20'

⊘ SINGLE MOUNT AUTOM. AA (GUN SIZE 20MM-40MM)

⊘ AUTOMATIC AA EMPLACEMENT (EMPTY) DIA. 5'-6'

◣ ARTILLERY EMPLACEMENT

◉ ARTILLERY EMPLACEMENT (COVERED)

◤ PILLBOX

⊗ DUAL PURPOSE GUN EMPLACEMENT (EMPTY) DIA. 22'-36'

◆ BLOCKHOUSE

◡ ARTILLERY EMPLACEMENT (EMPTY)

○ MACHINE GUN EMPLACEMENT (13MM OR UNDER)

◔ RADAR

⊐ SEARCHLIGHT

▬ EARTH COVERED STRUCTURE OR BURIED STORES

⊙ UNIDENTIFIED INSTALLATION

○ EMPTY EMPLACEMENT

⌇⌇⌇ TRENCH

⌄⌄⌄ ANTI-TANK TRENCH

△△△ UNDER WATER OBSTACLE

▣ RADIO DIRECTION FINDER

▲ RADIO TOWER

❋ LIGHTHOUSE

▪•• RADIO STATION

NOTE: DOTTED SYMBOLS INDICATE POSSIBLE INSTALLATIONS

DEFENSIVE INSTALLATIONS AND BEACHES FROM G-2 SECTION 10TH ARMY, 24 JAN. 1945 was like a gully. As long as you didn't stand up there, they couldn't shoot you in the crossfire because they couldn't see you. It went a good fifteen feet or more deep, in some places less. They had Jap marines there. Once you stick your head up, they cut you down like flies."

It was now early afternoon.

As they neared the top of Hill 27, the First Platoon was all spread out. They faced a row of the dangerous tombs where the machine gunfire had been coming from.

"We were told not to go near it—intelligence had told the lieutenant," Palmasani said of those particular tombs at the top of Hill 27. "We were warned to check it out first before you blow anything out. We knew that they were keeping their ammunition somewhere."

Palmasani spotted some of the First Platoon members right at one of the tombs. He thought, "What are they doing there? Those guys aren't supposed to be there!"

The word from intelligence was to pass the tombs by to be dealt with later safely. Did everyone get that word? Combat is never flawless, and in the Okinawa operation, the battle was so gruesome and protracted that it was easy to imagine the word not getting around. And there had been machine gunfire coming from the tombs.

"What happened was they went over to the catacomb and started throwing hand grenades," Palmasani said about a double turtleback tomb with two entry doors. "There was this big one that was loaded with ammunition."

"And who ordered the grenades to be thrown in?" I asked.

"Not the lieutenant."

"So my dad and the guys went on their own?"

"They went on their own. They weren't supposed to go near that place."

"Did you see it blow up?"

"Yeah! Unbelievable! Nothing went out the top. Everything come out the doors. It was loaded with Japanese ammunition. Grenades, bullets, artillery shells—you name it."

"So it was a slow explosion?"

"No, it went *ZOOM!*" Palmasani exclaimed, motioning with his hands how the blast punched out sideways. "You'd swore it was like they had dropped the atomic bomb there. God-darn smoke and you could see arms and legs and everything going up in the air. I was no more than a hundred feet away. You had to get out of the way or you'd get killed. The concrete roofs on them was two feet thick. That concrete comes down on you, it would squash you to death. Damn right, I was running. The whole outfit moved."

One report that I'd read estimated that there was one ton of explosives in the tomb.

Mulligan was exactly thirty days shy of his twenty-second birthday that day he neared the tomb. He stood five-feet-six, weighed 135 pounds, and had blue-gray eyes. Mulligan was a fire team leader, which meant he was the head of a subunit of four marines; three fire teams were part of the squad that consisted of a thirteenth man—Steve Maharidge, the squad leader.

"Did you see Mulligan get hit?"

"I didn't see anybody. Nobody saw anybody. Not with that smoke. They were in the wrong position, wrong place."

"Was my dad a squad leader at that point?"

"I believe he was, yeah."

I wondered: Did my father order Mulligan to throw the grenade? Were both of them throwing grenades? Or did Mulligan act on his own?

I asked if he thought the officers blamed my father for the explosion.

"I don't think they blamed him. I didn't hear anybody mentioning his name. I'm talking about the people that investigated it," he said of a new lieutenant who looked into who made the mistake.

"What happened to Mulligan?" I asked.

"He was buried in the rubble. The grave people don't like to mark that down on paper."

I mentioned that I wanted to identify his remains so that his grave could be marked.

"Don't bother. Take it from me. Believe me," Palmasani said. "I'm telling you the truth. I was there. I seen it."

Palmasani figured a dozen marines were killed. But records for the unit that day only list Mulligan killed. Those arms and legs Palmasani saw flying may have been those of Japanese soldiers.

One other man I'd interviewed suffered a severe blast concussion that day. I asked if Palmasani thought other guys did as well.

"There must have been seven or eight that got shell-shocked. They didn't even know where they were. Their eyes—they weren't straight out. They went in this direction, that direction. They looked goofy. We couldn't stay there too long. We had a job to do."

"I'm going to show you these marks," Palmasani said. He pulled down his pants to reveal his lower legs, thighs, buttocks, then he exhibited his arms. All were embedded with black specks of shrapnel from Japanese mortars and grenades from at least five different battles. "This is the fungus, the jungle rot. I still got it," he said of blotches on his legs. (My father was always putting bleach on his legs, trying to kill fungus from the Canal.)

"Thank God for the water canteen. The .25 caliber bullet went into my canteen, come out of the other side, and went into my leg. They couldn't stop the bleeding. I had to get that sewed. Oh, their marines were darned good. They used to dummy the bullets on the .25 caliber so when it come out of you, it would blow you wide open. See, if they were pointy, they'd go right through you. But when they come out of you if they were filed down, it would blow you out. I think they would have had to cut my leg off. That was a dummied bullet."

After two hours Palmasani announced that he was done talking about the war. His son Mike, seated behind him, asked why I was doing my research. I explained about my father's likely blast concussion, both from the tomb and from Sugar Loaf Hill, and how he was messed up by the war. Mike bobbed his head, rolling his eyes toward his father, who couldn't see this.

"You know, I don't think we had 37 people left in L Company at the end," Palmasani said about how so few of the 240 guys who'd landed on April 1 were still present in the unit.

One year later I telephoned Palmasani to see how he was doing. He didn't remember me. "What are you talking about!?" he said. I explained, but he didn't recall my visit. He did remember the flag.

"I want to know who took my flag!"

"I think my dad did—"

"What did he take it for!? It wasn't his. My name was on it."

"Yeah, I know, he—"

"Goddamn it! I would have shot him if I caught him now! That's my flag! I got that flag off the Jap I shot! I shot him in the head! It was under his helmet! He didn't have to steal my flag! That was mine! I shot two Japs in the goddamn head, and I took the flag! It belonged to me!"

A year and a half later an e-mail arrived from Rosanna Palmasani, telling me that her brother-in-law Mike died at the age of sixty-one on September 1, 2012. On September 5 Frank died. He was eighty-seven.

Laughridge's Gold: Laughridge

The 1992 Chevrolet Caprice in the driveway of the suburban home had seen better days, even though it only had thirty-eight thousand miles on the odometer. The vehicle, with faded and sun-blotched paint, had been purchased at discount when James Palmer Laughridge retired in 1991 after thirty-six and a half years at the General Motors Lakewood Assembly Plant in Atlanta.

I approached the screen door as a chill March rain fell. Jim Laughridge (pronounced Lock-ridge) had left a phone message after I'd sent a

Jim Laughridge in 2010

letter because his telephone was unlisted. When I rang back, the television news about a Chilean earthquake was blasting so loud that I had to hold the phone away from my ear. When he shut off the set, I had to shout. Because Laughridge was hard of hearing, I'd have to yell my questions on this visit. But I didn't need to ask very many questions. Laughridge, I would later realize, was ready to talk about the war and his life.

The interior was cluttered. Cigarettes had burned everything: the faded and soiled carpet, a couch, an easy chair, the countertops. Laughridge had a rough gray stubble of beard, and he wore a US Marine Corps cap. He spoke slowly with a strong Southern accent.

He was born in Forest City, North Carolina. His father, Willie Jay, was the manager of a cotton mill. "I was in a military school in Oak Ridge, North Carolina," he told me, when he was drafted "right out of high school, right into Parris Island. Hell, you haven't even really lived. We'd just seen a lot of John Wayne movies and all that kind of bullshit.

"When World War II started, I wanted to be a pilot. Joining the Marine Corps had not entered my mind. I wanted to fly. I had just turned eighteen, was just an ol' small town boy. Hell, I wasn't used to no Yankees and gang fights and all that kind of stuff.

"I got overseas in December of 1944. That was right after the First Marine Division had hit Peleliu and they lost their ass on that deal. About that time they started forming the Sixth Marine Division. They pulled us out of the First and they put us into the Sixth and sent us to Guadalcanal. Guadalcanal—that was hell, even after the fightin' was over. The weather. I really didn't form any close friendships with those guys because I hadn't been there long enough.

"When we got to Okinawa, they took twelve of us, sent us to supposedly protect the supplies. And here comes this damn lieutenant— Lieutenant Krantz. He was built like a bulldog. He was crazy as hell. He was another Sergeant York. He started taking us on patrol. And we spent about three weeks out in the boondocks, setting up ambushes. He wasn't authorized to do that. We just kind of lived [hand] to mouth. We were under no real direction except his.

"For scenic beauty, Okinawa was a pretty little island. If there was no damn war going on, it would have been nice. A place when we was pushing north, it was kind of like a school building. There were bicycles there. We were holing up for a day or two. A bunch of us got them damn bicycles, and we were just like fifteen-year-olds. I mean the war was another world away. We was just having a good time ridin' them bicycles. And this damn colonel come out, and he got every damn one of us and lined us up, says 'You're acting like kids. I want you to stack every one of them damn things over there against the wall and get your trenching tools.' During that march north they had dropped a lot of 60-millimeter mortar shells. He said, 'I want you to fill every goddamn hole that's in this place.' So we filled all of them holes and he said, 'Okay, now dig them out again.' So we dig 'em out again. Then we filled them back in. Anyway, we didn't ride no more bicycles, I tell you.

"Anyway, right at the northern end, that's when they put us in the 22nd [Love Company]. That was sometime around the first of May. That's where I really got to know some of those people for a very short time. Hell, we had . . . I don't what our percentage of casualties was, but it was over 100 percent.

"At that particular time I was carrying a carbine. We lay around up there three or four days. Then they loaded us on trucks real early in the morning. It was black. We rode all day to the south. By that time I was put in the 60-millimeter mortars."

Love Company fought its way to Sugar Loaf Hill, flanked on either side by a mound called Half Moon and the other by Horseshoe. I pulled out a picture.

"See the ridges on the right of it? Sugar Loaf was in the middle. These other two was on each side," he said. Their position was on the western, China Sea side, flank. "They had interlocking fire from each side. That's why you couldn't stay up on the damn place. None of them hills looked impressive, as far as size.

"But goddamn they had that thing laced with caves. When they'd lift our artillery, the Nips knew the marines was coming. They'd come out of them damn caves right in the middle of a bunch of marines. There was a lot of guys who cracked up on that damn hill.

1-4 TAKING OF SUGAR LOAF HILL — VICINITY OF NAHA

Sugar Loaf Hill, courtesty of USMC

"When we first moved south, there was an army tank that took a hit. Three or four of them guys went into a small cave. The Japanese got them. I don't know what the hell they was doing to 'em. All night long you could hear them screamin'," he said of the Americans being tortured. "But you couldn't get to them. That gets to you, that kind of thing. It gets you pissed off. They mutilated a lot of the dead Americans. Hell, they cut off their hands, their feet, their eyes, tongue, ears, guts.

"I had a real good friend of mine, named LeBough. He was Italian [American], a flamethrower man. He went up on the side of Horseshoe with that damn flamethrower. And all of a sudden there was one big burst of orange flame and smoke, and they never did find him. They just blowed him to hell and back and cooked the rest of him. Another little happy story.

"I was dug in one night with them platoon dogs. I said, 'Boy, I'm safe now. I can go to sleep.' I woke up real early the next morning, just so it got to where you could see. Them frickin' dogs over there were just lying sound asleep.

"Anyway, every day we was taking a lot of casualties, and one morning I answered the damn phone. I don't know who the sergeant was, he said, 'Laughridge, go up to the CP' [Command Post]. The truck brought in an extra load of water, and they came in five-gallon cans. 'You can go up there and take you a whore bath. And when you get through, we can send somebody else.' I got up there and stripped down to the waist and dumped some water on me, got all soaped up. I was going to rinse. I picked that can up to pour the water on me. A bullet hit that damn thing. Those cans, on each side there was an "X." That damn sniper bullet hit right in the middle of that "X." He had to do that intentionally, because he could have put that between my eyes just as easy. I always figured it was a sniper with some kind of weird sense of humor. Lot of crazy things went on.

"Most of the guys was always souvenir hunting, like Captain Haigler. Haigler, that souvenir-huntin' bastard. Mentally, I guess he was the kind of marine they needed. He didn't give a shit for nothing or nobody. He was kind of reckless, particularly with other people's lives.

"I had but one run-in with a combat officer. It had been rainin' for so stinkin' long. Everybody stunk like hell. I had gotten that chance to clean up a little bit. I'd picked up a pack and found a khaki shirt, all folded up, just like it came from the laundry. I had a brand-new pair of socks. I put all that clean dry stuff on. And I was sittin' back, really comfortable for the first damn time in weeks. I was a member of the 'you-you-and-you' squad. A lieutenant from Alabama, kinda a big slow-talkin' boy, he comes along and says, 'You, you, and you, go back and pick up some ammunition.' It just hit me wrong. I knew I shouldn't have done it. I said, 'Look, you want some ammunition, go get it!' I pulled my helmet down over my eyes, then looked up. He said, 'Boy, get out of that damn hole.' So I got out of that damn hole, put my shoes on, and the first step that I made out of that hole, I stepped in a puddle of water. There went my dry shoes, my dry socks. I'd really found some comfort, and I stepped in that damn water, and that was it."

Dry feet were the least of his worries. Sugar Loaf was the heaviest combat he had yet seen in the war. "That damn Sugar Loaf. They went up that damn thing thirteen times before they could stay. You get up there, they'd kick your ass off. Get up, kick your ass off. The Marine Corps had more casualties and psychopathic jobs off that damn one battle. We were wondering: why can't we just go around it? We were smart enough to ask that once in a while. We didn't ask no officer or nothin', talked about it when we were sitting around bullshitting."

He said the Japanese would yell things. "'Marines, you die!' 'Roosevelt eats shit,' all kinds of damn stuff like that. They was always hollering something about being wounded real bad. They wanted somebody to come out there. You hear one holler something over here, another over here. It was kinda spooky in a way because there was always that little doubt that it might have been a damn American, you know."

And they would pretend to be dead.

"We had to kill them twice. If you didn't, they'd raise up and nail you. Sometimes you cut their throat. Most times you take the .45—if you had a .45—and stick it in their ear. They had suicidal grenades. They was blowin' themselves up."

By then Laughridge had a .45 semiautomatic Colt pistol.

"One guy in the outfit, I don't remember his name, his daddy fought in World War I. He apparently stole a damn .45 at the end of that war and brought it back. And this boy carried that same .45 with him. The damn thing, the bore, it was almost completely wore out. You could just shake it, and it would make all kinds of noise. When he got killed, I got it. When I was on that damn island, my world at night, it was what was in front of me, on the side of me, and in back. And you slept with a goddamn grenade in your hand. That's the reason I like the .45. A rifle in a hole can be unwieldy. That .45 give you a great sense of security at night, particularly."

It could serve one other purpose—it could be used to commit suicide.

"I was always scared of something happening to my eyes. That's the reason I wanted the .45. I knew if I was blinded, that .45 would be strapped to me, and I could get to it. Now whether I would have done that or not, I don't know. But, uh, I just couldn't see being blind.

Worst thing in the world. 'Sides, I wun't nothin' but eighteen. I hadn't seen nothin' of the world. I wanted to see all these damn women. I was just introduced to them not too long before that.

"While we was trying to go through Naha, they sent me and Greene back to pick up some mortar ammunition. When that damn artillery landed somewhere behind me, or to my right, I was carrying [the ammo crate] on my left shoulder. It blowed me up against the edge of this tomb. God, it rung my bells for I don't know how long. I got up when I come to. I shook my damn head and started getting my vision back. I started looking for that damn ammo. I found it and got back up. I bled a little bit around the eyes. I couldn't hear a damn thing for four or five days after that."

I yelled, "Did they put you on the hospital ship?"

"No! Shit, man, you had to be bleeding, in bad shape, or completely lost your mind.

"We was going through Naha, a place we called The Factory. It was a great big ol' long buildin'. That night it was rainin' like hell, and these explosions kept going off. I got up to take a damn leak. I was standing there about half-asleep, and every once in a while them flares went off. And here comes four or five Japanese soldiers. I nailed one of them. They was runnin' low, you know. I nailed him right on top of the head. In the morning before I could get to that son' bitch to get the souvenirs, somebody else got there and got 'em."

Laughridge was not only interested in a sword or flags—somewhere on the march south he began ripping gold teeth from Japanese cadavers.

"I'd been watching guys do it. I figured I could do it too. I knew a guy, he had a bunch of these damn bags," he said of khaki canvas bags that hung from a belt. "All of them full of souvenirs. He had eyeglasses, gold teeth. You take a butt stroke," he said of using his M-1 carbine on the jaws of the Japanese. "Bust 'em, take the KA-BAR [knife] and pry 'em out. We had one guy that was a corpsman, and where he got a pair of dental pliers I don't know, but he'd bust them and take them dental pliers and pull 'em out."

"How many teeth did you have?" I shouted.

"Oh hell, I had a handful of them damn things."

He paused for one the rare times that afternoon.

The body of a Japanese soldier on Okinawa
whose teeth appear to have been taken

"It got so that if I killed five one day, I'd say, maybe I'd do better the next day. I got to where I enjoyed it. Instead of shooting one where I knew it would kill him outright, if I had a choice, I'd shoot him in the gut and let him die a slow and painful death. That was my frame of mind. When you live like a goddamn animal, you gonna act like a damn animal, you know—

"I don't know. Maybe one of these days I'll get it figured out. Anyhow, as they say, once a marine, always a marine. I still feel that way.

"A lot of guys don't like to talk about it. I don't like to brag about it. I didn't do anything. You just do what you're told and survive. I wasn't no damn hero. The thing that bothered me the worst was the damn odor. All them dead marines lying around, rotting. Maggots and flies all over. And the damn body lice. You'd be on the line at night. You can't move. Them damn things would start itching and biting. You got to scratch but you can't really scratch—

"Not just the movement—noise. When you're lying up there and everything's really quiet, all noise is exaggerated. You want to get up and scratch so damn bad you can't stand it. That really got to me, I tell you. You get them in between your crotch and under your arms. You'd give anything to be able to get up and just dig at them. That DDT, when they'd shower you down with that, that would take care of it."

Laughridge vividly recalled the day Love Company moved out of Naha, when they crossed the canal on May 30, 1945. They faced Hill 27. Laughridge described the ascent exactly as Palmasani had told me: "It wasn't a sudden rise. It was kind of a long sloping thing. After you got up to a certain level, it leveled off, and it went down again. It wasn't like Sugar Loaf—one big lump that went up."

Near the summit he went around Knob Hill, shown in the picture of bomb-damaged radio towers, taken by a US Marine combat photographer.

Laughridge and his fire team went by the tombs in the hill to the left, out of sight in the photograph. They moved north and went among the school buildings around the hill near the second tower from the right.

Just before the tomb exploded, Laughridge saw Malcolm T. Lear get shot in the head; Lear looked dead to Laughridge, but Lear survived. (I spoke with Lear several times by phone, but he told me that he had no memory of events from the war.)

"I ran right by it," Laughridge said of the double-doored large tomb that Palmasani had explained to me. Like Palmasani, Laughridge had been ordered not to throw grenades into the tombs. "I wasn't about to throw a damn grenade in there because like what happened, happened, you know. Right after we passed that place is when we started a big, long, downhill slope, and that's when we run into all them towers that had been blown up. That's when the explosion hit. The biggest I heard on that whole damn island. I saw ammo dumps go up on the beach

7-4 RADIO TOWERS EAST OF NAHA

Photo courtesey of USMC

when those kamikazes come in. This was bigger. I mean it looked like a volcano going off.

"I said to myself, 'Somebody done throwed a grenade in that damn son of a bitch.' They must've had a tremendous amount of ammunition in that damn thing. It filled the sky with boulders. I was huntin' for a hole, but I couldn't find one. I tried to duck inside one of those Okinawan tombs. It had a wall about four or five feet high on both sides. I remember looking up and hugging that damn wall. And all that shit started falling. Big ol' boulders, three feet in diameter, were coming down all around us. I didn't hardly believe it. I looked at a damn boulder, big around as that table. It hit about as far away as that wall over there."

After this, the unit crossed the Kokuba River.

"Everything started moving south, southwest," Laughridge said. "It was kind of a screwed up affair. One day I'd be in the 2nd infantry platoon, then one day I'd be with mortars. Hell, they couldn't or wouldn't get anything to us. We got into a warehouse. I know you've seen pictures of World War II Japanese officers, where they had those slick, shiny boots. I found a pair of these damn Japanese officer's boots. It was like 5th Avenue walking around in 'em. They was uncomfortable, but they was better than nothin'. Damn hobnails in the bottom of 'em."

On June 7 L Company was moving toward the Japanese Naval Headquarters on Hill 53. This hill was just across the Kokuba River from Naha, almost directly south of where Mulligan was killed.

"We had an airdrop. Trucks, tanks—nothing could move" because of the mud, Laughridge said. "It was right after the heavy rains. This damn navy plane come over and they dropped, and they missed us by about a thousand yards. The damn lieutenant come by and said we got to go pick it up. He started naming off the names to go get it and then he said to me, 'Hey you, bring up the rear.'"

Tall hills overlooked the area.

"There was Japanese dug in at the top. And they had taken a bunch of aircraft cannons, 20-millimeter cannons, and fortified that whole ridge. Down here was the flatland where we was," he said, pointing to a photocopy of Captain Haigler's battle map. "They was looking directly down on us. We started out to get that stuff, me bringing up the rear. There was a little rise down there. Just as I got to that rise, they zeroed in on us. That goddamn 20-millimeter stuff was falling like raindrops. I got hit, and everybody else kept on going. I don't blame them for that. It was wide open. They couldn't miss.

"I crawled about thirty yards. On one knee and two hands and elbows. And that damn stuff was coming under my arms and between my legs. Finally one hit me again. It just blowed me. When I went over, I could see the sunlight. I crawled until I got behind a little knoll. Funny thing, the night before we had a guy that got hit—I believe it was by our own men. We didn't have any stretchers, no transportation. We took a door down off this damn house, put him on it. There was six of us that carried him back to the first aid station. We must have carried him six or eight miles. Got back at daylight. I said, 'The next son of a bitch that gets hit, if he has to be carried out, I'm gonna shoot him right there.'

"So the next morning is when I got hit. One of the guys that heard me say that, he walked up and pulled the slide back on his .45 and he said, 'Lock, you ready to go?'

"When I got hit, man, they came on me like a damn bunch of buzzards. I had two canteens of water, the C-Rations, some K-ration candy bars, the .45—gone."

"They took everything?" I asked of his buddies stripping him.

"Oh shit, they picked me clean."

That World War I .45 was now in its third ownership on the island. I suddenly had an understanding of how my father ended up with Mulligan's .45. Laughridge didn't blame the guys—he would have done the same. "It was just kinda survival is what it was."

"What happened to your Japanese teeth?"

"When I got hit, I had a pocket full of 'em. And a damn corpsman come up and cut my britches off, and when he did, he cut my pocket out with it."

Gold teeth scattered on the earth.

"I don't know if anybody in the outfit got the gold teeth or not."

Laughridge spent three weeks in the hospital. A quarter-sized bullet was left in his leg; it was too dangerous to remove.

When he was released, the Battle of Okinawa was over. Laughridge's war also should have been over.

But it wasn't.

I'd listened for a few hours, barely asking questions. I showed Laughridge my father's division history book. He discovered a picture of himself, taken a few days before he was hit, passing mortar ammunition.

"That's me right there!" he exclaimed.

"If you can sign this book, that would be great," I said. I'd been asking all the guys I met to sign. When I looked up, Laughridge's eyes had rolled back in his head, and he teetered at the edge of the couch.

"You okay? Mr. Laughridge?!"

Silence.

"Are you okay?! Can you hear me? You want to sit back?"

He remained rigid—only the whites of his eyes were visible. It appeared he was dying. I frantically searched for his land phone to call 911. I didn't see it. I pulled my cell. Suddenly, he mumbled.

He shook his head, dizzy and out of sorts.

"That happens to me once in a while. When it comes, it overwhelms me. Then when it leaves—"

"I was ready to call 911—"

"When it leaves, I'm all right. When it starts, I can hear everything you say, everything going on around me. My motor part, I can't move. If I'm sitting here, I can't get up. If I'm standing up, I can't move to sit down because I'll lose my balance. I cracked my head open one time."

"What do the doctors say about it?"

"They've done these scans. They can't find it. At times I can go for six months and not get hit. Then I can get hit two, three times in a week. They don't know what causes it. I'm all right now."

He continued telling me his story.

"Right after I got out of the Marine Corps, from '47 to '49, I was at North Carolina State. I'd been an honors student in that military school. Hell, I could just read anything and pick it right up. No problem, including math. When I got back and took that test at North Carolina State, it lasted over four hours. All kind of damn subjects. I ended up with a rating having completed sophomore year and part of a junior year and part of some senior year in college in other subjects. Now, I didn't even have a high school diploma because I went into the Marine Corps before I graduated.

"But, uh, I couldn't settle down for some reason or other. I'd just get enough credits to hang in there. Anytime I'd meet a new gal, if she was good, hell . . . and I did a lot of drinking. Just a big old time. I had a C average on everything. That was a tough school at the time. You didn't get a grade on attitude. You got a grade on what you put on paper. Then I was asked to leave.

"I kind of preferred to hang around home. Finally, my daddy said, 'Boy, you gotta go.'

"'Go where?'

"He said, 'I don't know—just go.'

"So I packed my bags and ended up here in Atlanta. That's when I enrolled in a branch of Georgia Tech. And, uh, I had a good old time out there too. When I was asked to leave out there, I had a C-plus average."

"Was it the war?"

"I don't know what it was. All I was interested in was something to drink and pussy. I guess it's '49. I run into a woman, a damn good-lookin' woman. I thought she was old at the time. She was about, I guess, thirty-seven or thirty-eight years old. Had all kind of damn money, man. Lived in a great big old four-column house, two-story job. And she kind of like adopted me. She started buying my damn clothes. It got where I couldn't do nothing without her approval. I had to account for everywhere I went, everybody I saw, everything I did. I had to dress just to suit her. I couldn't take this no more. So one day I just took out all my old clothes she had stashed away, put them on. Put everything she had given me and left it on the damn bed. Never looked back. She was good in the bed, though, I tell ya'. Shit. I was happier undressed in her bed than I was anywhere else.

"Then I met this gal I got married to," he said of his wife, Beverly. "I went to General Motors in, I believe, August of '53. I was everything from a sweeper to a general foreman. And the best job I had was as a sweeper. Keep the place clean, that was my responsibility. As long as I did that, nobody fucked with me. They closed that damn thing down twelve or fifteen years ago. That's when General Motors started going into the tank."

In 1959 "I took on—I believe it was six Atlanta policemen. I had drank so much liquor. It started off with beer. Then blended whiskey. Then went to 100-proof Smirnoff. Fight just got started, and I was in it. The man I worked over, I likely would have killed him. I broke his damn jaw, popped his eye out, broke his ribs, his shoulder, cracked his head—you name it. And the other guy, I threw him through a plate-glass door. We was all friends—it was just three of us. Somebody called the cops. I remember the one that got me. He got behind me, he took that damn billy club and put it across my neck, and I went down. He worked me over goin' down to the police station. Woke up the next mornin', my head felt like a sack o' doorknobs. Don't remember to this day what the hell it was about. I wasn't thinking. Just a damn machine, I guess.

"It was a humdinger. You should have seen my apartment. Goddammit, it looked like World War II hit it. Blood all over the fuckin' walls. Furniture teared up, goddamn. My wife had a friend that was a lawyer, that knew the judge. They grew up together. Anyway, if he hadn't known that judge, I probably would have got some time out of that. My old lady was gonna leave me. If she'd been real smart, she probably would have. We worked it out somehow."

I asked, "Did that happen because of the war?"

"I don't know. Somebody was telling me here a while back about PS—posttraumatic, what's that called?"

"PTSD."

"PTSD or whatever. It don't have to happen right after the war," he said. "It can go for years."

Then the United States entered yet another war. Laughridge went to the US Marine recruiting office in 1965.

"I tried to get back in when the US first got involved in Vietnam. That damn recruiting sergeant said, 'You're too old, too beat up.' I told him all you got is a bunch of fat, pimply faced kids who don't the left from the right. I said, 'Look at me! I'm trained!' He said, 'Well, we can't use you right now.'

"I guess I got to a point in life where I just kinda got bored. I don't know if that's natural or not. Working at the same job, day in and day out. I was on the assembly line then."

"Were your kids still small?"

"Hell, they must have been twelve and eight. It was selfish on my part. I guess I was trying to run away from something. I don't know. Unless you ever worked on a damn auto assembly line, it's hard to explain what it's like. We was making Chevrolets and Chevrolet trucks. They got a federal prison over there. They had us on one side and the prisoners on the other. Sometimes you couldn't tell the difference.

"I went to the damn company doctor one time. 'It's like a goddamn never-ending monster,' I said. 'If you cut off its head, it comes right back. I do that day after day, and it's driving me up the damn wall.' He put me on sick leave. I mean I wasn't cuckoo or nothin'. I just got fed up with it. And I think I was out a month. Come back, it was still the same old stuff."

He laughed, sadly.

"Thirty-six-point-five years. I'd gotten tired of all the rules, regulations. I guess I got tired of discipline, I don't know."

"What happened to your wife?"

"Oh, she died in '77. Her family on both sides had a tendency for manic depression. She'd go for a long period of time, perfectly normal, then she'd get real depressed and go way down. She'd quit eatin'—or she'd get real happy, kinda like a happy drunk all the time. She did that, she'd go on shopping sprees and whatever. Enough to drive you up a wall. Anyhow, we put her in the hospital three times. And the last time when we took her out, they said she's in good shape. We think we've got this thing under control.

"I brought her home on Easter Sunday morning. Carried her baggage into the house. I said I need to get some screen wire to put on the back door that leads into the kitchen. And, uh—I wasn't thinking of all the stores being closed on Sunday. So I stopped at the drug store and got four packs of cigarettes, and I came home. We had a dachshund and two more dogs. When I pulled up in the driveway, all of them was standing up there in the window howlin'. Soon as I got out I said, 'Damn, there's something wrong here.' I went runnin' into the house. She'd taken my .45 and put it to her chest. So that was—"

Laughridge paused.

"—pretty tough to take." His son, "Jimbo," also killed himself six years previous to my visit. I couldn't bring myself to ask for details.

I was a set of ears Laughridge had been waiting to tell his story to. It didn't feel like an interview—what I was hearing was more of a confession. He was a screw-up, but a reflective and smart one. He was telling many bad things about himself. I respect people who do that; it makes me believe all the other elements. Despite all the dark aspects to his life, I liked Jim Laughridge.

"Well, I figure I've earned all the bad luck I've had," Laughridge said. "And I've earned all the good luck I've had. I can't complain."

Then:

"I do kind of wish I'd understood things more," he said about all the bad things that have happened to him and how, perhaps, his life might have turned out differently.

He sold the house where his wife had shot herself, then moved to Marietta, a suburb north of Atlanta.

"I moved up here on my sixtieth birthday, twenty-three years ago. Anyway, this gal moved in with me. I was screwing her, her best friend, one other good friend, and two old gals I knew before. Oh, hell, I was having a big time. Variety is the spice of life. I don't care what they say. Someone sees a good-looking woman and says he doesn't have thoughts, he's a lying son' bitch.

"I've just about cut off all the good things in life. I still have a drink of Smirnoff once in a while. And women—it's mostly look. But I have a good fling every once in a while. But the next morning—yew. Achy, breaky chest. I have to take them damn nitro pills and all that kind of stuff."

"You've had heart attacks?"

"Oh hell, I've had . . . one, two, three . . . four . . . five . . . I've had about four majors. Triple bypass. You name it. The woman I married, she had a baby at the time. She's just like one of my own. She's the one that's been taking care of me. Every time I have a heart attack, she takes me to the hospital. All of my kids, all of them graduated from college. Grandchildren graduating from college. All in all, I had a bang-up time. I wouldn't—well, there might be a few things I'd recall."

He showed me the scar of his leg wound. And shrapnel beneath his skin from other injuries.

"That damn shrapnel. It could range from the size of a grain of pepper to big stuff. I had a lot of it. It was in my hands and both legs. Every once in a while it would start working out, and your britches would pick it up. Little bitty stuff. It would aggravate the hell out of you."

"You think about the war much?"

"I watch the History Channel and they have World War II stuff on there. Then I'll have nightmares. Now this is after sixty years. And I'll probably have some more now after talking to you. Somehow or other I believe you don't ever get over something like that. Okinawa—I think it's done something to my mind that makes me have nightmares. If I can wake up, I'd call this gal I knew and talk to her. She'd say light a cigarette. Walk down to the kitchen and get a drink of water and come back up. By that time you'll be wide awake. When I dream about the war, it's realistic. And I wake up and, shit, I'm just washed out, man."

"What do you think of the Japanese today?"

"We didn't kill enough of 'em."

Laughridge laughed somberly.

"I have no sympathy for them at all. They're just in competition with us like everybody else. No, they didn't drop enough of them bombs as far as I'm concerned. And when the day comes that they come back—they'll be back. Germany will too. Now, that's an opinion. People in both of those countries haven't yet acknowledged defeat. They were jealous and hated us before that thing ever started, you know."

Laughridge seemed to be growing tired, so I packed up my stuff. He walked out into the misting March rain with me. We stood by the 1992 Chevrolet, and he kept talking. I realized that he really didn't want me to go. We were getting wetter and finally shook hands. When I was about halfway to my car down the street, he yelled, "Hey!"

"Just remember—shit happens!" he shouted when I turned to look back. "That's the way it is."

That summer I was in South Carolina and felt compelled to drive over to Atlanta for another visit. Laughridge appeared tired.

"I've been living a lot in the past for some reason or another," he told me of the few months since my previous visit. "I woke up clean out of bed the other morning yelling, 'Grenades! Grenades! Grenades!' I looked around and saw where I was. Mind is a funny thing.

"Before I went into the service I was a goddamn honor's student at a military school. And somehow or other, when I enrolled in North Carolina State, I really couldn't concentrate. It was easier to lay the books down and go get a beer. Before then, hell, I made As and Bs in military school. Something happened to my head. Well, they said all the marines was crazy anyway. Part of us was, I guess. I kinda had a hard time settling down. No particular reason that I know of. I couldn't get focused. Then by the time I got focused I had a damn house full of kids, grandkids. Too late now.

"Well, I'm not saying I'm that different than anybody else. Different things affect people differently. I ain't makin' no excuses. What happened, happened, you know. All in all, I've had a pretty good life. I can't blame General Motors for a damn thing."

As he showed me a picture of his grandson who had just graduated from college, Laughridge said, "You've been talking to all these guys. Are they any different than me?"

"No, not really," I said of the other Love Company members I'd met or talked with on the phone.

I wasn't being fully honest. What I really wanted to say was that I didn't know. Not all the guys from Love Company were as graphic or open in recalling the war and their lives afterward. A few seemed very well adjusted and didn't have issues. Some told me they'd forgotten the war. It's what my father would have said. Some of them surely had thoughts akin to those of Laughridge and simply didn't reveal them to me. I know my father had dark memories from those rare times he shared them with me, and that between 1946 and 1950, Steve Maharidge and James Laughridge lived the same drunken numb existence. My father also mirrored Jim in that he tried to go to business college, a junior college of its day, but he dropped out. My mother admonished him for not sticking with it. But it wasn't just a lack of drive like Mom thought. It was blast concussion or PTSD, or a little bit of both. My father eventually buttoned down a whole lot more than Jim, but just beneath the surface was that war-crazed marine I saw in Laughridge. If my mother had not been in Dad's life, he may have continued the drinking, brawling, and gambling. Like Laughridge, my father despised his factory job. Dad knew a guy he worked with who ran off to live in a tar paper shack in Idaho. Dad fantasized about that many times.

I didn't say any of this to Laughridge partly because I would have had to shout it, and partly because I didn't think I could have logically conveyed what I was feeling at that moment. (In a few months I'd write pretty much the preceding to Jim in a letter, after I got a phone call from his stepdaughter, Melody, the one who always helped him. I felt guilty for not answering honestly that afternoon. Melody told me that she'd moved in to care for her stepfather because he was going downhill.) Laughridge was smart enough to understand what I meant.

"I'll tell you one damn thing: you get to thinking, you wonder how anybody lived through it," Laughridge continued that afternoon, speaking of Okinawa. "The older I get, and I'm not a philosopher or nothing, but you look back and the whole damn thing was kind of stupid. It happened twenty years before—World War I. Then World War II. And it's been going on since World War II. What's the point in all of this? So you win a battle today. You're gonna lose one tomorrow. I don't know why people want to, as a country, just kill every damn body. It don't make sense. Not to me.

"Take all that money that they could be spending for something good here in this country. But they take it over there and blow it on some damn country you never heard of. People who have never been civilized, never will be. And as long as they live, they're gonna be fighting each other. And they just keep dumping that money over there. Hell."

I asked, "Was World War II worth fighting?"

"At the time it was, yeah. But we got a lot of propaganda what the world was going to be like afterward. It really isn't any different. You come right down to it, it's still the same old stuff. Europeans never get along with one another. Orientals sure as hell won't get along with one another. All them A-rabs is screwed up—the British moved in there after World War I. Split up all them little empires. That hasn't improved a damn bit. Somebody up there must be looking after us, if there is somebody up there."

"How do you figure that?"

"Because we've made so many friggin' mistakes. One right after another, one war after another. Same thing. Tomorrow it will be the same thing as last year. We just don't learn."

The sound of birds came through the front screen door.

"Somebody wrote a book that asked, 'What if they held a war, and nobody came?' Hell, I think it's all about money, misguided beliefs, ego. Whole lot of other bullshit. Even if you're another Audie Murphy or Sergeant. York, people ain't gonna know who you are thirty or forty years from now. Somebody told me right after World War II, 'You can take that Purple Heart and fifty cents and buy a beer in just about any joint in town.' And that's really about the way it was."

Laughridge clearly had been reflecting on our first conversation—he was speaking to me for his life's record. Also, he may have been trying to come to peace with his demons: "I'm glad somebody is putting it down like it was," he told me.

I rose to go. Once again Laughridge appeared to want me to linger. We ended up standing next to his 1992 Chevy Caprice parked in the driveway. Without prompt, he began talking about pulling gold teeth from dead Japanese soldiers.

"I thought it was a big brave thing to do. Looking back, it was chickenshit. I mean, goddamn, the man is dead. Let him be. I don't know. I guess my mind got warped somewhere along the line."

Jim Laughridge died at his home a little over a year later, on November 3, 2011. In 2012 I telephoned Melody. She said that her stepfather never discussed the war or other bad things in his life until just a few years before I showed up. She said that Jim told her that our talks and the letter I sent helped him understand more about what he went through. "You came at an important time for him," Melody said of her stepfather sorting out his life before it ceased. Not long before Jim died a doctor told them that his blackouts, like the one I witnessed, appeared to happen when he recalled emotionally troubling events. Melody and I wondered if this was due to PTSD, the effect of blast concussion, or both.

"We're an Aggressive Nation": Price

Tom Price was born on a farm in Springfield, Missouri. As the Great Depression came on, his maternal uncle had moved to California; the uncle returned to visit every few years, each time driving a new car. California represented a new life, a dream. Another uncle also moved west and found work. "And they told my dad, 'John you can get a job in California. There are jobs to be had out there.' We ate good on the farm. But we didn't have any money."

In 1937 the family picked up and drove west. Tom was twelve.

"When we left, there was snow on the ground, ice all the way across. We got into Pasadena, and there was big oranges hanging on the trees. Everything was green, and my mother says, 'This is paradise . . . we're never going back.'"

The family settled in Bell Gardens, then a rural farming center southeast of downtown Los Angeles. Many of the farmers were Japanese. Tom became friends with kids who were Nisei—second generation, born in the United States. "They were beautiful people," he said of Toshio, Toshiji, and Yaeko Watanabe.

"They had a little farm over there, raised a lot of stuff. Every Halloween they'd put straw in a truck and we'd go on a hayride. They was the richest ones in the city. They had more money than anyone else, but they worked hard."

In junior high school Tom met Vivian, who would become his wife. By high school they were sweethearts. Tom was sixteen years old and driving when a bulletin on the car radio announced that Pearl Harbor

Tom Price in uniform

Tom Price in 2011

had been bombed. "They'd been bombing China, you know. I said, 'Wait a minute . . . Pearl Harbor? I think that belongs to us.'"

Vivian was good friends with Yaeko, whose nickname was "Chuckie."

"She would come to my house and stay nights," Vivian said. "They'd bring us beautiful things from the fields, and my mother would fix apple pie, and we would have a big thing Friday night at the house. She'd stay overnight. There was no difference between Chuckie and us."

Chuckie lived in nearby Huntington Park. Before the internment order Japanese Americans were under curfew. "We would hide her in the car to get her from her house to my house so we could spend the night together," Vivian recalled.

The couple's Japanese friends were ordered to the Santa Anita Race-track, where they were processed for internment. Tom went to see them at the racetrack each Sunday before they were sent away. Vivian helped Yaeko and her family the day they had to go. "You could just feel the tension of the Americans, the white people. Here I am sitting with a Japanese girl—how could I do that? So that was a very antagonistic feel-ing. But I grew up with this girl. She was my closest friend."

The family was sent to a camp in Arizona, where they spent three years.

Tom and Toshio were too young for the war in 1941. Both wanted to enlist. Toshio ended up in the 442nd Regimental Combat Team, an all-Japanese US Army company that fought in Europe; it was a deco-rated unit and had twenty-one Medal of Honor recipients. Tom went into the Marines as soon as he was eighteen.

His first major battle was Guam. Lucky for Price, he landed after the beach was secured, bringing in ammunition and supplies.

"On Guam I got on the burial detail," he said, after the Japanese counterattack that left five hundred bodies in front of L Company the next morning.

"They were just dead all over the place. They dug a big hole with a bulldozer. We tied a wire around their leg or arm and drug them. It didn't take long to drag them over there, put them in a hole, and cover them up. It was very inhuman, like you know because they were . . . they was dead. But I didn't kill them."

When the company landed on Okinawa, Price believed the marines were sent north because the generals thought that "they would take the hilly part of the island. You know the southern part is more flat" and, thus, would be easier. The sad but true joke in the Marines is that they always start from the low ground—they're used for the toughest job of taking hills.

"Man, we covered so much ground in one day I couldn't even keep up, carrying the mortar. I was just totally exhausted. So I never dreamed we'd take that much ground that quick. I carried the tube, the bipod. My assistant gunner carried the base plate. That bipod and tube gets pretty heavy. Northern Okinawa, that's the only march I ever fell out of. Man, we were going over hills, and my legs were just like jelly. I couldn't go anymore."

Price finally made it into camp. It was his third day on the island.

When they got to the edge of the Motobu Peninsula, he watched as the captain's runner put field glasses to his face and "was looking over the hill. *Pow!* This Japanese rifleman hit him right between the eyes, man. So that was a bad omen right there."

There was an ambush on April 13. "Lepant got hit right away," Price said. "I looked, and he was lying on the ground." Price ran up a "little dry creek with willows on each side. . . . I didn't know where I was running to. I was just running." He dove into a low place. "Then I saw the grass cut about a foot away from my head. A bullet hit. And I'm thinking, 'I'm not hit at all!' And then, 'Somebody with a rifle knows where I'm at.' So I jumped up and ran behind a bank of a field they had irrigated. I feel something hot on my leg. I go, 'God dang! What's that!?' It was a bullet, laying right there on my leg. I don't know where it came from."

Then came Sugar Loaf Hill.

On May 15 they were braced for something bad to happen.

"The sergeant says, 'They're getting all sake'd up down in Naha, they got a bonfire and they're dancing. They're going to get all sake'd up, so get plenty ammunition tonight because they're going to pull a banzai attack.'

"Norman MacDonald, he was from New England. We was dug in together that night, so we dug a nice, deep foxhole. They was going to have to drag us out of here, I said to Mac, because we ain't going peacefully. All that night nothing happened.

"The next morning I got out of the foxhole. It was kind of cool. I just yawned, stretched, and looked up. And here's this orange thing coming through the sky, just like a giant bullet. It was orange colored because, though the sun was coming up and wasn't shining on us yet, it was shining up high. I said, 'Good God.' Man, I was just spellbound. No noise. It's floating through the air. It just seemed like I was frozen in time. And all of the sudden it noses down and it hit right up on top of the hill where our sergeant and the riflemen was. Down it come and *KABLOWI!* Big explosion, about fifty yards away. It killed a rifleman up there in a foxhole. They always said you'll never see the one that gets you, which can be wrong, man."

That night came the massive barrage in which my father and many other riflemen suffered blast concussions and were sent to the hospital.

"Our mortars was done wore out on Sugar Loaf Hill. We had fired them so many times that they were smacking the sides as they came out, so it was becoming pretty dangerous. They were supposed to come out smooth." There were no replacement mortars coming. "So we got rid of them. From then on we were just riflemen."

Price told me that the same lieutenant who ordered Jim Laughridge to get a bath also told him to get one. He then saw that officer get wounded by a Nambu machine gun. "That was his first and last orders," he said about the baths. "We never saw him again."

Of all the guys I found, Price was the only infantryman who went through the war unscathed. "Never got a scratch," he said. "The only wound I got was opening up a can of beer with a KA-BAR, and I missed the can of beer."

The company dropped into Naha, crossing the canal on May 30, and Price once again was staring raptly at objects in the sky when the tomb exploded.

"We were already past it. I'd say we were a quarter-mile away. We thought we were a long way from it. It just looked like the whole hill was going up. It just went, *BLEWIE!* We stood there and watched it. The blast kept getting higher and higher."

It was beautiful, in a dark way—the rocks seemed to be floating as they reached apogee. Price and others then saw the rocks were arcing in their direction.

"We realized we better start running. There wasn't anything really to hide behind. So we just hunkered down."

Price came home at the end of 1945. A recruiter tried to get him to re-enlist. Price told him, "Don't call me. I'll call you." He drank a lot at first, but that slowed, and in 1948 he and Vivian were married. They settled into a home amid orange groves in Norwalk, south of Los Angeles. They couldn't get a VA loan because the property was considered too rural.

In those early years after the war Vivian said she knew her husband was troubled.

"He would cry out at night in his sleep. Night after night he would call out his mother's name, or groan or half-cry. It wasn't good."

"Did he tell you what he was seeing?" I asked.

"No. Not a word."

"Why wouldn't he talk about it?"

"I don't know. Not until twenty-eight years later did I know."

"What happened twenty-eight years later?"

"He met with the fellows that were in the foxholes with him. The very intimate ones. The few. And when they started talking to each other, that was the first knowledge I had of the war at all, of what happened to him. It was better after we got together at those reunions. They were blood brothers, for sure. And it made a big difference in his life—and mine too."

The couple had two daughters, Robin and Lee, born in 1950 and 1959. At first Price worked for a fire extinguisher manufacturer, then the Studebaker auto company for ten years until it went out of business. A construction job followed for another decade. Then he bought a truck and hauled asphalt. "Worked for myself the last twenty years."

Tom and Vivian described having had good lives. They took vacations around the West in a motor home, flew to the Caribbean. "I'm not a very religious man, but it looks like somebody's looking out for me," he said.

His grandson was gung ho to join the Marines to fight in Iraq or Afghanistan.

"I told him, 'Go to school,'" Price said. "Get your education. I was glad I served. That was the 'good war.' But the boys dying over there—I wonder if it's worth it. Join the Marines, you can get yourself killed.

You see these boys in the paper every week, young boys, coming home dead."

Vivian explained to her grandson, "'Tom still knows you don't come back the same. You don't come back a free-hearted, loving, caring person anymore.'"

The grandson listened. He didn't enlist.

Price is befuddled by today's wars.

"Over in Iraq and Afghanistan right now, that's a losing proposition. We're just killing people, losing young boys over there. I say we should get out of there. It isn't necessary, the way I look at it. There's just nothing to win there. They've been fighting amongst themselves for centuries, and we're not going to change that. We're not going to change their way of thinking.

"I think we're an aggressive nation. It looks like that to me. We were fighting the British for our freedom. We fought the Indians to take their land. We fought the Mexicans. We wanted California from the Mexicans; we took it. We've been fighting all of our existence. As a nation we are aggressive—let's face it."

The Collector: Haigler

I'd heard a lot of uncomplimentary things spoken about Captain Frank H. Haigler Jr. Most vehement was George Niland. Ed Hoffman vacillated. "The captain wasn't there to ensure the personal comfort of George Niland," Ed once said. Other times Ed was less charitable.

The gulf between enlisted troops and officers is huge. I've tended to side with people on the bottom, but as I got to know Haigler over the years, I grew to like him. Among the reasons was that he fixated on the welfare of the families of the men who died under his command. He corresponded with many of them—in some cases for decades. Another reason was that he was extremely open and friendly.

Still, the captain was a most curious man, obsessed with the objects of war and death to the point of pathology. How could he have such passion for the inanimate objects of war and yet be so concerned about the survivors of the men killed in Love Company?

By the final time I met with Haigler in April 2011, with one exception, all of the family members with whom he'd corresponded were dead. He was the only high-ranking officer from Love Company still alive whom I could locate. He was a last man standing. In that ultimate meeting he was a mentally strong and physically able ninety-two-years old. Then that summer he faced a decision: he had a severe abdominal aneurysm; if it burst, it would suddenly kill him. An operation would be risky at his age, but if successful, he could live many more years. Haigler opted for surgery but died from complications that July. I learned of his death when I got a letter from Lynn Haigler Baker, his daughter. I knew it was bad news before opening it. Whereas once I could always call or visit Haigler when I was stumped about details of events on Okinawa, suddenly I couldn't call him anymore.

Haigler was the son of a career US Navy captain who was a medical doctor and, in 1916, was made one of the first navy flight surgeons. Frank lived in Tianjin and Tsingtao in China as a boy as well as Hawaii and Manila, the Philippines. Back in the States, he went to the Manlius Military Academy in upstate New York. He entered Northwestern University in Evanston, Illinois, and joined the Navy Reserve Officer Training Corps. He planned on the military as a career. He was on campus when he heard that Pearl Harbor had been attacked. When he went on active duty, the six-foot-two officer was assigned to a battleship, the *USS Nevada*, which had been sunk at Pearl Harbor and then rebuilt.

"We went to the Aleutian Islands for the Battle of Attu. When that was over, we went around to the Atlantic Ocean to prepare for the Normandy landing. I was at the Normandy landing on June 6, 1944."

Two weeks later he came home to Chicago on thirty-day leave, "one of the first back after Normandy." He had planning documents about the landing: these were his first wartime collectibles. He went to the *Chicago Tribune* with them, but when the newspaper checked with Naval Intelligence, the story was censored. Haigler got in trouble, but

Captain Frank Haigler in uniform

Haigler in 2010

not too much, because the Navy then put him in the US Marine Corps staff school.

He had to leave in a hurry after completing training and was only allowed fifty pounds of duffel. Rather than scramble to buy needed things, he purchased a case of expensive whiskey, which he discovered weighed exactly fifty pounds. He was rushed onto a transocean Boeing Clipper airplane to Hawaii, then transferred to a DC4 to Guadalcanal, where he joined Headquarters Company for the 3rd Battalion of the 22nd Marines. On the Canal he used the whiskey to barter for clothes and other items he did not bring with him and, later, for souvenirs on Okinawa. "I knew that whiskey would be better than gold," Haigler said.

When the division landed on Okinawa, "we crossed the island and we still had not seen any combat." They went north on the Pacific

Ocean side of the island. On April 6 and 7 Haigler's diary notes that they walked twenty-eight miles in one day. They then crossed to the China Sea side, moving north to the Motobu Peninsula, "where we did encounter quite a bit of action. We were stationed in that area several days and sustained quite a few casualties in combat." These days are shown in his diary for April 9 through 13:

"The combat involved Item Company and King Company and Love Company," Haigler said. Then the 3rd Battalion was ordered north: the brunt of the Motobu operation was done by the 4th and 29th Marines as well as the 1st Battalion of the 22nd. The next few weeks were nearly idyllic. The company encamped on the Okuma Beach, eleven days after landing on the island.

Haigler by then had gotten to know other officers in the companies of the 3rd Battalion. Love Company's Captain John P. Lanigan warned Haigler about Lieutenant Colonel Clair Shisler. Lanigan related the horror of that night of the counterattack on Guam's Orote Peninsula.

"He told me Colonel Shisler ordered them to go down the road—at Road Junction 15," Haigler said of the marines stopping in front of the trapped Japanese. "The captain then was Hedrick. Hedrick was very mad. He felt that that was almost suicide to do that. He went down there and *wham!* Shot right in the head by a Nambu machine gun. I got all this from Lanigan."

Captain Harry D. Hedrick was killed July 25, 1944, the same night my father was hit with mortar shrapnel. Hedrick wanted tank support, which Shisler would or could not provide, or to locate in a different position, Haigler recalled Lanigan telling him. Shisler didn't listen. He commanded Hedrick to put his men smack up against the Japanese.

Fenton Grahnert's story resonated—why did the tanks lead them to that spot, only then to be withdrawn? After all, had the tanks remained, the power equation of that battle would have been dramatically altered. A lot of guys might not have died; my father might not have been wounded. Some accounts of the battle, without naming Shisler, said there was competition with other Marine units to advance fast and get to the peninsula first.

Shisler's order made Love Company into a suicide unit.

(Lanigan, who went on to become a colonel in the US Marine Corps, died twenty years before Haigler told me this, so I was never able to confirm the account with him.)

Haigler also recounted what Lanigan told him about a prisoner who Shisler wanted killed.

"He ordered, 'Take that man out there and just straight stone him to death,'" Haigler recalled. "So the men took the guy, put him in the middle of the street, and then they started throwing stones at him. And they killed him! When division had heard that [Shisler] had ordered killed a prisoner, they had to do something. They transferred him out of the battalion. He should have been court martialed. . . . Instead of sending him back to the States, they put him on the staff of the Sixth Division to keep it quiet. He only came back to the 3rd Battalion when, as a result of Sugar Loaf, we didn't have a commanding officer. They put him back in command of his old battalion."

Haigler's diary has this note for April 13, 1945: "Shisler first seen." Haigler clearly had a wary eye on that officer.

Amid this period up north, Haigler's obsession with collecting once again got him in trouble. He'd kept, against orders, a top-secret copy of the battle plan for the Okinawa operation shown him before the landing. He gave it to a friend for safekeeping, and then that friend's Jeep hit a land mine: the briefcase containing the plan burst open and scattered the contents to the wind. That would have been the end of the story, but an Okinawan was detained and the plans were found on him; Haigler's identification was written on them. Haigler was chewed out, but able bodies were in short supply, and the twenty-three-year-old officer had been otherwise successful, so there was no punishment.

After some two weeks in Okuma/Hichi the 3rd Battalion was trucked south. They came to the Asa Kawa River, where on the night of May 9, a footbridge had been built.

"Item Company got across," Haigler said. This happened at 3:30 a.m. according to the *History of the Sixth Marine Division*. Before dawn, "a couple of suicide Japanese swimmers blew it up," Haigler said of the bridge. I Company was trapped. "Hell, they couldn't advance, and they couldn't retreat because the bridge was out."

The next day they got more soldiers across the Asa Kawa, and the rest of the companies followed. They were now in the heights overlooking Naha. Ahead of them was the at-first inconsequential-seeming mound that came to be known as Sugar Loaf Hill.

"The Japanese had what to us was a new type of defense," Haigler said. "They were defending from the reverse slope. Before, you always defended a hill on the front. The Japanese would hide on the other side, and then as you'd get to the top, they'd come out. You couldn't get at them. They're in caves, all on the other side. The only way you could even begin to get them was with mortars, but direct fire, no. The tanks that we'd try to get in there to support, they were hit by artillery from the Shuri angle," he said of Mount Shuri, which had a deadly commanding view. "So we were getting hit from the side and the reverse defense of the Japanese.

"We'd finally get a few men up there on top, and they'd [the Japanese] be coming out from the caves and throwing grenades. We couldn't get around the sides because of the other hills," he said of Horseshoe and Half Moon hills that provided enfilading crossfire. Days of rain began. "Everything turned to mud," Haigler said.

"Sugar Loaf turned out to be a meat grinder. In spite of our aggressiveness and bravery or whatever you want to call it, we still couldn't hold that position. We'd start getting so many casualties. That night, the casualties were coming back. The aid station and the company command post were in a little-sheltered hill near Sugar Loaf. I remember that quite vividly because it was rather frightening. I took care of several badly injured men and sent them back to the regimental aid station. I was able to start, in two instances, intravenous plasma because I had been in some medical training before the war.

"That same afternoon, our lieutenant colonel who had the 3rd Battalion," Haigler said of Malcolm O. Donohoo, "he had a conference with the company commanders up ahead of us a few hundred yards. And then they were hit. All of them at one time. All of the company commanders and the captain [Lanigan] were wounded. They grabbed me and sent me up to take over L Company. From that point on I had L Company.

"After Sugar Loaf we went right down through what would have been the suburbs of Naha. There wasn't much left of Naha. My God, it was just flattened. We spent a night there, getting our casualties rebuilt. An outfit had just landed with a lot of men to fill in our ranks," he said of twenty replacements for the many men killed or wounded. Among them were Privates George Niland and Edward Hoffman as well as a lieutenant who had just graduated from Quantico, James R. Bussard, an Ohioan who would die in two weeks, his bullet-pierced helmet later ensconced in Haigler's basement.

"That first night that we were down there, getting our replacements, it was just getting dark. I had to interview these people in the dark, and all I had was a flashlight."

On the morning of May 30 Love Company crossed the canal bisecting Naha. Haigler went north of Knob Hill/Mount Jokagu. Regarding Mulligan, who was on the other side and out of sight, Haigler said, "At that point, I didn't know specifically that he was killed. I was just simply told there was a hell of an explosion, and one of the men had thrown a grenade into a cave."

It's likely that Haigler learned of the explosion late that night or the next day, based on records that back up his recollection.

"I was so busy at that time that I didn't have time to think, because right after that happened Japanese artillery hit right next to my point and killed three of my men, right there, right quick, right at one time," he said of the next day when they were near Hill 46, the objective just beyond Knob Hill. Among those dead were Sergeant Donald A. Booth and Private Frank A. Blackwell. "So I had to run over to take care of those three men. I didn't have time to think about anybody else."

Then came a big challenge—Haigler found use for Captain Lanigan's warning about Shisler.

"Goddamn it, he was a real SOB. He'd never come up forward and expose himself to look over the territory. He'd stay in the back. And so he had ordered our company, L Company, to assault this valley, after Knob Hill."

Haigler, remembering the fate of Captain Hedrick, told Shisler, "'We can't do that without tank and artillery support.' And he wouldn't listen. And I said, 'I'll show you!' I was so mad, it was about a mile away, and I ran all the way back that mile. The machine gun section was all crouched along the side of this hill, and they were afraid to go up this valley. I ran into a sergeant. I said, 'Get your outfit out here. We've got an assault up this hill.' And he said, 'No, no, no, I'm not going to. I've got a couple of men, and they're in there and they're wounded, and we can't get them out.' Goddamn it! I ran up that goddamn valley myself, all alone. I was going to show Shisler that you can't do it. In effect, I was like Hedrick. I was so mad I was almost committing suicide."

He went into the valley about one hundred yards. He came on the two trapped men who were crouched in a shell hole filled with water.

"One of them was shot. Not bad, but with a wound through the neck. I didn't know how the other fella was wounded. They were so scared they were paralyzed. They wouldn't get out of the hole."

They told him, "'No, no! We're going to get shot!'"

Haigler replied, "'But it's quiet.' And while I'm arguing with them a bullet comes whipping by my head. Then a bullet went right through my shirt," he said, showing how it tore cloth on his arm but didn't hit flesh.

"Then I suddenly got scared. It was no wonder these guys were scared. I was like, 'How stupid could I be as a company commander? You can't expose yourself like this.' So I hauled ass. I got out. Looking back, I should have somehow gotten hold of one of these guys and forced him out. But I didn't. I got back around the little hill and I told that sergeant to stay put, and I got all the way back to the colonel at the command post."

He showed his superior his bullet-torn shirt.

"I said, 'I can't expose my men. I can't go up that valley without tank support or artillery.'

"And he said, 'Well, you've got to do it.'

"I said, 'I can't do it. I'd lose my whole company.' I was frantic. I was so desperate. I thought of those two men there. They wouldn't move, and I'm not going to sacrifice any more men. And then I looked way off to my left with my binoculars a mile or so. The army was supporting us on our left. And I could see these figures running back. So I assumed—correctly—that they must have been under attack and they were in confusion. I couldn't attack with no flank protection. It was impossible.

"So I told the colonel, 'I have no protection on my left.' He finally said, 'Well, okay. Hold your men. Pull them back. I'll get tank support tomorrow and we'll make an assault.'

"I said, 'Fine, tomorrow with some support.'

"So the next morning, we got a hell of an artillery barrage up that whole valley. Several tanks moved in. We took off. No opposition at all. We went right on up through that valley, and nothing bad happened."

Someone else got the two men out. Haigler put in for that marine to be awarded a Silver Star.

A lesson from Guam, via Captain Lanigan to Haigler, surely saved the lives of men in Love Company.

The 3rd Battalion crossed the Kokuba River on a Bailey Bridge near the ruins of a multiple-arch stone bridge that had been finished in 1720 and had survived until the 1944 bombing of Naha.

Love Company came to the place where Jim Laughridge was shot. After that the company was involved in a fierce battle for Hill 53—the tunnel complex that was the Japanese Naval Headquarters of Admiral Minoru Ota.

"On the eleventh of June my company captured Hill 53 just south of Naha," Haigler said. "You know, I always picked up souvenirs. We had thrown a hand grenade into a cave. Then I had my demolition sergeant, Joe Rhodes, throw a dynamite charge. And I thought, 'That will kill them all, so I'll run into the cave and maybe I'll get a good souvenir.' So I go running in there, and all I've got is this pistol. Several

Japanese soldiers are in there, they were killed. But there was one Jap lieutenant, he was starting to get up. He's right in front of me and it's dark. So I fired at him point blank. God, I tell you, I went down. I thought he shot me at the same time.

"He had a sword, a samurai sword. I grabbed that sword, crawled out of the cave. I said, 'God, he shot me!'

"The men said, 'What happened?' I said, 'I got shot, right in the balls!' I look down and there's no hole in my trousers and no blood running down. By this time I'm able to stand up. They dragged his body out. My bullet hit his helmet and ricocheted right back at me. So I was okay in about five minutes. It was just like I was kicked. But I had the sword, see.

"I did mention the subject of souvenirs because that was one of my drawbacks. If anyone were to criticize me, they could certainly have reason to. I was really hung up on souvenirs. I'd get hold of a Jap rifle or something like that. I couldn't carry it because I was busy doing my job. So I would give it to one of my runners to carry. I was having some of my men carry my souvenirs—that's bad."

Haigler suggested to his superiors that they should have several men detailed to look after souvenirs for men of all ranks in the company.

I was puzzled. Haigler explained, "It was a good trading thing. The men would get rifles and swords and so on, and then they'd trade them to the Seabees or sailors that would come ashore. They'd get food and provisions and stuff like that."

But Haigler was collecting for a different reason—he was building his future museum.

"I attributed too much importance to that, and I should not have," he said. "That was a shortcoming that I had. You never hear of this aspect of combat."

Another element that is not heard about, he said, was how officers were at a disadvantage.

"When we were in a position where we were going to do an assault the next day, we as company commanders had to go out and make reconnaissance of the area, get together with the platoon leaders and discuss what the activity was going to be. That kept us busy clear up to midnight. So we get to our command post, and everybody has been fed.

They've dug their foxholes and all. Here is the company commander with no foxhole, no food.

"I thought they've got to change the system. British officers always had an enlisted man that took care of their food, and he helped dig the hole. I had nobody to help me, and sometimes I got rather frustrated. I didn't have time to dig my own. And I certainly didn't have any food to eat.

"The corpsmen that we always had attached to us, they carried litters, and then at night they'd lay the litter down and had a beautiful place to sleep. They were the only ones that had a bed. I remember one time I was just dog tired and I hadn't had any sleep for several nights. The corpsman had this litter and I said, 'I'm going to use your litter to sleep on.' He got really irritated. He said, 'Well, I've been carrying it all day, and now you're going to sleep on it?' And I said, 'Yeah, you're damn right that I'm going to sleep on that litter tonight!' I remember a couple of incidents like that might have made me unpopular with a couple of men."

At the end of the Okinawa operation, as the southern part of the island was falling, Haigler said this leaflet was dropped from airplanes on the Japanese soldiers and civilians. The opposite side was in Kanji characters.

Many Japanese soldiers held to the *bushido* code and would not give up. Others couldn't—their officers wouldn't allow them to surrender. And civilians had been fed propaganda that all women would be raped and everyone killed; civilians committed suicide, many by jumping off cliffs.

Some, however, did surrender.

"There was one thing that bothered me quite a bit, but there was nothing I could do about it. Right at the very end of the operation we had two Japanese soldiers as prisoners. I told one of my men to escort them back to headquarters. He came back in about ten minutes and he said, 'Well, that takes care of them.' And I said, 'What do you mean?' And he said, 'Oh, they tried to run away, so I shot 'em.' And I thought, 'No, they didn't try to run away. You killed 'em.' I felt pretty bad that he would do that. But what could I do about it?"

Tom Price also remembered that incident. Price had told me,

A couple of Japanese soldiers who just had loin cloths on came down the hill. Captain Haigler told the guy, 'You take them back to the rear

Surrender leaflet

TRANSLATION OF TEXT

LIFE SAVING LEAFLET

1. The American Forces will aid all who follow the instructions given in this leaflet.
2. Good treatment—food clothing, tobacco, medical treatment, etc., will be accorded in conformity with International Law.

HOW TO USE THIS LEAFLET

1. Come slowly toward the American line with your hands raised high above your head, and carry only this leaflet.
2. Come one by one. Do not come in groups.
3. Men must wear only pants or loin cloths. Sufficient clothing will be provided. Women and children may come dressed as they are.
4. Do not approach American lines at night.
5. This leaflet may be used by anyone—Japanese, Korean, Soldier, Civilians, etc.
6. Those who do not have leaflets may advance to the American line if they follow instructions as if they had a leaflet.

of the lines and you see that they get there.' They just went a little bit down the hill, and we heard this B.A.R. open up. Captain Haigler never said anything, nobody said anything. They brought up a Jeep with some hot coffee and we had to walk down this path. One was laying there still alive. His eyes were open; he wasn't dead yet. He [the guy told to escort the prisoners] just shot them right in the back. Man, I always wondered how he lived with himself the rest of his life. I've seen a lot. When we went into that ambush up in the north, when Lepant got hit . . . if I could have got my hands on one then I would have choked him to death. But I still wouldn't have shot him in the back. They didn't surrender very often, but these two knew the jig was up. They decided to give themselves up. But it was a bad move for them.

By the time those two prisoners were executed, almost all of the soldiers in the company were replacements. Haigler said of the original 240 men in Love Company who landed on April 1, only "seventy or seventy-one" were not severely wounded or killed by the end of June.

Love Company returned to Guam, where the unit trained for the invasion of Japan's main island. Then the atom bombs were dropped.

"The war was over at that point," Haigler said of those last days on Guam. "I had orders to take my company out on the rifle range and get them requalified [with rifle accuracy], so I took most of the company with me. We were running behind. We couldn't quite get going. I heard that Shisler was coming. He had all of us officers a little scared of him. I thought, 'Oh, Christ, I've got to get these guys going.' So I ordered the first row, I said, 'Get up on the line and start shooting off-hip.' We didn't have enough time to get the men in proper prone position. That's where you start zeroing in your weapons on the targets. Men were lined up with their carbines, shooting, and Shisler comes up.

"'What's going on here!?' he asked.

"I said, 'They're getting qualified.'

"He said, 'Don't you know how to run a rifle range?! For godsake, they've got to shoot prone first, then sitting, and then off-hip! You don't even know how to handle these men!' So he said, 'Take your men and leave. Forget about qualifying.'

"I was wrong, but it was such an insignificant thing. He took that incident and he wrote a letter to get me reassigned. He said, 'This officer has no business being in command of a rifle company.'"

Sixty-six years after the run-in with Shisler, Haigler was still amped about it.

"The war was over! It was over!" he shouted. "Goddamn it! I was debating about whether I wanted to get out of the Marine Corps and go to medical school. When that happened, I thought, 'Yeah.'"

He resigned. Was Shisler giving payback over Haigler's intransigence in that valley after Knob Hill? Or over the issues of Haigler's obsession with collecting?

Haigler returned stateside and took some premed courses at UCLA. He then matriculated to the University of Illinois Medical School. By then he had a wife and child. He became an obstetrician and did his residency at the Mayo Clinic in Minnesota. He was then awarded a Fulbright Scholarship and spent a year in Salzburg, Austria. In 1956 he moved to Sunnyvale, California, to open a private practice. In 1962 he relocated to Southern California. What his daughter Lynn called a "transition out of the brutal night calls as he got older," he took a residency in anesthesia. After doing that Haigler went into family practice and did a lot of work in nursing homes. He was a doctor into his eighties. "He reinvented his medical practice several times," Lynn said. In later life, she said, his "business card read, 'Eccentric Enterprises.'"

Haigler's income allowed him to expand his collection. He bought the house and land in Fullerton. At peak, Haigler had fifteen functioning military vehicles from both world wars. There was the thirty-two-ton Sherman tank that bothered a neighbor who'd been in the war—the unique sound of the throbbing diesel engine brought back bad memories for that man when Haigler drove it around. Haigler sold it for "tens of thousands of dollars" in 1987. There were the German Nazi motorcycles, an amphibious Jeep, various command cars from World War II; he also had a World War II bomb-fuse setter. ("Nobody today knows how it functions. It's a very complicated piece of machinery—we didn't have computers, and this automatically set the shell to explode at certain altitudes," Haigler told me. As far as he knew, no other such devices survived the war.) He had a 1918 Renault tank; over a hundred knives, pistols, and rifles; a Civil War sword that his great-grandfather had in the Battle of Shiloh that he was waving while riding his horse "and a Confederate musket ball took off his finger," Haigler said—the bullet also took a chunk out of the sword handle; a one thousand–book library on both World Wars; and so on. The collection was vast.

Yet Haigler was still collecting. A year before he died he confided to me that he'd spent $20,000 on a shrunken human head from South America.

He never quite explained his fascination with such objects. In a lot of ways he was like a twelve-year-old boy his entire life, focused on the things a boy that age finds fascinating.

One thing that he did answer was when I asked if the war bothered him.

"No," he responded fast. "I'm very fortunate, I guess. As I look back, I think I did a good job. Nothing great, but at least I did what was expected of me."

In his own way Haigler was as honest as Jim Laughridge had been. I believed him when he said he didn't have any nightmares or issues regarding the war.

He tried to mend the past. He went to division reunions. The first time Ed Hoffman saw Haigler at one, he felt the captain avoided him. But Hoffman later got a telephone call from Haigler, and they had a nice talk. Haigler even extended an olive branch to Shisler.

"I heard that Shisler had had a heart attack, that he had been forced to retire from the Marine Corps. So I sat down—I don't know what possessed me—and I wrote him a very nice letter. I said, 'You and I have had our differences, but that's years ago, and I've always thought you were a fine officer. I'm so sorry to hear of your heart attack and that you are being forced to retire from the Marine Corps. The Marine Corps has lost a fine officer.' He never answered. Never answered! He was such an ass."

Shisler died in 1994.

We descended to Haigler's basement. We studied the sword taken from the body of the Japanese officer he'd shot on Hill 53. Next to it was a Japanese rising sun flag.

"Many years later my telephone rings one night. And this man says, 'Is this Captain Haigler?' I thought, 'Nobody calls me that.' He says, 'Oh, I found you.' He says, 'I'm Joe Rhodes, your demolition sergeant. He said, 'Remember that cave where I threw that charge in, and then you went in with your pistol?' He said, 'You got the sword, didn't you?' And I said, 'Yeah.' He said, 'When they dragged his body out and took his helmet off, I got the flag that was wrapped around his head.' I said, 'How did I miss that?' He said, 'Well, you were too busy worrying about getting shot in the balls.' He said, 'When you die, can I have that sword?' I said, 'Sure, you can have the sword. But you give me that flag then if you die first.' He said, 'Okay.' Well, about two years later his son mailed me the flag. He died. So now I have the sword and I have the flag."

Rhodes had signed the flag.

Haigler had numerous Japanese rifles. He showed the chrysanthemum that was stamped near the chamber on the weapons he'd collected on Okinawa. Only rifles that came from the island battles had it— many guys got rifles for barter in China, but the occupied Japanese government ground off the flower, a symbol of the Emperor, before selling them. (When I came home and studied my father's Japanese rifle, there was a grind mark where the flower had been; he clearly did not get it off a soldier he had slain as I had grown up believing; it most likely came from China, as did the sword.)

Despite his obsession with the items of death, during each of my visits to Haigler's house he talked about the families of the men killed. Most were grateful for his correspondence. But after years of writing to one widow, she asked that Haigler not stay in touch—she wanted to forget.

"The thing that has struck me as I've gotten older is not the men that were killed. I consider the real tragedy of war the families that are left behind, the mothers and the fathers and the brothers and sisters. For every soldier that died there are hundreds of people that live, and the rest of their life is changed. When you die, it's quick and it's over. But it is not easy to be a survivor in a family. We always talk about the soldiers. We don't put up any monuments for the families, and yet they suffer far more than the soldier did. I think that so often people don't think of this aspect when they have their Veterans' Day parade, Memorial Day. They miss the real point. That's why I talk about that a lot. Right after the war I thought, 'Gee, I've got to let them know that somebody is still thinking of their sons and husbands.'

"I'm not necessarily antiwar. I'm not a pacifist at all. But maybe they'd think a little more about whether we'd go to war in Iraq or Afghanistan if they considered things like this."

In the summer of 2011 doctors had to abort the surgery on Haigler after hours of work because of complications. Lynn had traveled to be with her father and his second wife, Pat. There was a second surgery weeks later. Lynn is a nurse, and she wrote in detail about the many complications from the surgeries. She also wrote,

> The surgery sites were healing and looked good. However, he was weak from not moving and not eating and too many days of pain. . . . I think it was the combination of fairly severe weakness, depression at that point, and seeing that he would be sent to a rehab facility for an extended time to recover that led to his saying, "No more, I want to go home, call hospice."
>
> We knew he was not good at doing "rehab," that it would be long, and he might never get back to his pre-surgery self. He was very coherent and knew the score. . . . Out came the tubes, we took him home (ambulance) with hospice. He relaxed immediately and totally when he went through his front door.

I was ready for a few weeks. . . . Pat, my sister Joan, I and his dog sat by his bed. He was comfortable and breathing regularly. He died very quietly within 15 hours much to everyone's surprise. . . . I thought—a marine to the end—he set his mind on something and did it.

Joe Lanciotti in uniform

Joe Lanciotti in 2011

The Poet: Lanciotti

One day at Frank Haigler's house I leafed through the files of letters back and forth to the families of the guys who died under his command, including Ralph J. Krupkowski, a machine gunner killed on May 12, 1945, after Love Company had crossed the Asa Kawa River. They were battling the Japanese on the ridge overlooking the valley.

Most of the correspondence was with his father, but one from Verna Krupkowski, Ralph's sister, stood out. This is how the letter began:

CABLE ADDRESS: "WALDORF, NEW YORK" / ELDORADO 5-3000

The WALDORF-ASTORIA

PARK AND LEXINGTON AVENUES / 49TH AND 50TH STREETS / NEW YORK 22/

March 11, 1949

Dear Mr. Haigler -

     Before I go any further, please let me apologize for my very tardy delay in replying to your letter. You have been very kind in answering my letter and sending the photograph and this certainly has been a fine way of showing our appreciation. Let me say here and now that we do and always will appreciate your actions in this matter. It has meant very much to us hearing a little first-hand information regarding Ralph.

     Since there is always an excuse for everything I also have one to offer for my late reply. First of all, I have been in New York where I am now writing this letter, combining a little bit of business and pleasure for the insurance company for which I work. And then too, we have been notified that Ralph's remains have been brought to the States and are now awaiting a telegram which will tell us the date of the burial.

On the next page, she wrote, in part:

>   There is one phrase in your letter
> which I cannot agree with and that is: "Our
> men did not die in vain". Perhaps I have
> not gotten over my bitterness over losing
> Ralph, but I feel that he did die in vain.
> Nothing has been accomplished by his dying,
> or by all the other men dying. The world
> is not a better place to live in; on the
> contrary, it becomes a rottener place day
> by day by all appearances. Maybe this is
> the wrong attitude to take but I can't seem
> to shake it off. However, there is no
> point in discussing it because you could go
> on and on and never reach a conclusion to
> this problem. When I began this letter I
> had no intentions of sounding off like this,
> believe me, and so before I start off again,
> I want to thank you again for my family and
> myself for the wonderful things you told us
> of Ralph (although we knew that Ralph would
> always stand out no matter where he was) and
> for putting our minds at ease, knowing he
> didn't have to suffer at the end. It meant
> much to us knowing that,
>   Thanking you again, I am,
>   FOR AIR MAIL OR FOREIGN MAIL USE *Verna Krychowski*

I already knew a lot about Verna's brother, Ralph. In life he stood six-foot-four and came from a small city in Pennsylvania. In death, I knew what his body looked like:

> His big, left arm stretched outside the poncho and I tried to
> place it alongside his body but it would not move. It would
> not bend. I didn't know what rigor mortis was then, all I know
> he was stiff and his big, left arm stuck out of the poncho sadly.
> The large, silver Marine Corps ring with the globe, eagle and
> anchor were on one finger. He bought it in the PX in Parris Is-
> land. All of us kids wore that cheap, silver ring at one time or
> other with pride.
>
> I had thrown mine away a long time ago.

These words were written by a man in Love Company whose name I came across in the muster rolls: Emerico J. Lanciotti. When I telephoned, he was surprised when I asked for Emerico. "I haven't gone by that since before the war," Joe Lanciotti told me.

"I know why you're calling," he quickly announced after I explained I was researching my father's war and Love Company.

"Oh yeah?"

"You're going through midlife crisis. You're feeling your mortality. That's why you're doing this."

I couldn't argue. Lanciotti was curt but not caustic with me. He suggested that I read his book, *The Timid Marine*. That phone conversation hadn't lasted more than five minutes.

Someone in my father's company wrote a book about what the unit went through? I ordered his self-published book. It's about how Lanciotti "cracked up" in battle on that day my father, Bill Fenton, Fenton Grahnert, Frank Palmasani, and the others were hospitalized—May 16, 1945, after the Japanese shelled the men facing Sugar Loaf Hill.

The introduction to *The Timid Marine*, in part, said this about war: "One must be immersed in the blood, stench, fear and agony of it until he is almost insane, to approach understanding. . . . I intend to grab you by the scruff of your neck and stick your nose into the reality of it."

Lanciotti wrote that nearly 1.4 million soldiers were treated for combat fatigue, that 37 percent of the ground troops were discharged for psychiatric reasons in World War II, and that many thousands deserted. Just one man was executed for "desertion and combat fatigue during World War II. He was shot by a firing squad." Lanciotti went on, stating, "I, and hundreds of thousands of combat fatigued veterans could sympathize with Eddie Slovik, that frightened soldier. . . . I was a very frightened and timid marine."

Cracking up happened to a lot of men. But this aspect of World War II is seldom openly discussed. I devoured *The Timid Marine*, published in 2005, in one night. It was written from the soul. Lanciotti was brave enough near the end of his life to write about a forbidden topic of the "Good War"—losing it on the battlefield.

Like the vast majority of enlisted men in Love Company, Joe Lanciotti was a child of hard times. His mother abandoned the family just before Christmas 1938, when Joe was twelve. Christmas was a tough time, and during that holiday right after Pearl Harbor was attacked, Joe was home with just his brother in Lodi, New Jersey. There wasn't much food in the house. Their father, an Italian immigrant and World War I veteran, was alone at the hospital undergoing a hernia operation.

Young Joe was a reader. He wanted to be a poet. In 1942 he read Thoreau. He cites Thoreau as the genesis of his lifelong questioning and distrust of authority. He dropped out of high school to become a poet. But there were conflicting pulls in his life. Joe often went to the movies. "The Hollywood propaganda machine was already planning movies to excite young boys to join the military," he wrote. Those films amped him up; they inspired him to volunteer for the Marines. On May 4, 1944, he went off to boot camp at Parris Island.

After training he applied for "sea duty," the elite group of marines who stand guard at the tomb of the unknown soldier, on big navy ships, or at embassies.

"It took me a while to realize I was just a cannon fodder marine," he wrote. "A rifleman, the bottom of the barrel, the guys they send to face the enemy in person."

He was stationed stateside for a while, but by the end of the year he was on a ship bound for Guadalcanal, where he landed just before the New Year's Day 1945. He'd heard a lot about the island and was excited to be on the Canal, "when I had just seen the movie only a few months ago.

"That is the way the government planned it, propaganda movies and then the real thing. Soon after a battle was fought, Hollywood would have its version on the screen for the country to watch. Everybody was a hero, and more enemy died than Americans. Hollywood depicted a sanitized and romantic war where no one died anonymously."

He was placed in Love Company's third platoon. Lanciotti's nickname became "Poet" because he carried a book of verse. He became good friends with Krupkowski and a man named LaFoo.

"It used to be so hot when we went out on drills that the sun," he told me, "it would feel like it was right in the back of your head." Like my father, he got a fungus infection there "that bothers me up to this day in the ear . . . the jungle rot that attacks the skin."

Following the unchallenged Okinawa landing, as Love Company moved north, men, such as Tom Price with his mortar, collapsed after the twenty-eight-mile march that Haigler wrote about in his diary. "I made it through that night, but my night was coming," Lanciotti wrote.

He described going on patrol on April 12, 1945, into a valley at the base of the Motobu Peninsula. He was "point man," which meant he was out front. Lanciotti wrote about how the enemy could see the "skinny, teenage boy who kept looking back over his shoulder" at the men behind him. He thought of Tennyson's "The Charge of the Light Brigade":

> *Into the valley of death*
> *Rode the six hundred*

Lanciotti detailed how the Japanese opened up on them, the sound of bullets crackling past his ears, the cries of wounded and dying Americans.

"The enemy could see us and we did not know where they were," he wrote. The bullets were kicking up dirt as he ran. "It was the longest, hardest, most brutal, fearsome run I had ever made in my life. You couldn't see a single enemy soldier."

As dead marines were being stacked on Jeeps, an officer announced that President Franklin Roosevelt had died. The next day was when Charles Lepant was hit.

In the book he tells of coming on Japanese camps with tea still boiling on fires. "Frequently there were men with their toes on the trigger of their rifles, the rifle muzzles in their mouths and their heads blown open. They had tired of war."

One night on guard duty, he and a friend named Lee could see the silhouettes of women and children sneaking by in the night. They'd been ordered to shoot anything that moved. Lanciotti had been smoking

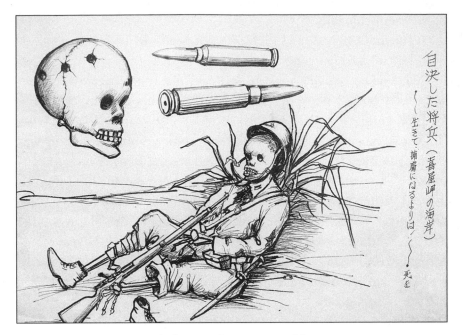

Skeleton of Japanese soldier
Courtesy of Shuri Heights High School Museum

a cigarette hidden in a cupped hand. Lee took it and made several "long drags" on it so that it glowed bright. The group of civilians scattered and ran away.

Later his platoon came to some caves. A few soldiers threw in phosphorous grenades. Civilians came pouring out, wounded. The burning phosphorus "could not be extinguished and ate through clothing into the flesh and into the bone. The pain was horrible to witness especially when children were the victims," Lanciotti wrote. The only way to extinguish the fire on flesh was with petroleum jelly. "Two marines were laughing, insanely excited by the brutality of their own fear. They laughed as a mother clutched her baby and tried to wipe the phosphorus off the baby's clothing. They had been calloused to the point of inhumanity. Were these my countrymen? Was I any better?

"'You dumb sons of bitches,' I shouted at the two marines. 'Look what you've done. They are only women and kids. Civilians.'"

He swung his rifle.

"'One more grenade and I'll blow your heads off.'

"They stopped laughing.

"'Are you becoming a gook lover, Poet?' one of the bastards shouted at me as I picked phosphorous from a woman's clothing with my KA-BAR knife.

"A civilian man who was bleeding from a stomach wound was moaning in terrible pain as marines milled around him," Lanciotti continued. "The wounded man pointed to the marine's rifles and then to his head getting his point across quite clearly.

"Smoke, stench, confusion, and fear" filled the air. The wounded man was ignored except by "LaFoo who took his .45 that he had requisitioned from a dead officer and calmly placed it to the suffering man's head as the man looked up at him thankfully.

> The look in LaFoo's eyes as he pulled the trigger, and soon after as his soul was ripped away, cannot be described. The society of men have never developed dictionaries containing those words. They are not words used to describe football games. So I offer, his soul was ripped away.
>
> LaFoo turned and smiled at us. It was a smile closer to a scream without sound. He said nothing and no one dared say anything to him. It was all said in the action. Bravery, fear, savage brutality and compassion. What exactly LaFoo felt in his heart no one will ever know. I remembered the story he had told us about tracking the wounded deer through the woods in New Hampshire until he could mercifully kill it. But this was not the same.
>
> Ever since that day he never tried to save himself from the shells that exploded near him. As we crouched and sought shelter in a hole from an incoming round, LaFoo would just continue a conversation as though nothing happened. . . . I believe he was a man who had partnered with death.

Lanciotti wrote about a "world of gunfire, urine and rotting human flesh. The latter so oppressive and intense that you absorbed it through your skin by osmosis. You tasted it in your mouth, over your tongue, after smelling with your nose. . . . We swipe away the fat, obscenely colored flies that feast on the corpses and then try to share our food, too. They are not easily discouraged. At times we swallow flies with our meals."

> The smell makes me think of the maggots I saw crawling out of the mouth of a young woman we came across earlier today. She had been stripped naked by a concussion that probably killed her and the maggots were crawling out of her mouth and vagina and some of the guys had laughs pushing a stick between her legs and pushed it into her vagina, in and out, in and out until the maggots oozed out of her mouth.
>
> They made God angry and I will die for it.

One night, near dawn on May 13, he heard that his friend Krupkowski "got it." Lanciotti reacted by running around saying he was going to kill Japanese. He wrote that later this embarrassed him. "The only reference points I had for mourning were movies that depicted a similar situation, so I played the role as I had learned it from Hollywood."

To keep a promise they made to each other, he wrote a letter to "Krup's" parents.

> What I really felt was that I was ashamed to be alive and able to write this useless letter to a mother and father who had lost their son, and his siblings who had lost their brother. But a promise is a promise, and I kept it even if I did not tell the story exactly as it happened. Civilians would never understand anyway. And who knows what happened? I didn't, and I was there.
>
> Each day took away more of our men so that we had suffered over two hundred percent in casualties. It was just a matter of time for the odds to catch up.

That afternoon, after learning Krupkowski had been killed, Lanciotti was sitting near LaFoo.

Two marines were busy near us pulling gold teeth from the mouths of dead Japanese soldiers and one was cutting off a soldier's ear. A thin trickle of blood traced where the ear had been cut from the head. The man pulling teeth had a small, cloth pouch with a drawstring that he put the teeth in, and the other had a similar pouch for ears. The man pulling teeth used a pair of pliers and the point of his KA-BAR knife to do his job. The other only needed his knife for his task. . . . When a tooth did not yield easily, the man would use his rifle butt to smash the teeth loose, and then continued his extractions.

LaFoo walked over to one of the marines who was cutting another ear from the corpse and kicked the man in the back, knocking him on the dead soldier. He did not say anything, not a word, and the stunned man looked up at LaFoo in surprise but did not complain. He recognized who had kicked him now and was not going to argue why.

Lanciotti wrote that LaFoo was "one of the psychos 'you don't fuck with' when you're on the front line." The men grumbled and left. (I wondered if one of those guys was Jim Laughridge.) Then Lanciotti noticed a bullet hole in LaFoo's helmet. It had gone in the front, spun around the liner, stopping harmlessly. LaFoo had the bullet. "That was the only souvenir he wanted to take home."

They now faced Sugar Loaf Hill. Lanciotti wrote, "Orders to take this hill come from a safe and distant place. Somewhere where it is dry, clean and comfortable.

"Our regimental commander was a cautious man when ordered to send us into danger. He was relieved of duty for his caution. 'Combat fatigue,' they said. He was given a medal and sent home by the big general who visited us on the top of the Naha Hill. . . . The commanding officer probably saved many lives, but he was too cautious for the top brass."

He recalled Emily Dickinson's poem about waiting for death; he repeated it over and over. He thought this: "Where I died, and my friends died, and the enemy died there would be a parking lot for a shopping mall."

The view from the top eastern flank
of Sugar Loaf Hill, 2011

"Each time we heard a shell coming, our muscles would tense in expectation of being hit. . . . At times, on a close call, the burst would send a pile of dirt, mud, and rock over us and we trembled and twitched as the bits of debris rained down. Some shit their pants, just a little, and I know I pissed in mine." For all I knew, Joe was just one foxhole away from my father. At most, he was within a few hundred feet of Steve Maharidge.

In that shelling on May 16, Lanciotti felt he could take no more.

> I stuck my foot over the edge of my foxhole hoping I would receive a good, honorable wound that would send me home. I aimed my rifle at my toes but could not pull the trigger.
>
> I stood up so the whole world could see me under the surreal light of the flares. Men were shouting for me to 'Get down, get down, you stupid, fucking bastard, get down.'
>
> But I was happy now and unafraid. . . . I was going to leave this madness.

I began to walk away from the insanity, exposing myself to death by standing while under heavy fire and going for a casual walk. . . . I shuffled towards what I believed to be the safe, rear area dragging my rifle by its muzzle. I was headed where there was less noise, less pain and less fear. I kept walking. . . . I expected to feel the impact of a bullet in my back. It never came. I didn't care. I was escaping.

He was stopped by a corpsman who wrapped a cloth on his arm. Was it yellow? He didn't remember. "I did not have to swim to Guam, which was one of my impossible plans."

They took him to a hospital near the line, where, he said, they kept enlisted men so that they wouldn't get too comfortable. The goal was to get him quickly back into combat. To remain longer, he put the lit end of a cigarette against a thermometer. It shattered. This was a common thing for the nurses to see. Shrinks asked if he was a coward—"yellow." They reminded him that he didn't want to let his buddies down.

"Most of 'my buddies' were dead or wounded," he wrote. "There were only strangers up there."

I realized that socially, economically, and intellectually, I belonged at the front. That was my destiny in life when war came, as it was my father's and grandfather's. We are a line of people who are used up in wars. Cannon fodder, food for cannons. And we face our counterparts on the enemy side. The losers fighting losers.

We had been duped by propaganda movies about the glorious war and the need to join up. I did, and now I felt I had done more than my share.

I felt like a fool remembering how I sat through those war movies getting goose bumps on my teenage skin. I remembered my father telling me it was all a fake. He had been in the First World War and did not enjoy war movies. Now I understood what he meant. By fake, he meant they were not honest.

Very few authors or experts question battle tactics in World War II. Lanciotti is one of those few who do.

I was curious how the Battle of Okinawa and the wider war in the Pacific are taught at the US Military Academy at West Point. I had questions about tactics. But my request to visit was turned down. I wondered why. I was left with the analysis of the rare writers to question how the war was fought. In particular, I was drawn to Frazier Hunt's *The Untold Story of Douglas MacArthur*. Hunt, a World War I veteran, understood about the horrible losses of combat from trench warfare in Europe. He became a journalist and covered MacArthur's campaign firsthand.

In writing about the "costly Okinawa venture" in which over 12,000 Americans were killed, 36,707 wounded, and another 26,000 suffered combat stress, Hunt in his overlooked 1954 book asked, "Why had American casualties been so high? Could they have been prevented? Had there been serious errors in tactics? There was some question, in the first place, whether Okinawa was an absolute essential objective. Smaller islands nearby might have been taken swiftly without serious losses."

In addition, Hunt noted that even if invading Okinawa had been a mistake, "Once the upper two-thirds of the 68-mile-long island had been secured, the lower tip could have been sealed off, and the [Japanese] troops there allowed to starve. Most of the American ground casualties had occurred in the exhausting series of deadly frontal attacks against this southern nest. The Japanese there might have been made prisoners of their own barricades. . . . The situation called for an over-all leader who had the imagination and expert know-how . . . to depart from staid, old methods of direct assault."

If the bottom of the island had been sealed off, one hundred thousand noncombatant civilians also wouldn't have died that June. Herman Walter Mulligan would not have been killed. And my father would not have suffered blast concussion on two different occasions.

Admiral Nimitz played into the game the Japanese wanted the Americans to engage in—head-on confrontation. Hunt noted that in three years of hard combat, despite the Navy and Air command starving MacArthur of resources (General Henry H. "Hap" Arnold had gleefully denied MacArthur use of the brand-new B-29s that had double the range and could carry twice the bomb payload of the old B-17s), far fewer soldiers had been killed under MacArthur's command than in the Navy and that he "by-passed and left to die on the vine" at least 250,000 Japanese soldiers. I did the math. There was a ten-to-one kill ratio between Americans and Japanese on Okinawa. If MacArthur had confronted those quarter of a million troops frontally like the Navy, some 25,000 Americans may have died. Instead, those men lived. And so did the Japanese men who were isolated and forced out of combat.

Hunt wrote, "The MacArthur strategy and tactics had paid off handsomely in American boys who came home."

Vindication of a sort came when MacArthur was made the supreme allied commander to receive the Japanese surrender on the battleship *Missouri* and to rule occupied Japan.

"The terrible losses in the Navy-controlled Okinawa battle had shocked President Truman, and this had helped influence him in favor of MacArthur," wrote Hunt. "Nimitz was the Navy's choice for the post of supreme allied commander."

At the field hospital Lanciotti ran into a friend from Love Company whose leg was amputated above the knee. The buddy asked why he was there.

"The words almost stuck in my throat. 'I cracked up,' I said.

"'Yeah? No shit? A lot of guys were cracking up when I got hit. Are they sending you home?'

"He showed no resentment that I was whole and he was without a leg."

Lanciotti told his friend that they were sending him back to the frontline.

"'I wish they would send you home, too,'" the friend said. "'Everybody should go home from this friggin' war.'" Then the guy began weeping.

A Jeep drove Lanciotti toward the front. Lanciotti wrote that he walked and took days to get back to the unit. Then the battle was over.

When Love Company returned to Guam, Lanciotti watched as thousands of sea bags were taken off a ship and hauled by trucks. Those bags were mounded in huge piles, soaked with gasoline, and burned—they were the belongings of the dead marines. Herman Walter Mulligan's sea bag was surely among them.

Lanciotti wrote in his book about being one of the twenty-six thousand psychiatric cases from Okinawa. "I learned that under enough stress, I would break down. I tried to comfort myself by rationalizing that there were thousands more like me, but found no solace in the crowd. And still I hear the voice of the young psychiatrist asking me, 'Are you a coward?'"

Back home, Lanciotti married Vivian, a few years older than he was, in 1948. He finished high school and went to college in Miami, Florida, studying journalism on the GI Bill.

When the couple returned north, Vivian was pregnant. Lanciotti worked for newspapers. The couple had two daughters, Vivian and Joanne. Then Lanciotti was hired on in public affairs with the Port Authority of New York and New Jersey. The family bought a house in New Jersey.

We finally met a few years after the first brief phone call. Vivian, nearly ninety, sat off to the side while we talked in the living room of the nice but modest home that reminded me of my parents' house.

"I still don't like authority. On Okinawa I was against authority. I was against systems. I was against governments. I wanted to get the hell out of there. I couldn't believe that I was with people doing things like this. If you read General MacArthur, the big guru of warfare, he says Okinawa was not necessary."

This makes Lanciotti bitter. But he is a curious mix—at the same time, he is proud of his service.

Lanciotti knew even back then that the United States would be trading with Japan. "I knew that was coming. I mean, what's all this agony for?"

He sent a copy of *The Timid Marine* to the Sixth Marine Division Association. Someone reviewed it in the newsletter. Lanciotti exchanged e-mails with the reviewer.

"He says, 'You were some piece of work.' He never heard stories like that from Okinawa. He heard people charging through caves, raising the flag, and killing the enemy with gusto. He says, 'I wasn't going to continue, but I couldn't put it down.' There, he was giving me a compliment; he didn't realize it. It was a negative review. I wasn't gung-ho. I'm not all-Marine Corps, although there are parts of it that are very patriotic. I waited so many years before I wrote a book about it. I never expected to write it."

The Battle of Okinawa and the wars in Afghanistan and Iraq are "the same," Lanciotti declared. "Nothing has changed. It's not because of the horrible things that happened back then but the question that it keeps happening again and again."

I asked if he stayed in touch with LaFoo.

"I saw him once. He came to visit many years ago. Then he disappeared. I don't know if he's still alive. We had nothing to say then, and that was only a few years after the war. But I still love him."

I was surprised when Lanciotti told me that he never killed anyone. He didn't mention this in the book.

"Unless I killed somebody by accident, I never shot a Japanese solider. I'd always miss."

"On purpose?" I asked.

"I never saw a Japanese soldier I wanted to kill. If the Japanese soldier was in the rocks, I'd shoot at the rocks."

He recalled that the day Krupkowski was killed, a marine named Roland A. Ludwig also died.

"I can still see this guy, his name was Ludwig. Bald head, blonde, from Wisconsin. That's sixty-five years ago, whatever. He had a little cloth bag, and he would go around with pliers. He opened the mouth of the dead people, pulled out the teeth. Only a small percentage of guys did that."

Lanciotti laughed sardonically. I thought of my father smiling and nearly laughing when he described the terrible things he saw.

"I don't know why I laughed there," Lanciotti said. "He kept that bag of teeth. There were quite a few. When I saw him dead, his mouth was open, and he had gold teeth. I always remembered Ludwig laying there. He was collecting teeth, and then his teeth were shown for collection. I did not agree with what he was doing or the cutting of ears. And how LaFoo reacted to certain things. LaFoo may shoot somebody through the head to relieve him of his pain. But he would not defile a corpse. He would make a corpse; he won't defile it."

Tears came to Lanciotti's eyes.

"I have to stop from being emotional because in talking to you I can remember what I wrote in the book and I can become very emotional about it, and I really don't want to."

I assured him it was okay and suggested that if he wanted to stop talking, he should. He didn't.

"I know as I get older and closer to packing it in, I never had this before, but I'm having more visions of what happened then. One of the first Japanese I saw dead with his head blown off, and that was the first time I ever saw what brains look like. I will remember that Japanese fellow, and I will remember the Japanese fellow who was run over by a tank track until he was like a pancake.

"As a young boy, when I was eighteen, I knew that after a few months, a year, everybody will start to forget the war. But I did not forget it. I don't know why. I got a feeling that a lot of other people did not forget it."

Not in Kansas Anymore,
May 16, 1945: Fenton

Bill Fenton, who was in the Second Platoon, and I talked by phone a few times after my father died. Ten years later I drove to visit him in Abilene, Kansas, population seven thousand, two highway hours west of Kansas City. Most vivid was his description of that barrage of Japanese artillery from the Shuri Heights, when Love Company was dug in, facing Sugar Loaf Hill.

Bill Fenton in 2010

"An artillery shell landed too damn close. It was delayed action. Thank God." Apparently in the second or seconds it took to explode, the marines had time to hunker down. "It blowed dirt all over everybody. It knocked a bunch of us unconscious—concussion. When they go off right close to you, it kinda makes a difference. It'll shake your eardrums, your memory, and few other things. Your brain rattles around. I couldn't hear anything for three or four days. I was wondering where in the hell I was."

Like all the other guys who were hit by blast concussion who I talked with, Fenton echoed them all when he said, "I just don't exactly remember" more detail.

The description of May 16, 1945, in the *History of the Sixth Marine Division* sounds sanitary compared to the stories I heard from Love Company members: marines "were forced to cling to their positions under particularly violent artillery and mortar fire. That May 16 was as bitter a day as the Sixth Division had seen or would see."

"I'm kinda hazy about that time," Fenton told me. "That blast going off, it kind of shook things up a little bit. I wound up in the hospital after that for a while. They were going to send me back up to the line, and the doctor who was looking at me, he said, 'We're so close to the end of the operation, you don't need to go back up there. You have combat fatigue.' He was being really good to me. He gave some other fellas the same thing."

My father and six other men I met with in my search were taken out of combat that day—and many others were also sent to the hospital. This is compiled from the May 1945 muster roll:

FENTON, William A., Jr.	16-27, sk 6thMedBn; 31, sk 6thMedBn.
GRAHNERT, Fenton A.	16-31, sk 6thMedBn.
LANCIOTTI, Emerico J.	16-21, sk 6thMedBn; 27-31, sk 6thMedBn.
MAHARIDGE, Steve	16-31, sk 6thMedBn.
MARKOVICH, Henry	16, WIA, shrapnel, face, evac to 6thMedBn; 17-31, sk 6th MedBn.
PALMASANI, Frank J.	16-31, sk 6thMedBn.

It's not noted why they were sent to the medical unit, with the exception of Markovich. Markovich lost part of his jaw and an eye because of shrapnel from a Japanese Shuri shell, he told me over lunch with George Niland in Naples, Florida, in 2010. (He seemed reluctant to meet, so I didn't ask any questions.)

Hank Markovich in 2010

Joe Lanciotti emphatically chose not to differentiate between concussion and the horror of battle. Bill Fenton surely had blast concussion; so did Fenton Grahnert, with a shell landing that close to his foxhole. But Grahnert wasn't as lucky as Bill: he was put back on the line. I don't know about my father and Frank Palmasani (his memory was sketchy about May 16), but evidence points to their having suffered blast concussion.

As I sat in Bill Fenton's modest home, I wondered where my father was between May 16 and June 21, the end of the Okinawa operation. The muster roll shows Steve Maharidge out of the company the rest of May; June's roll has him back in the unit on June 7, the same day it shows Bill Fenton returning. I had found, however, that the rolls were often in error. Bill clearly was not back.

Ed Hoffman was certain that he didn't see my father in combat those last three weeks on Okinawa. Ed was in the same platoon as my father, yet Ed told me, "I didn't see him until July, just before we went to Guam." That's when Love Company boarded the *USS Golden City* on July 8 and left Okinawa behind.

Still, I was left with a puzzle: when the tomb blast took place on May 30, was my father with the unit or on medical leave?

I continually wracked my memory about the one time my father told me about Mulligan. I vividly remember him saying, "They said I killed him!" I'm certain he was talking about Mulligan's death and not the time his friend was wounded in April.

I believe that, despite what is noted in the muster roll, my father must have been put back into combat just before the tomb blast and was taken out again after the second concussion, when a doctor may have ordered that he not return to the frontline. (Palmasani clearly was put back into the company even though the roll shows him in the hospital, the same as my father.) What happened those last weeks is a piece of the war my father never talked about. When he said they "blamed me," he may have believed that the rear duty, were he given it, was punishment when, in fact, it possibly saved his life during those brutal final weeks; with his brain damaged from multiple blasts, he may not have been able to react rapidly in combat.

Fenton told me that he was transferred to the headquarters battalion on June 7, and perhaps the doctor also sent my father there. "I was out of the company for quite a while. I didn't get back to the unit 'til we got back to Guam."

William A. Fenton Jr. was born in Kansas. His parents divorced when he was small, and he never really got to know his father.

He entered the military before he finished high school, in 1943. He trained at Camp Elliott in San Diego. He told me that he rapidly learned one thing about war: don't become friends with anyone.

"A kid by the name of [Clarence] Cole from Wichita, Kansas, we got to be pretty good buddies. He got killed on Guam."

Cole died July 25, 1944, that night of the Japanese counterattack.

"See, I was kind of a loner after the Marshall Islands. I had that feeling that I'm never going to get too well acquainted with somebody and have 'em get killed. I'd be friendly and all that, but not in a real buddy-buddy type situation."

Fenton, like Palmasani, was a flamethrower man.

"I had to dig two holes every night. I didn't want to sleep with it," he said of his fear of the tank blowing up if hit by a bullet. "A lot of times I dug a hole for it first. Actually, I only used the flamethrower three times," he said of Guam and Okinawa. "The only time on Okinawa, I had them charging out of the hole [a cave] burning up. One joker coming out of there was screaming and hollering, which he naturally would."

On Guadalcanal, after the Battle of Guam, he lived a few tents down from Mulligan. "Of course, we always used to kid him about being half-Irish and half-Jewish. He was always pretty good natured. He was always joking around." Mulligan used to affect a stereotypical Jewish accent and go into a riff about being cheap. "He'd always say there's an old Jewish saying, 'You always tear down the wallpaper when moving'" so that it could be used again. (Mulligan appears to have been the only Jew in Love Company, and I wondered how much of his self-deprecation was used to deflect anti-Semitism.)

I asked about the battle strategy that led to them being hit so hard at Sugar Loaf Hill.

"It was ridiculous. There's things we shouldn't have been doing. We often wondered at different times, 'Why the hell couldn't we just bypass that god-damned thing?' Isolate it. Set up a perimeter around it, where they had guards twenty-four hours a day, seven days a week. It would have been hard to do, but they still could have isolated it. When [General Simon Bolivar] Buckner made that [rear] landing, that should have been done earlier. We would have been a lot better off. There was a lot of places we shouldn't even have went. Not only us on Okinawa—a lot of the other islands, especially."

Fenton went with the division to Tsingtao, China, and was told he could go home on December 7, 1945, about a month before my father. When he got back to Kansas, a girlfriend urged him to finish high school.

"So I graduated in the class of '47. I should have graduated in the class of '43. I'll tell you what. I had problems for several years—nightmares and stuff like that. Not anymore. The more you talk about it, the less it bothers you."

"Why do you think that is?" I asked.

"You get it off your mind. I always try to look at the funny side of life, and I try to do other stuff."

Fenton first worked at a Ford dealership in Abilene, then he went into the trades.

"I was a commercial industrial electrician. We used to work on seed mills, big concrete elevators, and stuff like that."

He traveled around Kansas for that job.

"I got to know the western part of the state like the back of my hand. I know all the back roads and little bitty spots in the road, wherever there was a seed mill, an elevator."

Later he worked for a company that made electric wire harnesses for commercial trucks and farm machinery. The company built a plant in Mexico, then went bankrupt, forcing his early retirement.

He lived in a white clapboard house in Abilene that he had bought with his first wife after the war, where they raised their three girls. They divorced and he remarried. His ex died and so did his second wife; he'd just moved back to the Abilene house that his daughters now owned. We went outside for a picture. It was a big-blue-sky Kansas winter day. He told me that he returned to Guam in 1994 for the fiftieth anniversary of the battle. He got hugs everywhere he traveled.

"They celebrate the fourth of July, then they celebrate the twenty-first of July as liberation day."

"The tour took us all around. We were on a bus. A retired Navy fella, he was driving. He said, 'We're going to do a little detour.'"

The bus drove on, then stopped.

"He said, 'Approximately this is about where you made the line that night where you had the big banzai attack.'"

Fenton could only look at the site through the window. Because it was part of a US Navy base, for security reasons he and the other men who almost died there on July 25, 1944, were not allowed off the bus.

Our Secret: Rosplock

After hundreds of phone calls I worked my way down the list to this name from the muster rolls:

ROSPLOCK, Joseph P 1, sk Combat Fatigue.***

The fact that he was taken to the hospital on June 1 indicated that he might have been at the exploding tomb.

There was just one Joseph P. Rosplock in the databases. I tensed, as always when I suspected a good contact. I stared at the phone's keypad for a long time. A few days earlier I'd talked with a widow who burst into tears when I asked for her husband, dead for many years; the phone listing was still in his name. I took a deep breath and punched in the number. A male voice answered.

"Is this the Mr. Rosplock who was on Okinawa in World War II?"

"Whadya want him for?!" he said with hostility.

I blurted about my father, Mulligan, the explosion when a tomb blew up. When I ceased speaking there was a long silence. Had he hung up?

Then—

"I was there."

Rosplock spoke in nearly a whisper. A tenuous conversation ensued. There was tremendous pain in his words—about the explosion, about his life. I gingerly asked questions.

"Everybody's gone," Rosplock said. "I probably would have been better off if I was gone. I've had a lot of health problems. I worked forty-eight years and nine months, and I ended up without a pension. The company closed. I had to rely on my kids to give me a place to live. My wife died. My kids take good care of me, but, you know, fathers like to take care of themselves," he said near the end of the brief conversation.

Gently, I asked if I could mail him a picture of my father and Mulligan. Perhaps it would help him identify my father's friend. Rosplock agreed.

Two weeks later I rang again. "I sent you those pictures. I'm calling to see if they jogged your memory at all."

"All it brought back was sorrow. I gave a lot of thought to what happened. All I can pass on to you is what I passed on to you. There's a lot of things I don't remember because, when I was near the explosion, I was goofy. My mind is a blank when it comes to names and to areas, and that's probably because of the concussion. I spent many nights thinking about it after you called me and wrote me that letter."

Yet Rosplock talked on, motoring out more of his story without me asking many questions. We were on the phone for an hour. At the end he confided, "You know," he said, "this is the first time I talked about the war with anybody."

Those calls began a long phone and e-mail friendship. We often talked for as long as two hours at a stretch. On each occasion more layers about the war peeled back. I kept asking to meet in person. Rosplock wouldn't have it. We would never meet.

Rosplock was the son of Polish immigrants. His father's name was Rozplochowski. Because of discrimination against Slavs, his father shortened it to sound more "American." Joe was born in February 1925, in upstate New York, one of eight children. In 1931 he recalled seeing his parents sitting in the kitchen crying because there was nothing to eat.

Rosplock tried to enlist when he turned eighteen, but he was turned away because he had "flat feet." He went to a doctor who taped his feet so that the Marines would accept him. He did his basic training at Camp Lejeune in North Carolina and then went to Camp Pendleton. He was put on a ship bound for Guadalcanal at Christmas in 1944. He wasn't in Love Company then; he was transferred into the unit on May 1, 1945, after his company suffered casualties and was no longer viable. He remembered only one other name from Love Company—everyone else was a stranger to him.

In one early conversation he told about crossing the canal that bisected Naha town on the morning of May 30, 1945. A radio man under fire had jumped into a well to save his life, and they were trying to rescue him. A US flame-throwing tank was approaching as Love Company waited next to a creek, near a village or group of homes still standing.

"There was one of these spider holes the Japs used to hide in. They covered themselves up with bushes, and they would pop up and shoot the guy that was running past them. Nobody would know where the shot came from. One of them jumped up in front of me about twenty feet away and ran into this village. Everybody in the creek shot at him. Evidently, the Jap heard the tank coming with the flamethrower on it.

After that [the tank] burned the village down. Right after that is when we started walking up that hill and the tomb blew up.

"When that hill blew up, all the mausoleums blew up with it. It was such a loud blast. I could feel it on my face when it went off, and when I looked up I couldn't believe the stuff that was coming down at us. Some of those pieces were big as a car. They thought it was just an ordinary mausoleum. It was part of an ammunition dump."

Rosplock hurled himself behind a wall, which may have saved his life.

"Before I went behind the wall, I got peppered with rock," he said of smaller stones that blasted his body. "I dove. I landed on a rock, hard. Or I don't know if in the explosion, I got hit with a big piece of rock. Fortunately, I ducked behind that wall. Otherwise, I probably would have gotten seriously injured."

Rosplock watched a piece of the tomb roof come down on a guy, whose name he didn't remember, 50 or 150 feet away—he used both distances. "He had just come back up to the lines after being in the hospital, and he got killed because a chunk of it landed on him."

Herman Walter Mulligan had been in and out of the company. He was wounded on April 10 just before the Motobu Peninsula, suffering a gunshot wound to his right leg. He returned to the company May 17— if the muster roll was correct—after the devastating losses on Sugar Loaf. A few days later, on May 20, he was again sent to the medical battalion for an unspecified reason. He came back to Love Company on May 26. Four days later he threw the grenade into the tomb.

Rosplock, unable to hear because his eardrums were shattered, was asked to carry the man hit by the concrete; Rosplock and another soldier put him on a stretcher. "He was dead," he said. They took that man to a truck. Corpsmen told Rosplock to get on the truck as well. He and the dead marine rode off to the medical battalion. Rosplock didn't remember names, including Mulligan, because the blast rattled him. But only one man was killed that day—Mulligan.

I mentioned what Frank Palmasani believed—that men were buried by the blast.

"I don't think anybody was totally buried. I had to help carry guys back on stretchers. They loaded them on trucks. Ever since you had asked me for help, the last thing I can remember is putting the stretcher on the flatbed truck. They said, 'Hop on the truck and go with him.' I was out of my mind practically. The concussion from the explosion."

The truck with Rosplock and Mulligan's body went downhill to the rear area.

"When I got there another doctor took a look at me, and he put a tag on me and sent me to the encampment like they used to have that program on television where the helicopters would fly in—"

"Oh, *M.A.S.H.*," I said.

"*M.A.S.H.*, yeah. Well, I went to a place like that. Then the next thing I know they examined me, asked me a lot of questions. They put me on another truck and sent me to another area. The guy said, 'Why don't you come with me?' I got on the boat and went down the river with him. The next thing I knew I was in Hawaii. They flew me by air from Okinawa. I have no memories until we hit Pearl Harbor. I remember the first thing was them saying you can have all the eggs, pancakes, milk, sausage, eat it until it comes out of your ears. But whatever you take, eat it. Make sure you don't have to throw it in the garbage can. I ended up in a hospital in San Francisco. They were trying to keep me from going nuts."

In his file it noted that Rosplock suffered from "blast concussion" and that he was "nervous, jumpy and has battle dreams." After San Francisco he went to Portsmouth, Virginia. He had a huge mark below his left breast the size of a tangerine from where he hit a rock when he dove or was struck by a flying boulder. They kept X-raying his lungs because of this. Though he'd carry that scar the rest of his life, that wasn't the real problem.

"I had to go through a lot of tests. We would sit down, maybe fifty or sixty guys at a time, and the doctor would lecture us. They'd invite us into these rooms, and they would tell us to close our eyes, and this guy would talk to us. For weeks the only thing we did was quilting," he said, among other arts and crafts exercises. "If it wasn't for that, I probably would have lost all my marbles. I had to get my senses back together.

"For a long time, if somebody just whispered behind my ear, I'd jump a mile high, you know."

He was sent to the Philadelphia Navy Yard. He worked in the base post office. He was discharged on July 2, 1946. He went home to the Finger Lakes region of upstate New York.

"**When I first came home** everyone said, 'You're so hard to get along with.'

"My brother John, my father, my brother Larry, my brother Bernard, they all worked at the [foundry], owned by General Electric. Larry, he worked there about thirty-five years, but he had to quit because they had an accident where they were lifting this casting on chains. It broke loose and it hit my brother. They amputated his right leg.

"I worked there nine months when I came out of the Marines. I gave my father a big hug and I said, 'I'm sorry, Dad, that's it, I can't do it.' Then I ran a crane for the American Bridge Company. After that I got a job at a furniture store, where I worked for fourteen years thinking that I was on a profit-sharing plan. When I approached the owner of the store, I asked her how much I had in profit-shares. And she says, 'Well, I don't think I'm going to be paying any profit sharing.' See, in those days you didn't have any help from anybody to fight when you were mistreated by an employer.

"So I moved to Rochester, New York, and went to work for a big retail furniture/carpet company. I ended up having a job in the carpet department as an assistant manager. That was 1963. I had a nervous breakdown. I was married with two kids [Nancy and Rita], and I had a total breakdown, just a total breakdown. My father died. I lost my good job. I had just bought a house. I'd have what they call a panic attack. I had my first panic attack taking my family on the New York Thruway for vacation. It was like somebody sat on my head and my chin was poking into my chest. We had to turn around and go home. The doctor at that time said, 'You're just suffering now what you should have suffered when you were on Okinawa.'

"I couldn't even go to work for three weeks. I was scared to death to walk out the front door of my house. I couldn't drive a car. Too many things came to my mind when I was driving. I couldn't hold food down.

"The way I got over it, after all the talking with different doctors, is I went to see one of my parish priests. I said, 'I just can't get a hold on things. I'm worried about losing my job. I'm worried about supporting my family. I'm having too many things come back in my mind about the war.' This is exactly what he said to me: 'Joe, I want to tell you something. If you don't make up your mind to get that stuff out of your head and go back to work, you're going to keep getting sicker and sicker and sicker, and you're going to die. Your family's going to cry like hell for about a month. About five or six months later people will say, 'What was that guy's name?' That's how quick it happens.'

"He knows because he's dealt with a lot of guys," Rosplock said of other veterans in the parish. "He said, 'That's how quick people forget what you went through in the Second World War.'

"One day it was raining like hell, and my wife said, 'Come on, you're going to drive the car.' She made me drive around the block for hours. It took me several months to get over that. I was lucky I kept my job. You know, my life has not been a barrel of honey bunches."

The second phase of Rosplock's postwar life didn't get easier.

"There were five owners," he said of the company that was kind enough to not fire him during his bad period. "I was one of the owner's golf partners on Sundays. Dumb people worked there. We were all making pretty good money. They voted in two unions. So the furniture man couldn't help the carpet man, and the carpet man couldn't help the furniture man. They closed the doors.

"I didn't have enough vested rights in a pension. So I went to work for another carpet company. I knew there wasn't a pension plan, but I was already in my fifties. I had to worry more about a suitable income. I worked for them about fifteen years before my wife died. I didn't even get a watch when I retired. I had to retire because I had a bleeding bowel."

In January 1996 Rosplock's wife died. He was now in the third postwar phase of life.

"I tried to live on my own with just Social Security, but I couldn't make the payments. I sold my house in Rochester after my wife died. I moved here and used the equity from my house as the deposit on this townhouse," he said of where he now lives. There wasn't much profit on the Rochester house. His youngest daughter and her husband pay the mortgage on the townhouse.

"Fortunately, I have Social Security. And fortunately, I have two wonderful children. Otherwise, I would be a street bum. My son-in-law said, 'You just pay the utilities. If you have any problem with that, let us know.' My daughter helped me buy a very expensive keyboard because I play keyboard. I've got a beautiful organ. I play at nursing homes and hospitals. She said, 'Dad, you are not going to die of a broken heart like your father when his wife died.' I figured that since my wife died, that was the only way I could keep my head on straight was to go to nursing homes.

"I went through a training course. I was taught how to work with Alzheimer and dementia people. I was volunteering five, six days a week at the nursing home after my wife died. That was the way I got through her death—getting everything else off my mind while I was trying to help these people. If you're down in the dumps, go to an Alzheimer's nursing home for about five minutes, and when you walk out of there, you'll think you're the luckiest man on earth.

"I used to play under the name of Sylvester Metamucil. You know, Metamucil, that older people take. That was my stage name."

Concussion from the tomb blast impacts his playing. "I am still feeling some of the effects, because I've always had a tremble in my hands. Sometimes when I'm playing the keyboard, instead of playing the D sharp, I play flat.

"My keyboard weighs sixty-five pounds. See, if I lift it up, pain goes right to my feet. Where I was playing four and five times a week, I cut it down to two. I've been very sick lately. I had cancer. I had stents put in my legs for poor circulation. I take eight different medications. One of my medications, Plavix, for my circulation, if I had to pay the regular price, is $585. I get it for $11 because I'm on an assistance program."

He lives in fear of the assistance ending because of state budget cuts.

In each phone call the tomb blast came up—even if I didn't mention it, which I stopped doing. And there were two major scenes that he repeated from the war.

> I saw marines stacked head this way, head the other way, head this way, like they were a pile of lumber. You know how they stack logs? I saw bodies of marines stacked like that so they were able to come and take their bodies away. There's a lot of things that happened to me on Okinawa. It's not something I'm too proud of, you know?
>
> See, it was customary for any mausoleum or any cave that you passed, you either threw a hand grenade or an incendiary grenade. One time we were along the China Sea side at Sugar Loaf Hill. We were walking along this trail, and they had already thrown an incendiary grenade in that mausoleum, and after we passed it, evidently this Jap couldn't stand it anymore because when he came out he had a blanket over his head and that was all burning and this guy ahead of me said, 'Duck!' And when I ducked he shot over my head. The guy in front of me put about twenty bullets in him. That was one of the things that I've been dreaming about ever since you called me.

He didn't mention until a few years after we began talking that this last incident happened at Sugar Loaf Hill, on the extreme flank of the China Sea side. He would have been with Love Company then. "I have some memory" of it, he said, but most of what happened before the tomb blast was hazy. "I got hit a couple of times with rocks from shells exploding. We were lucky. A lot of the shells the Japanese fired were duds. One time I was with a group of marines, and if the shell had gone off, we'd have been killed. We all got splattered with mud and rocks and everything." This probably happened on Sugar Loaf, but Joe wasn't certain.

The later calls grew to be more like therapy—for both of us. My understanding of what my father experienced deepened. It appears that Rosplock was probably as close to the tomb as my father had been. Rosplock and my father may have suffered similar blast concussion.

Rosplock's stories of how he jumped when someone made a sudden noise behind him offered some explanation for my father's outbursts when, as kids, we would spill things at the dinner table.

Rosplock always apologized for not knowing more details. I reassured him that he was helping. After our conversations he told me he sometimes had nightmares about the war.

"I don't want you to feel that you cause any bad memories coming back to me," he said when I expressed concern. "I want to thank you. This is the first time I've been able to talk to somebody about it. See, you have made me feel better because you let me talk about things that I never told anybody else. You gave me an opportunity to get things off my mind that had been sealed up. I don't talk about it with my kids. I've never talked with any of them about what I went through. They want to know. I said, 'Oh, things were tough.' I said there were guys that went through a lot more than me.

"If my brother Genie was still alive I probably could talk to him about it. When he first came home from Iwo Jima you couldn't even walk near him. He was on the invasion of Bougainville, Guam, and Iwo Jima. The only thing I could get out of him before he died, he told me that when they hit the beach on Iwo, for two days he lay face down with the bottom half of his body in the water because those guys had been sighted for death. And then he said when he felt it was safe to move, he moved. He told me how many different times that he wished he got killed rather than stay alive.

"He was a couple years older than I am. I always said that it was easy for me to follow in his footsteps. I got his old shoes when he got new ones."

When Rosplock was hospitalized after the blast, doctors told him, "'You have to talk about your experience. You can't hide it. It happened.'"

He waited a lot of years.

"This is the best conversation you and I have had," he said one time. "There's a lot of things that I saw. You know, when you've got to bend down and take the rifle out of a dead marine's hands because the one you've got doesn't work—that breaks your heart. I ended up carrying his B.A.R. I'm lucky I got home. There were so many times that I can tell you I was lucky I'm not a dead man."

"I want to thank you back," I said, "because all these conversations we've had have helped me understand what my father went through. I wish my father would have had the help you got."

"I was one of the fortunate guys, that I had help. I wasn't just discharged. I was evaluated, I had a chance to talk to psychiatrists. I had very good meetings. It took me a very long time to get over the shakes. They were examining me because I was a wreck. I couldn't sleep."

Because of the corpsman who wisely put Rosplock on the truck after he'd carried Mulligan's body, Rosplock got help. If my father had stuck around, maybe he would have too. My father must have moved on with the First Platoon, because he told me that when he came in that night (at Hill 46, as I would later learn), he carried Mulligan's .45 caliber pistol.

"A thing that upset me—and I'm not saying you did it—when you sent me the roster, I took a look at it, and I'm seeing 'this guy got killed,' 'this guy got wounded.' When I got to my name, it says, 'battle fatigue.' Why is mine the only name on there?"

Out of the hundreds of men no one else had that term used to describe their injury. I didn't have an answer.

Rosplock often fretted that maybe it meant that people would think he was "yellow." I always assured him otherwise.

"You had traumatic brain injury."

No matter. Rosplock had doubts.

"I don't want to get too heavy on me getting concussion. . . . I don't know if I was close enough to know if I got concussion."

He was surely close enough.

"Now, I wasn't a coward, though."

"No!" I said. "It had nothing to do with being a coward! My father had the same thing you did."

I repeated what Frank Palmasani told me—no one's eyes looked straight. It was concussion.

"The reason I'm saying that, we have a clubhouse up here," he said of his townhouse complex. "I was the oldest guy here until last year. A guy named Frank came here. He was at Iwo Jima. He's two years older than I. He said, 'Do you have a Purple Heart?'

"I said, 'No.'

"He said, 'I thought you were on Okinawa.'

"I said, 'I was.'

"He said, 'How the hell did you get off of there without a Purple Heart?'

"'Because I didn't bleed.'

"'What do you mean by that?'

"I said, 'It's none of your damn business.'

"He was saying about, 'These goddamn battle fatigue guys! They want Purple Hearts. They're crybabies.'

"I thought, 'Hey buddy, you got a wound in your right arm that's healed, but the guy that got shell-shocked, he's still walking around nuts.'" Rosplock grew emotional.

"I didn't ask to leave! The doctor—he's the one who told me to jump on the truck. I wasn't a crybaby marine. They put me on the truck and told me to get out of there."

After many conversations I asked about using his name. He mulled this over and was inclined for me to change it. "Use 'Rossy'—that's what everyone used to call me. When I get off the phone, my daughter's not going to know I talked to you. None of my kids are going to know I talked to you."

"Okay," I said. "It'll be our secret."

"Because if I say I talked to you, they're going to say, 'What did you tell him?' They don't know nothing about me. I showed them my discharge papers, my beautiful picture. I was a handsome, young marine. I just said, 'This is all you're going to know about me. I'm home, and that's all that matters.'"

"I understand."

"Oh, Dale, I love you. I'm sorry I can't be more helpful."

"This is between us," I said.

"If you call me and my daughter answers, don't tell her who you are. Just say you're a friend."

"Okay."

"I have shoe boxes filled with tapes. Cassette tapes. I made them when I was driving. I had a stuffed doll I talked to set on the seat. But I was really talking to my children. I had a microphone and I spoke into a recorder about what happened to me in the war. It's all in there. The box is in the closet. When I die, they can listen to them."

Later that year, without my asking, Rosplock told me to use his name.

"What's making me feel good is because maybe what I'm saying to you is going to help somebody else. All these young kids are coming home from Afghanistan and Iraq and are committing suicide. They discharge them; they don't give them any help. Some of these guys have an arm and a leg off.

"I'll tell you, if I could go stand in front of Congress right now, I would say, 'You bastards have got to take care of those guys!' Now, what's going to happen to these seventy-five thousand guys when they come home and there's no jobs for the guys that are living here? All the money that the United States is spending over in Iraq. They're building schools and hospitals and fixing roads and bridges. Why the hell don't they do it here? If they started fixing roads and bridges here they could hire five million guys tomorrow. The congressmen that let all of the jobs go overseas, they're the criminals."

For a few years after the war, he had a disability payment, but the government rescinded it. I insisted that he re-apply. "Joe, we owe you!" I told him that George Niland appealed and got his payment increased. But Joe would have none of it.

"I consider myself very lucky. I managed to get married and have nice children. I'm having a problem now because I don't have a pension."

When we talked in the late summer of 2011, Joe said, "I wish I could help you. You know, it's been sixty-six years since it happened."

"Oh, Joe, you've been such a wonderful help."

Early the next year Rosplock wanted to get his military records from the National Archives in St. Louis. I found the address. Weeks later I got this e-mail from him at 2:20 a.m. that in part said,

> Still no words on my records. Is there any way you can help me
> to get them? I wanted to talk about my service in the Marine

Corps with my children before I go. I also thought my records would help restore my memory about Okinawa. . . . now my nights in bed are spent trying to finish certain situations that I remember, but can't complete the memory of that situation, when I should be sleeping. It is amazing how little I can remember. . . . I can remember carrying the stretcher after the explosion, then my mind goes blank.

[He went on to detail numerous health problems.]

I can feel my strength and energy slipping away. The peripheral artery disease in my legs is worse. I was told there is nothing more they can do for me. Too dangerous to go into my arteries again. . . . I would really like to get those records because I cannot stop thinking of certain happenings that don't have endings.

Your friend, JOE

I dropped everything and wrote an impassioned e-mail to the press office at the records center, asking for help; the wonderful people there sent Rosplock his records the very next day. We talked after he got them.

"The thing that made me cry the most is when I saw the letter they sent to my mother," he said of them informing her that Joe would be hospitalized for at least six months. "She probably cried her eyes out for a month."

The files prompted him to call his sister-in-law. His late brother Albert and other family members had visited him when he arrived in Portsmouth, Virginia. Albert, she told Joe, "said your condition was so bad, they didn't know if you were going to get over it."

Joe Rosplock finally began to talk with his family about the war. He was about to go stay with his daughter Nancy for a week.

"I'm going to walk in the house and show her the envelope and tell her this is my service history. Do you want to talk about it now?"

"That's good you're going to do that," I said.

"Well, the way I've been feeling . . . any doctor I talk to about this peripheral artery disease says you can have a stroke or a heart attack, so I figured I'd better talk to my kids now. You're the only person I really opened my heart to. You know how reluctant I was to talk at first. I can tell you lots of stories that would make you shit your pants. There are some stories I could tell you but I will never tell you."

Just before we said goodbye, he insisted, "I've had a happy life. I know my wife is waiting for me when Jesus calls me."

Finding Life: Hoffman

Edward F. Hoffman was born in September 1927 in St. Paul, Minnesota. He went to Catholic grade school. When Pearl Harbor was bombed, he was in ninth grade at a public high school. His older brother, Phil, joined the Marines in 1942 and fought on Guadalcanal. Hoffman wanted to follow him—he enlisted when he was sixteen. He trained at Parris Island and was at sea in April 1945. In May his ship was "greeted" on arrival in the Green Beach landing area of Okinawa with a kamikaze attack by a Japanese Zero, but it missed. Hoffman and the others then went over the side of the ship.

"Climbing down that net, I thought, 'What am I doing here? My class hasn't even graduated high school, and my ass is here.'"

A group whose names began with "H" ended up in Love Company. A truck drove them south to the ruins of Naha town, where World War II began for Hoffman. He and George Niland had to carry a wounded man to a medical station while under machine gunfire. Then at night he and another new marine killed "four or five" Japanese soldiers. "All of a sudden this is real. I realized that this is the way it is. It's kill or be killed." In the morning a sergeant took them to Captain Haigler, who said to them, "'I wish I had more guys like you.'"

On May 30 Hoffman crossed the canal and went left, while Mulligan and the others went right.

"I don't know who my squad leader was that day. He's hiding behind a rock wall so that he doesn't get nailed, and he told us to run across this open area, 'Two at a time and space yourself.' In other words, make it irregular. And as I'm running across that field there's

Ed Hoffman in uniform

Ed Hoffman in 2010

machine gunfire. I looked down, and here's this guy that just minutes before was telling me to run across in groups. He was shot through the head. It was just a fleeting second, but it seemed like an eternity. I'm thinking, 'This guy was just talking to me, and now he's deader than hell.'

"I ended up hitting the deck. I think this happened around ten in the morning, and I was still there maybe four in the afternoon. Every time I practically took a breath, that machine gun was chomping the ground around me. He had a hell of a clear view on me from I don't know where. Finally, somebody threw smoke around there, and then I was able to get the hell out."

On June 3 Fenton "Gabby" Grahnert returned to Love Company after being in the medical unit from the shelling on Sugar Loaf Hill.

"Gabby was my fire team leader," Hoffman said of the four-person unit in a squad. "That was my world. Gabby'd tell us what to do, where to go."

One night Hoffman bedded down inside the walls in front of a tomb. Something was poking him. "I pulled my poncho back. I started digging—I uncovered a face. It was a nose. I was lying on top of a Japanese soldier they had buried there. He was just barely covered."

Love Company crossed the Kokuba River and made the assault on Hill 53, the headquarters of Japanese Admiral Minoru Ota.

"We went off to the right, along the edge of the estuary. We were pinned down there at the beginning of the hill. There were some Nips hiding up in there. They bolted and ran. The B.A.R. man, a guy by the name of [Roy] Hollenbeck, a Jap jumped right out of a tree and rode him piggyback for about twenty feet. Then he jumped off and started to run. He said, 'You guys, there's a Jap! Somebody get him!' He's screaming, he's got a rifle in his hand. But he didn't react. Somebody dropped the guy anyway. Then we started doing the caves, blowing them up as we went along.

"This is right around noon. Maggie [Pio Magliaro] was our squad leader. So I'm lying out in front of a cave that we'd already blown. And the other fire team was working on the one in front of us. I'm lying there with my rifle across their point. Gabby's off to my left, maybe thirty feet away. Obviously, I'm looking ahead because I'm watching where they're working. All of a sudden I get this dirt flying all over my face. I thought, 'That's strange. What the hell was that?'

"I look, and here's this Japanese guy raising his head out of the cave with a pistol. He'd just taken a shot at me from about twenty feet and missed. It hit in the ground about eight to ten inches from my face. He's heading for a second shot. I squeezed the trigger and nailed the guy right in the head. Bang. Just like that. The only reason he missed was because we'd blown the cave already. Concussion had got him—he was pretty well dazed up. It was a Japanese major. Gabby took the pistol. I didn't want the pistol. I just wanted to get my ass out of there. I was so close to being shot.

"We moved on to the cave after that. We would set down a base of fire with the automatic weapon, and we'd get one guy to run across the front of it. We would try to make it safe for the flamethrower man. Maggie ran across there, and he got shot right through the chest."

They worked their way around the hill and took "friendly fire" from the 29th Marines that had finally been landed behind Japanese lines on the Oroku Peninsula.

The unit moved south. "So about one in the morning they stopped us, held up the line. It was dark. I thought I could sit there and smoke. I sat on a log. Only it wasn't a log. It was a Japanese soldier who had been dead about two weeks. All that moisture went into my trousers. Did I stink."

They entered Itoman town at two o'clock in the morning to replace First Division marines on the frontline. The men were headed for the Kunishi Ridge, then the Mezado Ridge and Hill 69.

"We moved up about eight, nine in the morning. I took a bullet through my canteen that morning on the way up that hill, and I thought I'd been hit because all of a sudden, liquid is running down my leg. They said you never really feel it if you get hit. It's shock. I didn't even want to look. I just put my hand down there. I thought it was blood.

"And that's where Gabby got hit," Hoffman said of Grahnert being shot in the face. "We were in the assault about halfway up the hill when Grahnert got nailed. I yelled for the corpsman. I never saw so much blood in all of my life. Just gushing.

"We had to keep going. Only about four of us got up to the top of the ridge. Guys were getting hit left and right. We had another good guy by the name of Marion Rounds, and he died that day too. We got up there and had to be replaced almost immediately—they brought another company up. Remember that guy I told you about who had the Jap jump on his back? He was up on top and yelled, 'Look at the Nips!' And I looked down, and there was all these Japanese brass, high-ranking officers, running. He had a perfect shot, if he had opened up."

From Okinawa, Hoffman and Love Company went to Guam to train for the invasion of mainland Japan.

One of the guys who had signed my father's Japanese flag showed Hoffman a tobacco sack filled with Japanese gold teeth on Guam.

"It was half to three-quarters full of gold teeth that he pulled out with his bayonet. He [said he] boiled them in a ration can, boiled the hell out of them to disinfect them."

He described the guy with the teeth as having gone "Asiatic," which meant "too far East for too long. He was in my tent. Early on he got some bananas on Guam. They were green. He would just sit there and stare at the bananas. I think he was waiting for them to ripen."

Some of the guys who'd gone Asiatic had been in the war since 1942—they weren't used to civilization. They had a different outlook. "To some of them, everybody was a gook. Didn't make a difference if they were Japanese or Chinese. People in the States were called white gooks."

After Hiroshima and Nagasaki, Love Company went to Tsingtao, China.

"A bunch of us went in first," he said of landing and meeting the Japanese soldiers. He preferred working with the Japanese than the Chinese nationalists.

"They were a bunch of thieves and crooks," he said of the nationalists. "The Japanese were very, very respectful, and they maintained order until properly replaced by us. The surrender went beautiful. They worked with us, we worked with them. And then they started to collect the families, the dependents. Then I got the chance—I considered it a chance—I rode in an LST with fifteen hundred of them back to Sasebo. Prisoners—soldiers and women and children.

"It was just wonderful, their behavior. Here I was, a seventeen-year-old, sitting on the deck with fifteen hundred Nips. Most people might have been bothered, but I wasn't. They were great. It was enlightening, and it was good because everything was working out. There was no bitterness."

The prisoners left the ship cleaner than when they had gotten on, he said, after the voyage that took them past the Korean Peninsula to the Japanese port of Sasebo, fifteen or so miles south of Nagasaki.

"That's when I got to see Nagasaki. I stood on a hill above there and looked down on it. It was flattened out. It was ninety days or more after they dropped the bomb. It was amazing. The next day we were heading back to China. I stayed in China until the late spring of '47."

The government was trying to downsize troops and gave Hoffman an early discharge.

Hoffman entered college in early 1948 and began doing construction, traveling to California for work. In short order Hoffman married and had a son, Stephen. In 1950 his brother, Phil, convinced him that to make some money—twenty bucks a month—he should join the Reserves. By then he was a corporal. "I went to two meetings, then the Korean War started. All of a sudden, my ass was back at war."

He was called up in June. By December 1950 he was in Korea.

"I blew out of a hole with one of the Chinese 122-millimeter mortars. Those were the big ones. They supply a big shock. It hit near me and took me right out of the hole. The mortar is the one thing that scared the hell out of me. They can reach you regardless where you are."

His eardrums were shattered and took time to heal. In April 1951, while still in combat, his second son, Craig, was born. In June his unit was hit by friendly fire. Air Force pilots in Corsairs thought they were Chinese. "The first napalm took the air team out. They made seven passes—four napalm bombs, four 500-pound bombs, thirty 2.5-inch rockets, and then all of the .50 calibers. When I went over the top of that ridge I started firing my M-1. I could see the son of a bitch in the Corsair."

"You were firing at him?" I asked.

"Damn right! We all shot at him. They unloaded on us completely. They killed twenty-five to thirty men."

He described the napalm dropped in a container.

"I watched it kind of waffling down. It hit some trees about thirty feet above my head," he said. It then careened down the mountain. He made a whooshing sound to describe the inferno below him.

"Korea sounds worse for you than Okinawa," I suggested.

"Oh, no. It's all the same.

"I got back from Korea on Labor day of '51," he said. His marriage was over. "I walked out of the house the next day. The whole thing went down the tubes. In eighty-nine days I had a divorce. Being Catholic, it was a tough thing to do.

"I kept plugging away at school because I had a year in between China and Korea. I got pulled out of school to go to Korea. I worked at the Hamm's Brewery in St. Paul, 'til 3 a.m."

By the early 1950s he was constantly going back and forth to the Golden State for construction jobs. "I would run out to the West Coast to work."

In 1955 he was passing through Cleveland. He called my father, and they had a beer in a South Side bar.

He traveled to California through 1960. "I'd go out and work nine months to get money to keep above water. There wasn't a job in geology being offered. And oil companies were done hiring. So I went out back to the coast."

A friend was studying for a contractor's license. "I realized that with all those years of laboring on brickwork and masonry, I knew quite a bit about it. So I took the test ten days later, and I passed the damn thing." He went into a partnership for a year. It didn't work out. "Finally, in 1962 I took a gamble and went into business for myself." He did tract houses—rough-and-finish work on fireplaces—and custom work.

"I was doing four and five million dollar houses back twenty-five years ago. I waited twenty-one years before I married again. And then I met this girl," he said of Susie. "We got married in 1972. And all of a sudden we ended up with a daughter, Catherine, in 1975."

The couple owned a home in Reseda, in the San Fernando Valley. In 1992 they relocated to Minnesota for family reasons. They moved to

Stacy, north of Minneapolis, buying a house on five acres, in the country. "We love it, except for the snow."

After the 1994 Northridge earthquake, he loaded up his truck and worked for nine months in California.

Immediately after my father died, a lot of my energy went into an off-the-grid house that I was building. I lost myself in hard labor—one job in particular: digging a long trench by hand for a septic pipe. Not long before, I'd telephoned Ed for the first time. It must have been the third call when I started the ditch. "Have you got a laser level?" Hoffman asked. I had a line level, maddening to use to achieve the required slope of one-quarter inch per foot.

After purchasing a laser level, I easily did the job with precision.

Over the years I talked more with Hoffman than any other guy from the company. He was always upbeat. He kept up with the times—we also e-mailed each other a lot. The war didn't seem to haunt him. Then we got the chance to meet. I drove to Minnesota. I pulled into the drive of the address he'd given me. A man on a riding lawnmower halted the machine and bounded toward me. This couldn't be Ed, I thought—he was too young. But it was. He had an infectious smile and a young man's eyes. Susie was also far younger than her years. Both keep busy.

We spent the afternoon talking. Come evening, we drank whiskey. I mentioned that Hoffman and my father were living in California at the same time for a half-dozen years.

"Damn it. I can't get over your dad being out there and I didn't get to see him. To see him—that would have been wild."

He showed me an M-1 carbine that he bought after the war. I sighted the rifle at the wall. It was the first time I'd held an M-1. Hoffman pulled out pictures and other war memorabilia.

"I had pictures of maybe eight or ten people in a group, a little family picture, like they're out of photo albums. I had some pictures that I took off of a body, yeah. But the group picture I found lying alongside of a hut. I might have had a half-dozen pictures. That was a sad thing. My god, those people lost everything. About fifteen years ago I packaged them all up and I sent them to a newspaper in Naha and told them to do the best they could and try and return them to the people. I thought, 'They're not doing any good here.'"

"Did you ever hear back?"

"No. But I felt better about it, because I thought that just maybe somebody would find them. I'd be tickled pink if I had lost some pictures and somebody returned them."

I mentioned that some guys still harbor hatred for the Japanese.

"That's amazing," Hoffman said, shaking his head. "I think what's happened to Japan since the war has been a good thing. We're driving a Toyota and I've got a Suzuki in the garage."

We drank at the kitchen table until nearly two o'clock in the morning. We could have stayed up until dawn.

At one point I noted that "only 7 or 8 percent of the people in the military in World War II were in combat."

"I'm sure it was less than that," Hoffman said. "I heard 5 percent."

"How'd you guys get to be so lucky?" I asked.

"I think I'm talking to Steve. You even look like him. And you have the same sense of humor."

Ed went upstairs to sleep. I flatbed-scanned some of Hoffman's pictures. As I lay in bed in the guest room I felt sad that my father wasn't at the kitchen table drinking whiskey with Hoffman that night instead of me.

Hoffman wanted me to stay longer. But I had to be back in New York City. Being with Ed and Susie Hoffman was a lot like being with my parents. I was critically aware that I was at a point in life when the days were ending when I'd be able to chat with people of that extraordinary generation.

As I packed to leave, Hoffman told me, "When I was a kid, there were still Civil War veterans running around. They were one hundred years old. I want to be like that—one of those guys from World War II, a hundred years old, around to talk about it."

Hoffman repeatedly told me on the phone over the years—and again that night over whiskey—that he doesn't agonize over anything that happened in either World War II or Korea.

Out of earshot of her husband, Susie told me, "He never talks about it. It was the biggest thing in Eddie's life, though." She believes that he may have occasional nightmares, though he never mentions them in the morning.

"Sometimes when that happens, he kicks me in his sleep."

"What do you do?" I asked.

"I kick back."

Karl Brothers
in uniform
and in 2010

"There Are No Nice Wars":
Brothers

Karl Brothers had come into Love Company on Guadalcanal in late 1944. He was in the Third Platoon. He now lives in an upscale suburb north of Akron, Ohio. We'd talked by phone a few times, and then I drove to Ohio to visit. His house is atop a hill with at least a half-acre of front lawn. I grew up a twenty-five-minute drive away. We sat at the kitchen table. His son, Eric, was present.

"Do you remember Kennedy?" I asked Brothers, who was a youthful-looking and -acting eighty-four. I figured that he might have heard about the rape.

"Oh yeah? Well, I heard some rumors," he said about the rape, without further addressing my question, in an attempt, apparently, to avoid the answer.

Was this the brotherhood of the Marines, him covering for Kennedy sixty-five years later? I thought, "C'mon, Karl." He saw doubt in my eyes.

"Well, yeah, he was going to be charged with rape. Kennedy was accused of going in one of those civilian compounds. This gal claims he raped her, him and a guy from West Virginia. They kept moving them around so the AG, the adjunct general, couldn't find them— that's what I heard. I know that he was sweating that one out, him and [the other guy]."

Still, Brothers hedged. "Now, whether he did or not, I don't know."

"My dad said he did it. So did Fenton Grahnert and George Popovich."

"Really?" Brothers sighed. He seemed surprised the others had spoken. I asked about the night Grahnert and Kennedy were on guard and the civilian couple was shot dead.

"That sort of thing happened quite a bit. Some of the Japs wanted to move south. They [civilians] said the Japanese soldiers told them they'd kill them if they didn't take them through our lines. Sad. At night they'd force these women, children, and babies to walk with them. They'd use them as shields. We'd order them to halt. They wouldn't halt. They'd reach a certain point, you'd fire. We had light 30s and the B.A.R. The next morning you go out and see you've killed women, children, old people, and a few Japanese military trying to pass as civilians."

As for the babies Kennedy shot, he said, "Well, in a way, it might've been the best thing, because nobody was going to take care of them. Even if we got hurt, there were no facilities, except for a corpsman, within twenty miles. So what are you going to do?"

"Grahnert was bothered by that."

"It's easy to look back and say, 'You should do this or that.' But there wasn't anything there to do anything with. There are no nice wars."

Brothers **was born** and raised in Akron in the heyday of the town being the hub of the tire industry; his father worked for a stairway manufacturing company.

"I was going to graduate from high school. I wanted to be in the Marine Corps—I had a brother there. I enlisted when I was seventeen, on St. Patrick's Day. I wasn't eighteen until May 20, so they put me in a reserve status and said, 'We'll be calling you within ten days of graduation.'"

The call came three days after he got his diploma.

Brothers remained uninjured even at Sugar Loaf Hill.

"At Sugar Loaf you didn't dare raise up. They'd get you. On Okinawa those guys had that island gridded out with artillery. They could put it right in your pocket, and they did it. They had those high-powered Czechoslovakian artillery, and boy, they were good with it. Tanks didn't last five minutes. A tank would pull up, and *boom!* If I saw a tank coming, I ran. I didn't want anywhere near those guys."

Brothers's luck at not being injured continued as Love Company worked through Naha, assaulted Hill 53, and moved south through Itoman.

"At night a guy was coming towards the hole I was in, and I could hear him speaking something in Japanese. He was trying to get through our lines. I saw this guy, silhouetted by the moon. We tried to get him to stop. I could see he was reaching for something. He was getting close. So—*blam, blam, blam!*

"What he was reaching for? He had a couple of grenades. He was close enough—he could have thrown them right in the hole. I remember a guy named [Woodrow] Strang. He was a sergeant. He was in the hole next to me. And the guy, he was hollering. Strang says, 'Finish him off.' So I finished him off. The end of him.

"The next morning the captain [Haigler] come up and said, 'You killed him, you bury him.' Well, that was all coral rock there. With the entrenching tool you couldn't even chip at it. Forget him, we couldn't bury him. We left him there."

Before moving out Brothers searched the body.

"Here's a picture I got from that last guy, an envelope. Inside, he had forty yen and this."

Japanese family

"I wonder if it was his wife and kids," I asked.

"That's what I think," he said. He also removed a patch from the Japanese soldier's uniform. He showed it to me.

"That was when they were all trying to get back somewhere," he said of Japanese soldiers trying to flee to safety in the mountains in the north.

"So some wanted to escape—they all didn't want to die?"

"Not really. That was a myth."

Days later, on June 17, Brothers's luck ran out on the Mezado Ridge, the same day Grahnert was shot. A Japanese soldier popped up out of a spider hole and bounced a grenade downhill toward Brothers.

"I got a lot of shrapnel in the face and arms and neck and legs. I don't know if you've ever seen a Japanese grenade. When they went off, instead of splintering into big pieces, it went into little pieces. But they'd penetrate. I was really fortunate that I didn't get any in my eyes. At the time you feel like, oh man, you've got a thousand needles in you."

He was taken to a field hospital. By the time he was released the battle was over. The fighting in the south part of the island was intense, he said.

"We had no idea what was down there. General Buckner didn't either. Our intelligence wasn't good at all. They [Japanese solders] were concentrated, and they were determined. Every foot, there was somebody.

"It was wild. The Japanese—I'll tell you one thing, they were A-number one military people. We were up against a real enemy there. Those guys weren't a pushover. When a guy's willing to die, what are you going to do? And yet they did a lot of stupid things. I remember going towards Naha and these [Japanese] guys were drunk and laughing and shooting people. I mean, what's this all about? For any eighteen-year-old kid, this is weird. It makes a different impression on you now. They were expendable and they were used."

I asked about Lieutenant Colonel Clair Shisler. Brothers said he'd heard that he almost got court-martialed for killing prisoners on Guam.

The message was the same on Okinawa. Unlike Guam, there were no official orders. Brothers said the policy of not taking prisoners was "implied."

"How did they imply it?"

"You don't want to be quoted and court-martialed. That's what happened to Colonel Shisler. But what do you do if they tell you to take a couple of prisoners back? They take some private and say to him, 'Take these guys back to regiment.' When you don't even know where you're taking them back to? You're going to be out there walking around with a couple of Japs in the dark. I mean, they tried to escape. What else could you do? You had to shoot them, right? Well, that's what you did. It's just guts. That's something they don't like to discuss. But I mean—it's just—

"That's the reality of it, you know. I didn't do that, but I knew some who did. I probably would have." He added that he would have looked for a truck that took American bodies back. Sometimes prisoners were put on those trucks.

"Shisler, I think he did right. You don't want to see a couple of marines killed by friendly fire, walking back at night. They don't tell you how many marines were found, their bodies messed up and mistreated. They didn't take any prisoners either. So you didn't. You didn't want to get captured."

A guy Brothers knew from Akron, Joe Felber, was in the First Marine Division on Okinawa. "He was wounded. The Japs found him and some other guys they killed. They thought they killed him. They sliced his head with a rifle butt. But he survived. He had a big plate in his head. He said, 'Them guys, the Japanese, were having a ball, smashing everybody up.'"

Brothers came home and married in 1948, joining the Akron Police Department not long after. He and his wife, Marie, had two children, Eric and Randy. He was a policeman for forty-eight years until retiring as a sergeant in 2001.

I asked, "How do you feel about the Japanese today?"

"We've been driving Subarus for thirty years now." He laughed.

"I didn't know anything about them," he said of the Japanese when the war began. Since then he's read many books. He said he now understands more of the Japanese perspective. "The United States, all of Europe, Britain, we were in China. We wanted to throw the Japs out. I can understand the Japanese saying, 'Hey, why are you squeezing us out?' They wondered why they couldn't have a cut of the pie. Let's face it, that's what it's all about—resources. It's what wars are about."

"I hope we all learned a lesson," I said.

"Doesn't look like it. What are you going to do in Afghanistan? I think we're making a mistake. We're not going to win that war any more than we would have won it a hundred years ago. What are we fighting for?"

As we flatbed-scanned war photographs, Karl said that he never had any problems due to the war after it was over.

"I hear those guys talk about, what is it, delayed stress? I don't buy that myself. If you made it out, why worry about it? It could have been worse. You could be walking around like some of these guys with no limbs. Then you've got something to worry about.

"Concussion, now that can really cause some problems. Boy, some of those guys were way off. Nice guys, but they were subject to tremendous concussion. Most of those guys were kind of punchy. One guy kept smelling popcorn, and they thought that wasn't unusual. Your brain gets screwed up in your sensory area. I mean, the guys that really got severe concussions, there's nothing you can do about it. Like a punch-drunk fighter, there's no cure."

Brothers keeps active. He works out "three or four mornings a week." As I was getting ready to leave, the subject of Kennedy came up again because I'd just had an image of Captain Frank Haigler's diary on my computer screen. Haigler had written, "April 15 to 5 May: Investigation of civilian shooting and raping."

Brothers was now harder on Kennedy.

"I don't know whether they could have convicted him or not, but they didn't take any chances. I think Shisler was probably responsible for protecting him. If they'd been convicted, they'd have gone to either the firing squad or to Portsmouth Naval Prison for about thirty years. Better to be shot in those days.

"He came from money. I would say that he was a spoiled kid from New York. He just seemed spoiled."

"I Wanted to Stick a Jap with a Bayonet": Kennedy

In one decade of searching I'd avoided an obvious character—Kennedy. Perhaps I'd overlooked him because his was the darkest star in the universe of my quest. Odds were that he was dead. And his was such a common name. Yet a database search found three age-appropriate possibilities. I called two: one was dead, and the other was in the Army during the war. I rang the third.

"Is this the Mr. Kennedy who was in the US Marines, in the Battle of Okinawa?"

"Yes."

I leaned forward so fast that my chair nearly careened to the floor. I said my full name—

"Steve! I remember him. He was five-nine—"

Kennedy was spot-on about my father's height It was as if I were talking to an apparition. His voice, in a high and yet hard-edged octave, like that of a television cartoon character, was incongruous. I'd expected something deep and sinister like a cinematic cliché. Then, suddenly—

"Who is this?! Why are you calling?! How did you find me?!"

I explained that I was trying to learn more about Herman Walter Mulligan—

"I don't remember him! I don't remember anything!"

To jog his memory I said that I'd like to send the picture of my father and Mulligan.

"I don't remember! You're lucky you got me! My legs are bad, and I don't get around very well! I almost never answer this phone!"

I suggested that Kennedy humor me. I'd send the picture and call back in two weeks.

"I won't remember," he vowed. Kennedy went on about how "there were so many damn hills we had to go up" in both Okinawa and Korea, where he later served. (He'd been a twenty-year career marine man.) He insisted that he didn't recall specifics of people. He didn't join any associations. He didn't keep in touch with war buddies.

"Hey, it won't cost me but a stamp," I said about sending the picture.

"Okey-doke," Kennedy said sharply.

Afterward, I telephoned Fenton Grahnert.

"You're not going to guess who I just talked with," I said.

"I can't. Who?"

"Kennedy. I'm going to go see him—"

"Take a gun! Take a gun!" Grahnert implored, nearly frantic. Sixty-five years after watching Kennedy shoot the babies, Grahnert remained terrified of him.

How dangerous could it be?

Precisely two weeks after my first call, I rang. I expected that Kennedy wouldn't answer. He picked up on the second ring.

"Dale! I was going to call you," he gushed. He went on about my father and the picture. "You should come by sometime. I sure remember your dad. I had him pictured exactly. And he sort of had a funny-shaped nose. It wasn't fat, it wasn't a prize fighter's nose. . . . I pictured him looking exactly like that in the picture."

He sounded nervous. My letter noted that I'd talked with nearly thirty guys from Love Company—everyone who landed on April 1 was aware of the rape. I, of course, didn't mention it, but Kennedy had to know I knew. I sensed he was worried and wanted to assess what I had on him.

I told him that because my siblings and I were interring our mother's ashes with our father at Arlington National Cemetery in two weeks that I could stop by as I made the long drive back to California.

"I don't receive until one in the afternoon. Last night I didn't go to bed until five o'clock in the morning." Kennedy told me he never slept at night—he always went to bed at dawn. He lived alone. His wife had died years earlier.

I plugged Kennedy's address into Google Earth. A screen of green came up, miles from any town. I zoomed in on the barely visible cottage in a deep forest. The dwelling was lost amid the thickness of trees. He was in a wilderness.

I own weapons, perplexing some friends in the city. For half the year I live in the wilds of California. My nearest neighbor is a half-mile across a canyon. While on a moonlight walk in my meadow I once surprised two men illegally waiting to shoot deer at two in the morning. I ordered them in a command voice to leave. They sped off. At the barbed wire fence they'd cut to gain entry about a quarter-mile distant, they fired three rifle shots. When I phoned the sheriff's office, a bored dispatcher told me they wouldn't make the two-hour drive out from town unless there was a body. That was an educational experience about living beyond the reach of the law. So I have weapons.

But I wasn't about to go armed as Grahnert insisted. If Kennedy did something stupid, it would happen fast; I'd be dead before I could react.

Not going was not an option. I had to meet the apparition. I needed to look into his eyes and ask about the rape and baby killings. Meeting him would make me understand something, though I didn't know exactly what that might be.

After my mother's burial I drove through the night. The next day I left the interstate and traveled on winding mountain roads. I came to the turnoff to Kennedy's place, a gravel lane flanked by towering ash and white oak. On the road edge grew sassafras mixed with a snarl of ragweed and wild grasses that were a harsh green from early June rains. I vividly remember the flora because I stopped and took a deep breath before continuing.

The house was more like a cabin. In the drive was a jet-black SUV with a US Marines sticker on the bumper. I turned my car around and parked at the gravel edge, facing the distant paved road: I wanted the option of a quick exit.

I went to the front door. No answer. In the carport was a screen door. Out of the interior darkness, a voice barked, "Get in here!"

The door opened into a bedroom. Numerous stuffed teddy bears on a shelf and dresser surprised me; the room was clean, the bed tight-sheeted. In the center of that white bedspread was a brown revolver holster. The revolver was absent.

I passed through a hall. I emerged into a dimly lit room, the walls adorned with images of horses. Kennedy, who was balding, sat in an overstuffed armchair, his legs up on a stool. He was flanked by two walking canes. His hands were hidden beneath a blanket. On the brown leather couch to Kennedy's right, dead square in the center of a seat cushion, was a second holster, black, for a semi-automatic. It, too, was not present.

"I grew up hearing about you, and now I finally get to meet you," I said. I offered my hand.

Kennedy shook with his right hand—the left remained beneath the blanket.

I pretended not to have seen the holsters, the only items out of place in the otherwise spotless home, clearly stationed to intimidate. *Fuck you*, I thought, *I won't show being scared.* The weapons surely were beneath the blanket. Kennedy didn't attempt to get up.

"I'm out in the country, as you can see," Kennedy said, as I began to sit down without invitation. "Watch that holster—"

My left buttock was already half on it; I'd aimed purposefully. I remained seated on the holster.

"Now, I can't be a good host to you, because I can't get around. I live alone. That's why you see the shoulder holster there. At my age I'm pretty well crippled up as you can see. And, uh, at my age, crippled up, living alone, in the country, I'm not going to have a house invasion. Because right here is the big snake: Colt Python. That's the finest revolver ever made."

"I understand," I said about the unseen firearm. "I have a house in California. It's actually wilder than this. If I didn't have a weapon, I'd be an idiot."

I stared into Kennedy's eyes. I wanted him to think that I might be armed. Kennedy stared back.

"Is that the one you had in the war?" I asked nonchalantly about the pistol from the holster beneath my buttock.

"No, no. I had another one in the war."

It was a .38 caliber back then, he told me—the same caliber weapon that Grahnert said Kennedy used to shoot the babies.

"It's nice around here," I continued. "I used to come to this area to hike and hunt, back when I was a kid."

"Oh, did you?" Kennedy said.

"Do you deer hunt?" I asked.

"I thought I was going to hunt when I got out of the Marines. I was all prepared, had all the rifles. Then I saw the way they do it around here. They mostly drink and play poker. And they throw corn out in the bush. See, after I retired from the Marines, I went into law enforcement. I was a constable. I was a police officer. I was a bounty hunter. I was a body guard. I've done everything. It was all law enforcement. I'm better at chasing—at finding men. Man hunter. Not deer."

"You know," I said, "Hemingway wrote that the best hunting is the hunting of men."

"That's right. That's exciting. Because they can shoot back, the ones I go after. Now, I got your letter here."

He pulled out the picture of my father and Mulligan.

"The guy next to Steve, I recognize the face. And I recognize the ears. But I don't recognize him. In other words, his face brings back a memory. But I sure remember your dad. I had him pictured exactly. Can you imagine marines today looking like that in a common area, rolled up utilities, loafers, crap like that? Oh, we were a mess."

I mused about the .45 pistol on Mulligan's hip.

"Well," Kennedy said. "That means to me that he was either a flamethrower man or a machine gunner." He pointed to a photocopy of a map I'd sent. "I'll show you where I left the island. I left way back here."

"You got hit on Sugar Loaf?"

He didn't answer.

"Then after Oki—that's when we went to China. Tsingtao," Kennedy said. He looked at me coolly. "Now I got to be honest with you. I was just a kid. That's where I broke my cherry."

"Yeah, yeah?" I asked, dubious.

"Chinese girl. I think it cost a nickel." He paused. "And then the fleet pulled in, and the price went way the hell up to a dime, maybe fifteen cents."

I realized that he wanted me to believe that he never had sex before China. He was trying to deflect me about the rape.

His parents, he said, were famous professors, his mother far more famous than his father. She won awards and made the newspapers—she was among the first women in her area of expertise. (Sure enough, when I later did research, I found articles about her.) Kennedy grew up a block or so off Park Avenue.

When the war began he went to the military recruiting station at Times Square. He was too young.

"I wanted to stick a Jap with a bayonet."

As soon as he was old enough, the Marines took him.

"Did you have any college before you went into the Marines?"

"No, no—no," he said. "That disappointed my parents, of course. My sister, my God, was a Vassar graduate."

"Did you get pressure?"

"Sure. I was the black sheep."

"That's too bad."

"Oh, what the hell."

"Did you get along with your parents? Did they accept what you did as a career?"

"Never did," he said, fast. "Never. But they had a picture like this one of me up there."

He pointed to the wall and a portrait of him in uniform at age eighteen. He first went to New Caledonia, then to Guadalcanal in early 1944. He was in a rear unit that put up communication lines. He didn't want to climb telephone poles. He wanted to see combat. He asked to be put in the infantry. He was transferred to Love Company.

Kennedy talked about the Guam landing and the night on the Orote Peninsula, but with vastly less detail than Charles Lepant or Fenton Grahnert.

"Do you remember the bad stuff?"

"No, I don't remember any bad stuff."

"Where were you hit?" I asked.

"In the lower legs."

He wouldn't describe what happened, certainly not that it was self-inflicted. "Anyhow, I was evacuated to an Army field hospital. I was then evacuated to Pearl Harbor Hospital."

I thought about his luck at not hitting an artery when he shot himself. His luck continued. The surgeon at Pearl Harbor who worked on him was from New York City and knew his mother. This doctor helped expand his luck by introducing him to the chief architect of a new hospital being built.

The architect, also a New Yorker who knew his father, "had a fully equipped beach house right down from the Royal Hawaiian Hotel. When I got out and had my thirty days recoup, instead of going to the other side of the island where we had a recoup camp, he turned that over to me to use. And of course, I had a little Wave corpswoman that I got attached to at the hospital. She'd do her shift and then she'd come out to be with me for the rest of the day at this little house on the beach. Oh, I had it good."

As he laughed heartily, I thought of the girl he'd raped on Okinawa, Mulligan dying, Joe Rosplock and my father suffering blast concussion at the tomb, Jim Laughridge being shot at Hill 53, Karl Brothers blasted with shrapnel, and Fenton Grahnert shot in the face on the Mezado Ridge.

Records don't show Kennedy going back to Love Company. My father had a list of platoon members in China, and Kennedy was not on it; Hoffman didn't remember him in Tsingtao.

"When did you rejoin the company?" I asked.

"Back on Guam, uh, I mean back on the Canal again," he replied. But Love Company never returned to Guadalcanal. He was clearly lying.

Kennedy said that when he came home to New York after the war, "All my parents' friends said, 'We can get you a job' near my parents' summer place in Westchester County, like as a janitor at a small country school. 'Hey, that pays pretty good,' they said. I said, 'What, are you kidding me?' So I reenlisted right away."

The downside was the Korean War. "I was one of the 'frozen chosen,'" he said.

"I was pretty wild when I was young. In marine talk, 'A stiff prick has no conscience.' And so I overstayed my liberty a couple of times. See, I was a platoon sergeant in 1947. That's four stripes, three up and one rocker. And this one colonel took one stripe away from me. It took Korea for me to make that back."

When visiting home Kennedy remembered, "Me and a couple of my buddies from the corps, we got pretty well lit in New York one time." They went to the Stork Club, a legendary onetime speakeasy on East 53rd Street owned by former bootlegger Sherman Billingsly. It was sometimes a mobster hangout and always a celebrity scene. Each night Billingsly was seated at table number one; gossip columnist Walter Winchell often was at table fifty.

"So we went in there around one o'clock. We'd already been bar hopping. I guess we started a little trouble. And Sherman Billingsly came over and asked me my name. He said, 'You marines are causing— you don't quite fit in here.' And we refused to go. So he made a phone call." Not to the cops. He called Kennedy's father. "My dad got out of his bed, came over—this was two o'clock in the morning—picked us all up. My dad, he never heard the end of that, I'll tell you."

He went on with similar stories—he was plugged into the world of power in New York City via his parents. Why did he join the Marines? Surely not to be in the company of men like my father from Cleveland's South Side or Mulligan who labored in a textile mill in the South.

His life in the Marines ended as Vietnam was heating up.

"Well, I figured with three infantry wars, sooner or later, you're going to get it, see. Third eye," he said, pointing to his forehead and the bullet he imagined getting in Indochina. "I had a family by then. I knew what my military occupational specialty was—cannon fodder."

Yet he continued living on the edge after the military. He loved being a bounty hunter. "I'd still be out chasing people if I could walk. Most of my work was done at night. That's the way you find these people. Or early in the morning, while they're still in bed," he said, with a laugh of satisfaction. "I enjoyed the warrant work. Because that took some skill."

He and his wife and son moved around a lot that last decade he was in the Marines. "We owned three houses. This is the worst place I've lived in my whole life. But I enjoy it. There was nobody here but my wife and me. I'm a horseman. I had the barn built. My tack room is like a den, where I keep my saddles and stuff like that. That's where I worked out of when I was bounty hunting."

He hadn't been to New York City in years. He stopped visiting after his parents died.

I eased into the tough questions by first asking if he was involved, like my father, with making raisin Jack, bootleg booze, on Guadalcanal. Kennedy went on about how they fermented it in "Lyster bags." A bit later I changed the subject.

"Oh, there's something else I wanted to ask you that my dad mentioned," I said. "Something that happened to a woman on Okinawa."

Kennedy stared with winter eyes, slate gray and beady in that dim light. I stared back—hard. I imagined that these were the exact empty eyes that existed when he raped the woman and the eyes that Fenton Grahnert saw just before Kennedy pulled the trigger on the babies. A chill came over me. Yet I continued staring.

"Yeah, yeah," he finally said.

Our eyes remained locked. I did not speak.

"Yeah. I think some people, uh, either they beat her—or something."

A long silence.

"It happened on the northern end," he said.

Neither of us blinked.

"Yeah, yeah," he said. "Yep, yep. There were two guys actually."

I spoke, finally.

"You know who they were?"

Fast—

"Nah."

"Some guys were bothered by that," I said. "My dad was bothered by it."

Kennedy grew fidgety. His eyes looked away from mine for the first time since I brought up the rape.

"Yep, yep," he said. Another long silence. "Yeah, yeah, yeah, yeah."

Kennedy turned to telling about how he lost full use of his legs ten years before. He talked fast, on and on, nervously repeating, "Yeah, yeah."

I wondered if his crippled legs were caused in whole or in part by his shooting one of them to get off Okinawa. I then asked about the two babies being executed, and his response was the same as with the rape. I wasn't going to get anything out of him. I wanted to say, "Mr. Kennedy, I know you raped that girl and killed those babies. Don't bullshit me," but I was mindful of that Colt Python. I'm not that brave.

I drove away. I realized just how tense I was when I made the paved road—I stopped the car and had to walk in circles on the empty road to work off nervous energy, and I let out a primal yell. Once in a town I stopped at a roadside diner. As I savored an otherwise mediocre meal, I thought about the Park Avenue side of Kennedy my father lusted after his entire life: to acquire money, "class," power. I wished my father could have witnessed just how pathetic Kennedy looked. As much as Kennedy epitomized the banality of evil, he also represented an empty side of the American dream.

I'll never know if Kennedy remains up all night to avoid waking screaming in the dark from memories of the atrocities that he committed. His only visible worry appeared to be getting busted. And so as I stood to leave his cabin—he remained as I'd found him, with one hand beneath the blanket in that chair, never having moved—I had tortured Kennedy the only way possible: I announced that I was going to Okinawa and would visit that little town in the north where the rape occurred.

"She might still be alive," I said. "She's younger than you—she'd be in her early eighties. I'm going to try to find her and learn more about the rape. Maybe she'll remember who did it. I'll let you know what I find."

For the first time in nearly three hours, I saw fear in Kennedy's eyes.

Part Four

ISLAND OF
GHOSTS

The Land of Courtesy

The men of Love Company gave me a vastly better understanding of my father's war and of the burden they had all carried in different ways as a result of it. My father was haunted by the memory of Mulligan; others had different names and faces that stayed long in their thoughts. Each of them had been able to return, sometimes with staggering clarity, to the battle-torn islands of the Pacific in 1945. But this was not enough. After the long journey over the years of finding as many men as I could from Love Company, I still felt there was one group that I had neglected and needed to hear from, because I knew that the war did not end for everyone in America.

I wondered about the people of Okinawa.

As a child, when I snuck into the attic to study my father's chest of war memorabilia, the image of an Okinawan man from the booklet, *Nansei Shoto: A Pocket Guide,* given to him by the Marine Corps before he landed, made me feel sad. I knew nothing at that age about the fact that one-third of the island's pre-invasion civilian population was killed in the battle, but the drawing of this robed man always moved me.

Drawing of Okinawan man

I must have instinctively known that people like him died. In 1940 the population of Okinawa was 475,000, about 900 people per square mile, denser than Rhode Island. Most were farmers who lived in houses with straw roofs.

Drawing of Okinawan house with a straw roof
(*from* Nansei Shoto)

Okinawa is the largest of the Ryukyu (pronounced "you-kyu") chain of islands. The irregular-shaped island runs more or less north to south for sixty-eight miles and averages three to ten miles in width. It has more in common with a cross between Florida and California than the jungles that most Americans think of when conjuring the battles of the Pacific, though coral reefs fringe the subtropical island. It's beautiful—my father often said that if not for the war going on, it would have been a great place to vacation.

Okinawans are a mix of Malay, Chinese, and peoples from southern Japan—they form a unique culture. It had been a monarchy ruled by Shuri Castle. The name for their island in the native Luchuan language was *Shurei no kuni*, "The Land of Courtesy." In 1816 Captain Basil Hall, a British naval officer, wrote about "their aversion to violence and crime." Hall discovered that the Okinawans had no cannons, muskets, bows and arrows, or even daggers.

US Commodore Matthew C. Perry sailed into Naha Harbor on May 26, 1853, awakening the island into a maelstrom of world events.

(Perry had sailed west to force Japan to open trade with America—the first time the United States had angered the country, a move that caused Japan to begin militarizing to prevent further invasions.)

Okinawa was then a semi-independent nation that paid tribute to China and the Satsuma warlords just to the north. These extortions drove the island into poverty. After the Meiji Restoration began in 1867, Japan said the Okinawans were Japanese. China claimed the island in vain. In 1879 Japanese troops took over Shuri Castle, annexing all of the Ryukyu Islands.

For years Okinawans couldn't vote. They paid higher taxes to Tokyo than other prefectures. Mainland Japanese looked down on them. "Student digs [housing] posted prohibitions against Koreans, Okinawans and dogs," wrote George Feifer in *Tennozan,* of signs in mainland Japan. Yet Okinawans retained their "legendary hospitality," Feifer said.

Okinawans tilled small plots using "night soil"—human waste—for fertilizer. In many places escarpments were terraced. A favored food was yams. They also grew sugar cane and other vegetables. "They are simple, polite, law-abiding folk," the booklet, *Nansei Shoto,* told my father.

This was the background when Japan began militarizing the island in early 1944.

Ei Shimada, governor of the Okinawa Prefecture, was a puppet leader sent from the mainland. Yet he cared for civilians. In May 1945, as the Shuri Line was about to fall, Shimada went to the bunker of General Ushijima. According to Feifer, Ushijima said he was going to withdraw troops from the Shuri Heights to the south. This would buy time before the island fell to the Americans.

Shimada "voiced a passionate plea . . . not to abandon his main fortifications," Feifer wrote, "because it would mean that thousands of civilians would die." Shimada later accused the Japanese army of "needless slaughter" of civilians. "Had the 32nd Army held to its promise and remained in its main bastion for the final stand . . . a large number of civilians would have been spared because they were apart from the army and relatively safe."

Army General Simon Bolivar Buckner Jr., the son of a Confederate Civil War general, was in charge of the land war and made a huge blunder on the US side. Even if JICPOA's intelligence was bad, by

May it was clear that something else had to be done. Buckner stubbornly kept driving head-on down the island and didn't make a reverse landing until it was too late. If he'd done that sooner, fewer American soldiers would have died and a huge number of civilians would have been spared because the Japanese troops would have been contained at Shuri.

I was in Southern California visiting Captain Frank Haigler just months before he died. I told him that I wanted to visit Okinawa and that I would try to meet at least two families of men who I suspected my father had killed.

"Don't do it!" he implored. "Let it be!"

Frank knew about the outfall of war. He didn't say it, but I suspected from his response that he may have regretted keeping up the correspondence with the survivors of the men who died in Love Company. He'd learned: Let the dead be.

But I couldn't.

The Tomb

I walked the streets of Naha, following the initial course that Love Company traveled on May 30, 1945. A sprawling modern city of gleaming buildings surrounded me. Cartoon-like taxis, in colors of electric blue and salmon pink, raced past. Sidewalks teemed with people.

I came to the canal, green with stagnant seawater, that bisected the core of downtown. The tide was out. Somewhere within two hundred feet of where I stood, Love Company had faced this channel. I imagined the tide was also low that morning so that the men could use a plank bridge to cross. On the other side and to the right was the path taken by Jim Laughridge, Steve Maharidge, Herman Mulligan, Frank Palmasani, Tom Price, Joseph Rosplock, and the others. To the left is the route used by Captain Frank Haigler, Ed Hoffman, and the others.

It was my second full day on Okinawa.

I'd first "seen" Okinawa in 1985, when I flew out of Tokyo's Narita International Airport en route to Manila to report on the revolution that would overthrow Philippine dictator Ferdinand Marcos. The pilot announced that Okinawa was off to the right. I stared down at the irregularly shaped island thousands of feet below. It actually resembled a slightly tangled length of hemp rope: The kanji characters for Okinawa roughly translate to "rope in the sea." As the island vanished behind in the mist, I thought of my father, then freshly retired in California, and the war that was then forty years behind him.

On the very last day of March 2011 I spent a marvelous spring day in Tokyo before an early morning flight to Okinawa. Cherry blossoms were in bloom—the trees seemed to be everywhere. On the flight I'd been engrossed in a book about the war. I'd just read the account of how Japan's military leaders ordered the heaviest warship ever built on earth, the *Yamato*, on a suicide mission toward Okinawa to engage far superior US forces—there weren't enough planes to give the ship air support.

It had been a sunny day just like this sixty-six years earlier. The book told about how the young sailors in the Yamato group had stared at the cherry blossoms as the ship steamed out of Tokyo Harbor. Most wouldn't live to see other seasons of blossoming cherries. They knew the famed *Yamato* was doomed.

Early the next morning, April 1, I flew south. Okinawa appeared as the jetliner descended through intermittent clouds: reefs, an unbelievably blue ocean, stunning white beaches, steep mountains green with thick forest. The jetliner touched down at 8:36 a.m., six minutes after the US Marines had set foot on beaches to the north sixty-six years earlier.

I headed for Green Beach II, the landing site where my father and Love Company came ashore. The 3rd Battalion's code name had been "Blizzard," according to landing papers my father kept. I stared at the endless city racing past the van's window.

The freeway took me north to the village of Toya, where I saw my first *shisa*—ceramic statues of genderless half-dog, half-lion creatures that come in pairs. One snarls menacingly with a closed mouth: This keeps in good spirits. The other snarls with an open mouth: This keeps

Shisa statue

away bad spirits. Unique to Okinawa, they were everywhere—on rooftops or in front of houses.

Under the watchful eyes of numerous *shisa*, I used the 10th Army landing map that I'd scanned at the National Archives. Green Beach II wasn't difficult to find. I instantly recognized it from 1945 pictures—it was low tide, and the unique configuration of the reef's coral outcroppings hadn't changed. In 1945 the ocean would have been black with American ships. I stared at an empty horizon.

Walking to the water's edge, I stepped amid blooming vines of morning glories. These blue flowers were surely also present the day my father's company landed. Birds sang. Their cries seemed loud in the relative quiet. Broken coral and shells were blinding white. The water was warm. At a nearby resort a child played and cried out happily in the sand.

There's a danger of hubris when you study the past. Sources speak in cinematic detail. You read countless books and documents, study old maps, and form a mental picture. You can fool yourself into believing that you can "see" what happened in a place such as Green Beach II. I wish I could say that I really saw events of that long ago day. But I could not.

I only saw a beach that would have been great for swimming and fishing and making love in one of its secret coves if I had come to this island for any other purpose than finding ghosts.

And so on that second day on the island I stood at the edge of the canal in Naha. Years of anticipation lay behind the walk I was about to take to discover the spot where the tomb exploded. I had low expectations. Would anything be recognizable?

I knew exactly where to go, however. I had descriptions from the men of Love Company, a printout of Haigler's battle map (the major street grid was the same as before the city was leveled in 1944 and 1945), and Google Earth. While in New York City I'd "walked" this route numerous times using "street view." Yet I couldn't virtually find the tomb. If anything remained, it was hidden behind buildings that blocked the view on the computer.

I crossed the canal on a bridge. I deviated from the dog-leg route Frank Palmasani told me about and went in a straight line toward Mount Jokagu, a course that would have exposed me to machine gun-fire on May 30, 1945. Today, I was safe; even if there were machine guns on the hilltop, hundreds of buildings blocked a clear sight-line. The land began gradually rising, as had been described to me.

I came to a minor summit south of Hill 27. There were several ancient tombs, pocked with shrapnel damage from American bombs; they were surrounded by weeds. A sign in kanji characters announced that if their owners didn't claim them by January 1, 2013, they'd be demolished. Many tombs have remained untended because families that cared for them were killed in the war.

It was a wealthy area, as high ground with a view often is in any culture. I found myself on a footpath behind the smart apartment buildings and was suddenly thrust into another world—old Okinawa—not visible on Google Earth's street view. I came to a shack, dug into the hill, made of weathered gray wood that seemed from the end of the war;

I wondered if the wood had been salvaged from bombed buildings. Clothes hung on a line, and I had to duck beneath them to proceed. I paused at an open door. Inside was pitch dark. Wafting out was the smell of cooking *inobuta,* the black-haired pig famous to the island that is bred from a wild boar and a domestic sow, whose fat is so thick that it could keep a walrus warm. I'd eaten it for the first time the previous night, and I realized that when my father raved about the flavor of the pig they killed up north, he and the men probably were consuming an inobuta. Dad said the meat was tender because they'd beaten the animal to death with hammers until it was black and blue. Yet the pig I had eaten was soft as the flesh of cod.

I wanted to know who dwelled here in apparent poverty. But I felt like an intruder. I continued along the path.

I emerged at apartment buildings I recognized from Google Earth. To the left were turtleback tombs. The site of the Mulligan tomb was ahead—around the backside of the hill where it curved west. Despite my anticipation, I paused. The roof of one tomb had appeared mottled on my computer screen. I clambered atop and confirmed what I suspected: It clearly had been struck by an American shell and repaired after the war. (Charles Lepant told me, "Man they were built. . . . I seen the battleship shells bouncing off them tombs. . . . They'd just ricochet off.")

I went around the corner of Mount Jokagu.

On the left was an apartment complex; on the right, an office building. Trees and shrubs were visible behind. I walked between the buildings and came to face twin turtleback tombs made of bright cement.

The dual tomb appeared to be constructed after the war—the cement was better formed than the old tombs. On the immediate right was a tangle of feral philodendrons and other flora amid trees towering over the site. I went to the edge of this wildness. I made out where the interior walls of a tomb had once existed. It appeared not to have been impacted by a shell—the manner of destruction indicated that the blast had emanated from within.

I trembled. I moved on to the immediate right of the blown-out tomb and found square-style tombs.

Turtleback and square tombs on Hill 27 in 2011

The roof on the left, nearest the blown-out crypt, had been cheaply repaired with asphalt. The original concrete top was blasted away. The tomb on the right, suffering cracks from concussion, had this crude inscription from when the repairing concrete was still wet.

The patching was done on April 18, 1958. A man named Yomitan was interred here. I pulled out a picture of Hill 27 I'd gotten from Ed Hoffman. The pattern of tombs matched exactly.

I returned to the minijungle that had once been a crypt.

I now stood on the exact spot where Herman Walter Mulligan threw the grenade into the tomb.

I made the walk to the tomb every other day for nearly two weeks. One day I visited twice.

When I returned to the hotel at night I passed barkers for the "girl clubs" in the central district. These were not brothels, I was told. Men spent four thousand yen for an hour of talk with a scantily clad woman.

The women's hair ranged from blonde to henna; none was natural. Presumably, the clubs appealed to Japanese men with a Western fetish or Americans who desired Westernized Asian women. The barkers— young Japanese men with slicked hair, wearing suits—stood outside these joints, aggressively pitching each passing lone man. But every

night I was shunned; they looked away. I was puzzled but then realized: I had death in my eyes. The barkers sensed something more than lack of interest in my demeanor—there was something fatal.

I wanted to talk with the families whose dead were buried in the adjoining tombs. I didn't really know why, for certain. At the least, I hoped to hear anything I could about the tombs when the explosion happened.

I left notes in both English and Japanese on copies of the picture of my father and Mulligan, with contact information.

On one visit I went farther around the hill where there was a school, quite likely the one where Jim Laughridge had been when the tomb exploded. To the right was a lane that went into a minor forest. I followed it. Around a bend I grew lost from Naha town. No modern buildings were visible. Tombs flanked the lane that ended in trees. Visible through their trunks was a grand view. To the immediate west was Hill 46 and the valley where Captain Haigler had implored Lieutenant Colonel Clair Shisler to allow him to wait for tank or artillery support. To the south was the Kokuba River. Across it was Hill 53. To its left was where Laughridge was hit and scrambled to escape. On the hill itself was where Ed Hoffman was nearly killed by the Japanese major and

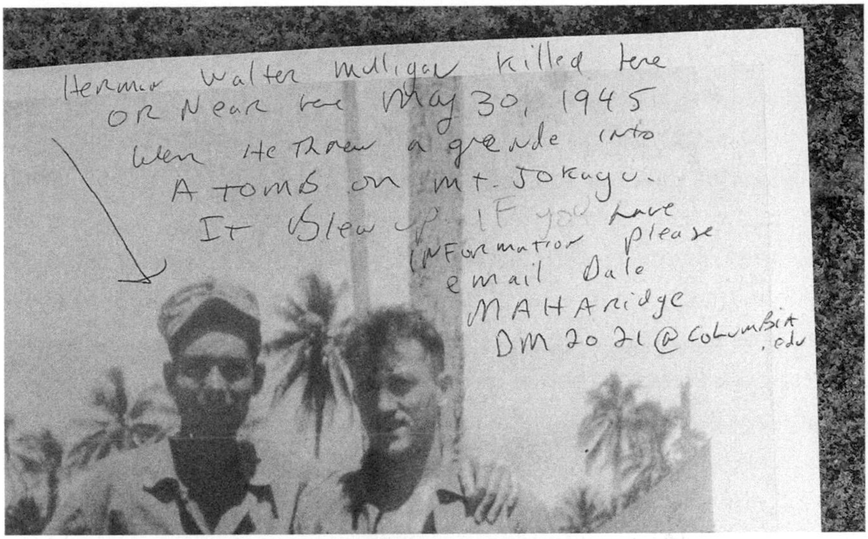

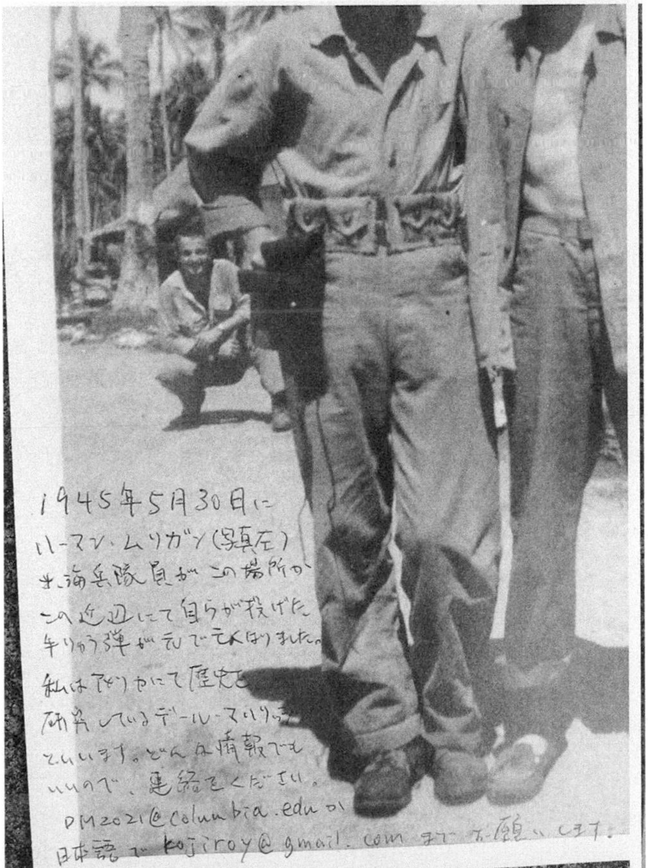

Notes on pictures that I left on the tomb

where Pio "Maggie" Magliaro fell dead. Beyond is where Lieutenant James Bussard was shot dead through his helmet, which was now in Haigler's basement.

I wondered about all the other men in Love Company who were killed who I had no connection with through the stories I'd heard from my father and the men of Love Company. There were plenty. Some had been blasted to atoms by direct hits from the Shuri artillery. Guys laughed sadly when they told me that Arlington National Cemetery is full of "remains" that were just bone fragments and gore—nothing really. In some cases men told me with assuredness that dead Japanese soldiers were often scraped up and sent home as Americans. "A lot of Japs are buried there," one said.

I thought about all the thousands more civilians and Japanese soldiers whose corpses rotted unclaimed in caves or were bulldozed into mass graves in the mud of that Okinawa spring of industrial-scale death.

In the twilight I backtracked on the lane flanked by tombs. I crossed a road and came to the spot where Mulligan died. Something told me not to get close. I went into the open garage beneath the apartment building. No one was around. I stared through pillars at the patch of jungle that had become a spectacular volcano on May 30, 1945.

I was on the spot where my father probably stood that day, or he was just to the right of me, where the office building was now located. I imagined him training his B.A.R. on the doors of the tomb to cover Mulligan as he ran up to throw a grenade. I knew Dad was a B.A.R. man until the end because he often lamented that he didn't put the B.A.R. he'd carried all through combat in his duffel bag to bring home. Officers warned him the bag would be inspected when he got off the ship. But no one ever looked inside.

I considered how this island impacted my growing up. When Susie Hoffman said that war "was the biggest thing in Eddie's life," it resonated. My father went from being a jobless kid in the Great Depression to a squad leader in charge of the fate of twelve other men, and then a sergeant. Split-second decisions could end up fatal; he was a cog in the biggest battle in the Pacific. It was a supreme transformation, from powerlessness to ultimate power over life and death, then a return to poverty at 798 Starkweather Avenue on the edge of that smoking valley of steel mills. Putting aside what he witnessed, if all that was not enough, my father suffered his first blast concussion at Sugar Loaf Hill, which the Japanese soldiers had nicknamed *Sunbachi,* or "cone hill." I'd visited it early today: The prefecture's government had flattened its top for a water supply tank. There was just a plaque of commemoration on the summit that looked down on a shopping mall. The Japanese desire to forget was equal to that of some Americans. But my father couldn't will away the blast concussion damage to his brain that happened where shoppers now purchase Prada and Dior. I looked up at Shuri from where shells had wailed in 1945 directly over the future site of the mall, to my father's position behind. Then my father endured the mother of all explosions here at the blown tomb.

Before coming to Okinawa I wanted to know about traumatic brain injury (TBI). I had talked with Douglas Smith, MD, director of the Center for Brain Injury and Repair at the University of Pennsylvania. "For absolute certain, like with your father, TBI can do that," Smith told me when I related how my father would go into raging fits. "Some people who sustain a concussion brain injury can become combative. It can almost manifest as emotional instability, an inappropriate emotional response."

Smith explained that the brain is "visco-elastic." This means the brain is built to endure mild shocks. "It's like a Jell-O mold," Smith said. "That jiggling and shaking stretches axon fibers." A little bit of jarring does no damage to the axons, which extend from brain cells and transmit electrical current. But in a concussion tiny structures in the axons break. In addition, salt flows in and short-circuits electrical flows, causing blackout.

"If I take Silly Putty and I make a cylinder and pull, it keeps stretching and gets thinner and thinner. But if I take the same Silly Putty and pull rapidly, it snaps very rapidly in the center." In the first microsecond pulse of a blast, Smith said, "Your brain might act like glass that is bent. The axons' internal structure breaks, which then stops axon transport of protein down the axon tube. It is akin to tying off a rubber hose; the axons begin to swell, which can lead to disconnection. Once an axon disconnects, it cannot grow back together. The brain is diminished. It's the kind of injury that keeps on taking. It initiates long-term nerve degeneration. It never stops in some people." Not everyone reacts the same way,

Smith said. It depends on which part of the brain is damaged. Repeated concussion might amplify damage. And it may cause Alzheimer's disease—my father was losing it a bit near the end. (I also thought of George Popovich Jr., who lost his mind at the end.) This may explain why Dad mellowed. Smith told me that as Alzheimer's develops, "some individuals become more aggressive, others more passive."

Dad's double-dose TBI ensured that World War II would continue at one house in North Royalton, Ohio. This was repeated at an untold number of houses all over America, from battles in all wars, from then on forward: *Okinawa. Inchon. Dak To. Tora Bora.* All were veritable factories churning out TBI and posttraumatic stress disorder.

I wondered if my father came home different from the war. In 2011 I visited my Aunt Helen (Kozak) in Cleveland. The Maharidge clan is not one for personal disclosures. For sure, that house on Starkweather Avenue was not an ideal place to grow up. But none of my father's brothers and sisters had the kind of sudden rage, at least to my knowledge, that my father possessed.

Aunt Helen was surprisingly open. She told me that she once asked my father about the war, and he angrily yelled at her to shut up.

"So we never asked about the war again," she said.

"Was he different after?" I asked.

Absolutely, she replied. She said he came back real quiet but with an explosive temper. Not long after he returned from China in January 1946, she went out with a girlfriend. They ran into some boys they knew; they hung out for a while with them in a public place. When she came home Steve asked where she'd been, wrathful that she'd been social with boys. "He slapped me," she said. This outburst was sudden and violent and shocking. Was he like that before going overseas?

"No," Aunt Helen said. "He never did anything like that before the war."

I often recall the day my mother placed all blame for my father's rage on his mother, in the immediate aftermath of his death. My grandmother had issues, for certain, but the truth is that the war-damaged man troubled my mother. I regret that I didn't finish this work before she died so she would have known about his traumatic brain injury. My father had a head filled with snapped Silly Putty.

A good friend, Jan Haag, would write that "you and I had, in many ways, the same father—mine was utterly ruined by being in the infantry in Korea. . . . He was wounded twice and sent back out to fight before a last shrapnel blast nearly killed him and got him sent to an American hospital in Japan. He, too, had that same explosive anger." Like my mother, her mother also fought back, "which meant that our house was a pretty constant war zone. . . . It is no accident that my sister and I avoid conflict and that we have chosen partners with whom we never fight." Her final sentence describes me. I've lived my life in reaction to the rage of the house I grew up in; in some ways perhaps this makes me a better man, in others, not.

A sudden buzzing past my right ear, *whoosh!* I ducked so fast that I fell, my left hand keeping me from going all the way to the garage floor. I sprung back up, ready for combat, certain that someone had swung a fist or a club next to my head.

No one was present. Was it a bat? The air was empty.

I spun around and looked at the site of the lost tomb. My heart raced. I ran away, downhill—fast.

A Surprise in Okuma: Zayasu

The Okinawa Expressway runs more or less down the center of the narrow island, coming to a long grade that took me to the edge of the China Sea and a view of the Motobu Peninsula that rose apparition-like out of the mist. After Nago town I passed the place where Charles Lepant was hit by machine gunfire. Now the road hugged the ocean. The land was wilder. Green hills plunged toward the sea. Ahead, using a 1945 military map, I easily identified a point of land jutting into the ocean several miles distant: the Okuma Beach that Captain Haigler's diary called Hichi, where Fenton Grahnert fished with "DuPont spinners" and where Kennedy raped the girl.

It had taken just an hour and a half after leaving Naha to reach Okuma. The Okinawa of one's imagination is far more vast than reality. There was a bridge over a ribbon of a river. A hill rose to the right—this is where Kennedy shot the babies.

Inside a Japanese version of a roadhouse, Restaurant Kuina, where one can eat traditional Okinawa food, including *ta imo*, yam ice cream, an older woman was extremely helpful. She made phone calls to the most elderly residents. It was my chance to find the rape victim.

I began at the home of Kogen Ota. The Japanese military had conscripted him at the age of fifteen in January 1945. They put him in an agricultural military unit. He carried a shovel instead of a rifle; his job was to grow rice. He didn't recall the date of the American landing; he simply remembered the sea thick with ships. He climbed a hill to get a better look. As he told this story, he offered me Acerola, fruit juice in cans.

He told how American Grumman planes strafed the village before the landing. A one-year-old boy inside a house was shot in the head and killed. Ota grabbed his sister and went to the hills. He was scared. They went deep into the mountains to get beyond the reach of the battleship shells.

"Was there a woman raped by one of the Americans?"

I described where the rape happened, up a hill above the town. He said there were many people from Nago town who were camped there to avoid the bombing. He said it could have been one of them but that no villagers that he knew of were raped.

I went to the home of Chiyo Tamaki, ninety-three. I knocked on her door and she yelled for me to enter the small dwelling. I found her in the bedroom, a tiny wisp of a woman with a deeply lined face enthusiastically smoking a cigarette—an ashtray contained dozens of butts. She told me that like everyone else in the village, she and her husband ran into the hills. She had been pregnant. She gave birth while in hiding. She reiterated what Ohta told us: There were many Nago town residents camped up on the hill.

One American soldier got fresh with her. She said she shook her head "no," and she grabbed her crotch to indicate what he could not have—an act she repeated for me, using the hand free of a third cigarette she'd smoked since I showed up. Then she lifted her shirt, bared her breasts (an act she did not repeat for me), and squeezed a nipple, squirting the man with milk. He ran away.

Compared with the Americans, "the Japanese soldiers were worse to the Okinawans," she said of such sexual advances.

By the descriptions from Love Company members of the "compound on the hill" and from the elders of the village, it was a woman from Nago whom Kennedy raped. Nago was too large a city to check out in the limited time I had—finding the woman, were she still alive, was a long shot, and I had to abandon the search.

This is also where Seiichi Zayasu lived, the man whose passport and wallet had been kept by my father. The address was just a few doors from Chiyo Tamaki's home. It was a vacant lot. Across the narrow road was a house marked by a name out front that read "Zayasu."

Without thinking, I knocked. A man in his eighties opened the door. I learned he was Seiichi's nephew. What did I want? Before I could answer, Seijin Zayasu invited me in.

Heart in throat, I began explaining the story, how my father might have killed his uncle—

Seijin looked puzzled. His uncle didn't die in the war, he said. He was too old to be drafted—he was forty-nine in 1945. He died in the 1950s. I stammered. How, then, did my father get Seiichi's passport, the wallet?

Seijin told me that Seiichi, his wife, and seven children fled into the mountains before the American landing. They lived in the forest for months. He explained that Seiichi's house was one of only a few left standing after the American shelling and bombing, and in fact, it existed until some five years earlier.

I realized that my father must have gone into the empty house when Love Company was stationed here and had filched the passport, the wallet, and other items sometime between April 15, 1945, and the first days of May. I wanted to laugh but restrained myself. I imagined my father laughing somewhere over this discovery I'd just made. It was the kind of thing he would have found humorous.

For decades I'd shaped a false narrative. I was very happy to learn that my father had not killed Seiichi. I realized that except for the guy who he talked about on his deathbed, perhaps he'd not killed anyone else on Okinawa, given that it appeared that he was out of combat after the tomb exploded.

I met with Seiichi's son, Moritake Zayasu, in Naha. Moritake was nervous. He wore a fine suit and tie. He was a quiet man. He talked softly and sparingly.

His father was mayor of Okuma village in 1944, Moritake said. He was also a farmer; the family raised rice, yams, and vegetables.

He was ten years old on October 10, 1944. That was the day the Americans bombed Naha and other parts of the island. The north was not bombed at that point—but they knew war was coming.

"The next year, in 1945, the aerial bombings got heavier around February," Moritake said. "We dug a trench at the base of the mountain and hid there during the day. We would go back to our house at night."

When the Americans landed, "we were in the mountains the whole time." The family believed Japanese military propaganda that the Americans would kill civilians.

"We would do what we could not to get caught. Information would come our way, and we would have to go deeper and deeper into the mountains. At first we made a simple shelter close to the village. There was a lot of food near the village, like fish and shrimp and crab, but there wasn't much in the mountains. But we would try to find things to eat. Food became scarce after three months or so, and we would eat leaves that seemed edible or tasty."

Moritake paused.

"Very difficult, very difficult. It was a hard time. It was really tough not having food to eat."

When they cooked, they were careful to minimize campfire smoke.

American soldiers discovered the family in June. He said his father was able to escape. The rest were taken to a village and held in a house for a few weeks. An American officer gave them a "certificate" so they could leave. They went back to the mountains to live with Seiichi. Finally, in July, the Americans forced all the people in the mountains to return home.

He described the Americans as "really friendly. We would get candy from them. Most of the homes burned down from the war, but our house made it without burning down."

He didn't recall his parents being concerned about missing items—they were happy to be alive. They were one of the few Okinawan families that Moritake knew to have had no one die in the war.

I told him that I came expecting to meet the son of a man my father killed, "and I'm very happy to know that he did not kill your father," I said.

"I was surprised today, but happily surprised," Moritake replied.

He said that after the war the Voice of America was building radio towers, and his father was a supervisor of construction. Moritake was attending a distant school when his father was killed in an accident on the site, at a quarry, in 1952. Moritake ended up working at a refinery for Nippon Oil until he retired.

Moritake repeatedly asked why my father kept the items from his father. He wasn't angry—just baffled. I tried to explain the American soldiers' obsession with souvenirs. Perhaps the items seemed exotic to my father.

"My father entered your house, obviously when you were gone, and took some things," I said. "If he had lived longer, I'd loved to have

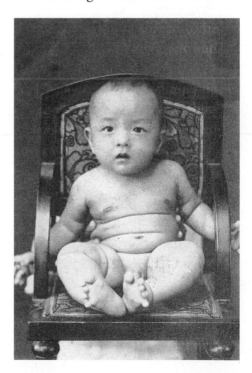

come here to Okinawa with him, and I'm sure he would love to have returned everything. I'm sure he would also apologize. So I apologize in his behalf and return them to you."

I set down the wallet, the passport, and a baby picture.

"I think this might be me!" Moritake said. He held the image and studied it in amazement. "I've actually never seen a baby picture of myself. If it is in fact my photo, then it would have been taken at Okuma back in the day. There was a photo studio there even before the war."

Yoshikuni Yamada
shortly after the war

Yoshikuni Yamada in 2011

The Ghost of Tatsuo:
Yamada

I held in my hand the Japanese military training manual signed by Sanemasa Yonashiro that my father brought home. Yonashiro was dead, and I couldn't find his relatives. But in the search for them I came to meet Yoshikuni Yamada, one of the *tekketsu kinno tai,* which translates to "Blood and Iron Corp" but more commonly has come to stand for the "boy soldiers" who were forced to join the military even though they were as young as fourteen.

I stood in the shade of a tree at the Himeyuri Monument to the war at the southern tip of Okinawa, waiting for Yamada. The eighty-two-year-old man came toward me at a brisk pace. We exchanged greetings, but he was in a hurry, so I pocketed the old manual and tried to keep up with him at a near jog. He had gray, thinning hair and an easy smile. He was the kind of octogenarian whose age you forget moments after meeting him.

Yamada was focused on getting somewhere. He carried a clear plastic bag with tangerines, flowers, and other items. When we came to the crest of a hill overlooking the Philippine Sea, he headed across a lawn to a wall of brush and a massive outcrop of coral rock thick with trees and vines.

In late-June 1945 he had fled to this spot. It was a blackened wasteland back then, trees blasted away by American shells and napalm. Yamada pointed to a ten-foot-wide crevasse, now obscured by cycads and vines, some fifteen feet deep. It was even deeper back then, he said, but in the intervening sixty-six years, decaying vegetation had filled in the bottom. Yamada had inhabited this crack in the rock with his friend Kozo Arakawa.

"Both of his eyes were damaged, so he couldn't see or move," Yamada said.

Being a buck private, officers ordered Yamada out of the crevasse at night to get water from a bomb crater just outside of the rocks' protection. Shells were constantly falling, so he had to work fast. In the moonlight he could see bodies floating in the water, which was thick with maggots that had come off the bodies.

"It would take too long to use a water canteen, so we would use a camping pot. Then we would all share the water. Then everyone would have diarrhea and amoebic dysentery."

On June 23, two days after the United States declared the island "secure," he said the bombing was fierce. Fires from napalm bombs burned everywhere. Then there was a lull. It meant the American Marines were nearing.

"Before the *kiri-komi* we didn't really have anything to eat. But since it was supposed to be the last meal, they made us eat a lot. I ate a lot of brown rice until I was full. I was so nervous, and the body is so strange. Everything I ate came out."

A first lieutenant then barked into the crevasse, "'If you're alive, get out of there.'" The officer ordered Yamada to commit *kiri-komi*.

"I didn't tell Kozo I was leaving then," Yamada said.

His blind friend clung to the walls of the crevasse, calling his name, feeling his way along and looking for Yamada.

"So I looked at his face one last time. I just wanted to say something." He said nothing. "There's nothing I can do now that he's dead."

Yamada crawled away from the crack amid the dead scattered all around. He ended up in front of all the others, living and dead. He had no rifle, just two grenades.

"I threw away my rifle in Shuri," he said. "The reason is that it turned red and rusted. It stopped working. If they saw me throwing a rifle away back then, it would be the death penalty."

Sixty-six years later Yamada lay belly-down on the ground where he had done so that night with his arms outstretched. Back then he held a grenade in each hand. One was to kill a US marine. The other was for himself.

At dawn Yamada said he glanced up and saw US marines in front of him. An American soldier in a foxhole some three hundred feet away turned his helmet upside down, filled it with water, and washed his face.

"He looked really young. He was probably my age. He had a real baby face. There was a small machine gun. I think it was called a Thompson."

The young marine then opened up with that weapon on the Japanese bodies in front of the coral rock outcrop. Yamada shivered with fear.

"*Bang! Bang! Bang! Bang!* Right in front of me. The amazing thing was [the bullets] didn't hit me."

When he again looked, he saw marines laughing. Then the Americans just watched.

"After some time a tank arrived. The tank was large like a mountain."

It was a flame-throwing tank. "The blazing flames went across the ground," he said. Some of the napalm landed on his buttocks.

Yamada, moments after showing how he lay on his belly,
waiting to die nearly sixty-six years earlier

"I panicked and used my hands to try and brush it off, but then it got on my hand." His buttocks burning, his hand burning, he noticed that "all of the guys alive started running away. That's when I went towards a boulder for shelter and a petty officer was shot in front of me, a bullet hit his head. His brain was all over my face, and it had hair around it."

To his right was a classmate from his school.

"I was in fifth grade and really small. He was only in third grade, and I have this impression that he was bigger than me. He got shot and was screaming. Then he died. That's when I was shot here," he said, grabbing the side of his chest.

"There was a hole right here. I saw my own lungs, and it made a hollow noise. I tried to run this way, but my body wouldn't listen to me and I end up going that way. Then I jumped into something like a cave, and we were being shot at all night there. The [people] who were shot would turn red and then black."

He said he got pushed deeper into the cave by more Japanese soldiers seeking shelter, until he was in its center.

"I was unconscious. I think it was the middle of the night when the soldiers started walking over me. It hurt really bad when they stepped on me. I realized I was alive and gained consciousness.

"After a while it was morning. I went crawling towards the brighter area outside. I was covered with shit and blood, and barely alive."

The next thing he knew, someone grabbed him by the collar and pulled him upright. It was an American. He expected to be killed. Instead, he was taken to have his wounds treated by corpsmen.

"He was an amazing guy. He did a good job and I'm very thankful. Usually you would leave someone that was covered in blood and shit, but he took care of me. If he were a Japanese [soldier], he would have me killed or left me alone to die." His fellow soldiers killed each other in such situations.

"Now that I think about it, I think that Americans at the time had the teachings of Christianity in their daily lives, or he wouldn't do such a thing. I was dirty and rancid. Thanks to him, I was the only guy to survive after the *kiri-komi*."

Yamada said there were eighty-eight *tekketsu kinno tai* who came south. Fifty-five of them died around him at the end. But thirty-three went AWOL and hid to avoid certain death by *kiri-komi*.

"This may be a bad way to put it, but there are a lot of survivors from the group that ran away. I'm the only one to survive the *kiri-komi* from the twenty-third to the twenty-fourth. I used to be the smallest back then. I failed at everything I did. I would get thrown back during bayonet training. I could never aim right with a rifle, and my grenade would only reach half way. Strange enough, I'm the only one alive and well. The bigger guys, even the guys that survived, most of them have died now."

Of the military leaders, he said, "They knew that we were going to lose. They would say it was for the Emperor," he said wistfully.

"It was stupid, really.

"I was a defeated soldier. We all were defeated soldiers. There were guys committing suicide, and there were others that would kill others with rifles. Humans are strange. When they would die, they would say 'mom' or 'mother.' Nobody would say, 'Hail to the Emperor!' But there was a veteran who put a gun into the mouth of a dying man and forced him to say, 'Hail to the Emperor!' I remember those kinds of things."

Yamada was sent to Hawaii. It was actually a work camp—he said he didn't feel like a prisoner of war. He had fun, and he learned some English. (He sometimes talked to me in English, most often in Japanese, which I had translated.) He believes he doesn't speak well, but his English pronunciation is perfect.

After a year and a half in Hawaii Yamada went to college in Tokyo at Chuo University. He thought he should be in Tokyo. During the war he wanted to be "a Japanese like those on the mainland. A good Japanese."

By this he meant loyal to the country in a time of war. He didn't mind risking his life to be a good Japanese.

He thought the rest of Japan was like Okinawa. "All burned down. Gone." (Tokyo, of course, was massively firebombed—but the destruction was not as complete as on Okinawa.) He lived in a Tokyo neighborhood where houses were still standing. Then he heard someone playing a piano. He was shocked. "This is the Japan I defended? People were still living in houses and had the luxury of playing a piano?" he recalled thinking. It wouldn't have been so bad, but the mainland Japanese looked down on Okinawans. "'You are dirty. You are no good,'" he said of what he was told many times.

He had had enough of the main island. Yamada returned to Okinawa in 1954 and began an import-export business.

Yamada now pulled things from the plastic bag—incense sticks, matches, a bottle of water, a cup, a tangerine.

"Dale, I am going to light an incense for my friend," he explained.

He ignited the incense and uttered words, nearly swallowed by a strong wind, to his long-dead friend, Kozo Arakawa. He kneeled and bowed.

"Kozo . . . there's a man named Dale-san here. I guess his father fought in the war, but he died in 2000. His son researched all these different things over the last ten years, and he's in Okinawa now, all the way from America. He wants to know about our perspective of the war here in Okinawa. That's why I thought I'd share my experiences with him. Rest in peace, Kozo.

"Dale-san, this is the end of my story. But there is something that I want to share with you. It's Tatsuo's place."

We traveled to the west of where Yamada had tried to commit *kiri-komi,* closer to the ocean. An even larger mass of coral rock rose before us. There was an ancient turtleback tomb dug into this hill, covered in jungle. In 1945 Yamada said the stone mountain was bare, burned and blasted of trees. When one has pictures from the war etched in their head of a blackened mud wasteland, the verdant Okinawa of today seems like an imposter.

This was the first place he'd come after fleeing from the north and my father's company and the other advancing US marines. He'd arrived on June 12.

"It was a sunny day. It rained the whole time before that. The birds were chirping, and it was a real nice, quiet place. We heard the *Bang! Bang!* in the distance, and it sounded like thunder. We were bombarded a couple days after that."

Once the bombing began, the officers moved into the concrete tomb in front of us. Yamada showed me where he and the regular soldiers were dug in—in the open. He was with another boy soldier, his good friend Tatsuo Miyagi. A shell hit, and shrapnel blew off Tatsuo's buttocks and the back of his legs. Yamada carried his friend toward a village on the ocean, but fleeing Japanese soldiers and civilians were running at them saying the Americans were coming this way. Yamada, still carrying Tatsuo, turned west. Others told him the Americans were also coming from that direction. So he carried Tatsuo deeper into the hill of coral rock, where he set him down. He was exhausted and couldn't carry Tatsuo any longer.

Before us was a major well-worn path leading into the smothering trees and vines covering the coral rock mountain. I figured it was a hiking route for tourists. Yamada, still carrying the clear plastic bag, headed down the trail. I followed.

The trail dead-ended in a thickness of trees. Sunlight barely filtered through the canopy. A wall of coral rock was before us; at the base, a lone boulder. This is where Yamada had set Tatsuo down. Yamada said he's been coming to this spot since 1954. In the early years he visited once per week. In recent years he comes twice weekly.

I suddenly realized that the trail was created solely by the feet of Yamada having trodden it for the past fifty-seven years. He was the only man to use it.

Offerings from earlier visits—dried flowers, papers, lay in front of the boulder. Yamada pulled newspaper and started a small fire to burn the old items. In the flame he lit sticks of incense. He set out a tangerine and a cup of tea and he clasped his hands. He bowed his head.

> Tatsuo, there's an American here today who says his father fought in the Okinawa War, and he was a marine. This man was a victim of posttraumatic stress and struggled from it. His son is here in Okinawa to find out about different things, and I am trying to share my experiences with him and that's it. He came all the way over here, and we will talk while we pray that you rest in peace. Tatsuo, please rest in peace.

He fell silent. It was quiet except for the sounds of four different kinds of birds that belted out jarring cries.

"Tatsuo was sitting right here," he said about the ground before the boulder. "And this is where I said goodbye to Tatsuo. I gave him a grenade. I told him to go first. To be honest, he was becoming to be like baggage to me. I thought I was going to die anyway, so I told him to go first. That's why it still bothers me now. Since I survived, that bothers me terribly."

That's when he fled to the crevasse we had first visited.

"There are still bones in the rocks above us," he said as we turned back on the trail. "After the war I think this area was all bones. It would be tens of thousands of people. It's a little too dangerous so you shouldn't go."

He may have been talking about the rugged terrain in which it would be easy to break a leg. Perhaps he meant the ghosts that would

Yamada praying

haunt me. Either way, I would let those ghosts rest on that mountain of wild rock.

We emerged from the trees into the blinding sunlight, next to the tomb.

Yamada continued to speak of Tatsuo.

"He said, 'Please take me to my mother.' I feel bad now. To do it, I would have to surrender. To surrender, the Japanese would have shot me in the back. Many Japanese were killing themselves. They were shooting those who tried to surrender."

He said he often dreams of Tatsuo. In his dreams he is carrying his friend north back home to his mother.

"If we surrendered, then I think the Americans would have treated him. There were a lot of American pricks, but there were a lot of good guys too. The good guys were a little strange though. They would treat injured soldiers. The Americans were really kind to the weak. What I did to Tatsuo is constantly on my mind. I wonder if I could've helped him. I asked a doctor and [he] said that someone hurt that badly wouldn't have made it. It was a bad predicament, and I couldn't do anything. So, please, let's go. You can't help it. It's in the past. Let's go home already."

I replied, "My father would have said the same thing."

"Let's go," he repeated. "Let's go." We quickly left.

We drove to a golf resort, a country club to which he once belonged when his business was doing well, not far from the Mezado Ridge where Love Company stopped moving south. Before the battle the resort had been a camp for Japanese soldiers. On the way we passed a rusting and slender Japanese anti-aircraft gun left as a monument to the war. Yamada remarked how it looked very small compared with the American guns. Indeed, it looked like a toy.

As we ate overlooking the rolling greens, I learned that Yamada had to undergo military training at age thirteen. I pulled out the manual my father had in his possession. Yamada thumbed through it, stopping on the pictures of how to hold a rifle or throw a grenade. "They would make us remember these things like crazy."

He stopped on a page. "The Imperial speech," he said, in which they recited allegiance to the emperor.

Yamada is blind in his right eye from a mortar that malfunctioned. Because he was a *tekketsu kinno tai*, he was not taken seriously. He was given that rusting rifle. After he threw it away he made up a story about how it was lost.

"I was a low-ranking soldier. They didn't give me equipment."

He pointed to an imaginary hole near his forehead. "They gave me a helmet with a bullet hole in the forehead and blood on the inside," he said of the helmet that had been salvaged from a battlefield. "But that helmet saved me when shrapnel hit it. It was dented, but I was not hurt. I didn't die."

To the Japanese soldiers, women and civilians were "a little bug," he said, meaning their lives were as inconsequential to them as an insect. They were forced out of protective caves. He said the Japanese officers didn't care what happened to civilians.

For most of the battle he was stationed at Shuri Castle at the headquarters of General Mitsuru Ushijima. His job, like many boy soldiers, was as a communications runner. Wires were down because of the bombing, so the boys were sent amid the battle to relay messages. It was an extremely dangerous job, and most did not survive. Yamada ran to and from Sugar Loaf Hill below Shuri.

The training manual that I'd just shown Yamada belonged to Sanemasa Yonashiro. This is a picture of Yonashiro that I got at the Okinawa Technical School where he had attended. He'd signed the booklet in 1936, when he was a freshman. He had to come from a family with money: Few kids went to school past the age of twelve. The school was for the elite.

Prewar picture of Yonashiro

He wasn't listed as a war casualty. He was alive in early 1945 and marked "dead" in 1955. The exact death date is unknown. He may or may not have died in the war. I couldn't find any family members. School officials said that over 200 students from the technical school were made into soldiers in 1945; of them, 170 died in battle.

Yonashiro's family was from Okuma, where my father had pilfered Seiichi Zayasu's passport from his empty house. School officials said training manuals were in short supply and that Yonashiro's copy may have been passed on to another *tekketsu kinno tai* who didn't sign it. My father may have picked it out of a ruined house. Yamada backed this theory. He said all the boys like him "didn't keep things like this." They were surviving and had no desire to carry anything that wasn't vital. But there is a chance that it was early in the battle and Yonashiro had the book on his person, that he was the guy Dad talked about on his deathbed.

I asked Yamada about both the Japanese and American battle plans. Did he think they were flawed?

"The Japanese military would tell us to fight until we die and to never become prisoner and live with the humiliation of being a captive. That's how we were trained, and stopping beforehand would not have been an option. The Japanese Army would take it to the end. If it was me, and I knew that we were going to lose, then I would order [the soldiers] to run and go to the US Army. That is why people like us shouldn't be talking about these kinds of things—

"These hard questions are too difficult for a buck private like me. Please ask people who were higher above. Please ask these difficult questions to the Ministry of Defense. This isn't something that I should be talking about. This conversation is too difficult. I have no opinion. There's no way I could have an opinion. This country called Japan wouldn't tell us anything about the outside world. We didn't know what kind of country the US was, and it wasn't until the end of the war that we realized how strange things were."

He spoke in Japanese, and I wouldn't know precisely what he said until later, when I saw a translation. But I didn't need that at the time to know that the thought of questioning the horror he'd lived through deeply troubled him. In ways, he was exactly like some people in the United States.

We returned to the safer conversation of his history.

In the final days of May they were ordered to leave Shuri Heights to retreat south. He was told to take a soldier with a severe leg wound to a hospital cave east of Naha. There was no anesthetic, yet a doctor sawed off the soldier's leg. Yamada said there was a bomb crater in front of the cave that was filled with rainwater where many arms and legs were discarded.

Inside the dimly lit cave was a pile of what he thought was stacked lumber. It turned out to be bodies. He worked at the hospital cave for a few days, hauling out human waste. At the end, before the next retreat, they stopped bothering. The cave was full of shit.

"What was life like?" he asked rhetorically. "Like an insect. Like a rat. I mean, it's pitch black. You couldn't move. We would get bombarded constantly in the caves that we were in."

As the Americans pushed south, Yamada said the severely wounded in the hospital cave were given poison to die or were shot. He described the scene of the retreat: men without legs crawling, dozens upon dozens of them, begging for help. "They would grab on to you," Yamada said. The Americans strafed and bombed the road, so he went cross-country with Tatsuo, ending up where Tatsuo was hit by the shrapnel.

As we finished eating, he told me that he had heard a voice today at the coral rock hill.

"It was Tatsuo."

I nodded.

"Do you believe you can hear such a thing?" he asked.

"Yes."

I told Yamada about how I'd been repeatedly going to the tomb where Mulligan was killed, about the fluttering sound racing past my ear, and how it caused me to duck for fear of something whacking me in the head.

"But there was nothing there," I said. "Yet there was something there."

He nodded knowingly.

"Do you think American spirits remain here on the island?" I asked.
"I don't know."

One time at Tatsuo's death site, he said, a butterfly landed on his
arm. He moved his arm and the butterfly remained, as if looking at
him. It would not fly away.

"That was Tatsuo. Years ago there was a mean dog there that would
chase people away," Yamada continued. "It never chased me. It just
came when I was there, and it would make a whimpering sound. Maybe
that was Tatsuo."

Caves used by Japanese soldiers remain on the grounds of the golf
course in the outcrops of coral rock that dot the greens.

"Players sometimes see soldiers coming out of them. The golfers run
away when they see this," Yamada said.

He looked out the window. He stared at the links for a long time.

After lunch I fantasized about what it might have been like if my father could have come to Okinawa with me and met Yamada. If my father were still alive, he would have been eighty-five. I suspect he'd be
like other guys in Love Company—he would have been more open to
talking about the war as an octogenarian. I imagined the conversation
between him and Yamada. Perhaps this would have healed wounds
and made things better, as I imagined as a boy of age seven, ten, twelve
years old.

Perhaps not. I would never know. But I did have one surprising
view on war from my father that I had discovered just ten days before I
left to fly to Japan.

I was in Cleveland and visited Glenn Haller, who still runs D & D
Tool Company in the building behind the house where I grew up.

Before going into the shop I inspected our old front lawn. The lilac
tree my mother had planted forty-five years earlier still grew; I kept the
bedroom window open even on chilly spring nights to take in its fra-
grance. Tiny saplings I helped my father plant were now towering trees.
As I neared the shop door, the noise of a wheel against steel grew
louder, changed in tone as Haller took a deeper cut; there was the taste
of iron in the air as I opened the door. I was home.

Haller was blackened with grime just like my father would have been. The shop was essentially unchanged, although work was slow. We talked about the business, and then Haller told me something I'd never heard from my father.

"'If there's a war,'" Haller recalled my father saying when he trained him after the sale. "'I'll drive my sons to Canada. I don't want them going.'"

As I absorbed those words that I never would have heard from my father himself, Haller gladly agreed to let me sharpen the flutes of an end mill on the same Covel machine that had been in our basement. I chucked the tool and moved it toward the spinning wheel. I paused, glanced at the LeBlonde and the empty space where my father would have stood; I looked over at the wall where the picture of Mulligan would have been posted. The tool touched perfectly—sparks flew; steel dust filled the air.

I went to dinner with Yamada and his daughter, Natsuko Nozaki, thirty-seven, who is a reporter for Ryukyu Asahi Broadcasting Corporation, the TV station in Naha.

"She is not my granddaughter. She is my daughter," he said proudly of his child from a mistress. He has another daughter who lives in Los Angeles.

Natsuko told me that her father, for all of her life, has been visiting Tatsuo's death site and sometimes his empty tomb at the north end of the island.

"He did not tell me the details of what happened. Just roughly what happened."

We ate courses of the meal that included sashimi salad, *hokke* fish, *umi budou* (a local seaweed known as "sea grape"), and *nankotsu no karaage,* deep-fried chicken cartilage. Natsuko told me that Tatsuo's father was in her high school history books—he was a famous sugar cane grower. Tatsuo was his only child.

Natsuko said that Tatsuo's family wants to forget. They don't like the fact that her father visits the death site and tomb. Once in a while, she said, her father goes to the far north to clean weeds from the vacant tomb of his friend, but he does so stealthily, without letting Tatsuo's family know.

"I'd go with him, and he would become way quiet. I sensed something very serious happened that he could not forget."

In mainland Japan young people are not learning the history of the war. Natsuko said it was different on Okinawa. Okinawans were invaded, and they grew up with the outfall of the war. And yet they feel the mainland Japanese forgot them. Some years ago, Natsuko said, she reported a story on a fierce debate about the wording of World War II in Japanese history books.

"One sentence, just one sentence, caused controversy. That sentence read, 'Okinawans were ordered by Japanese soldiers to die.'"

Some right-wingers in mainland Japan said that was not true. "The sentence was changed to 'Some Okinawans were ordered to die.'"

This caused a huge outcry on Okinawa.

"People came out. My father was one of them, as a witness to the experiences—110,000 Okinawans got together to protest. They wanted to prove the stories of their grandparents are true. What he experienced, he experienced. It is fact. He hates people describing his story as a good story. It is not a good story. It is a bad story."

Tetsu No Bofu: Ohnishi

In the third week of May 1945 fourteen-year-old Masako Ohnishi and fifteen of her family members fled Naha town, running south just ahead of Love Company after the United States broke through the Shuri Line. Thirteen of the sixteen were dead four weeks later, but marines didn't kill any of them. Her relatives were among the 150,000 civilians who died in the nearly three-month battle. June was the deadliest month, when an estimated 100,000 were killed, Feifer wrote in *Tennozan*, "most of them in the last ten days" on the south end of the island.

Ohnishi met me in a park just south of Sugar Loaf Hill, in the shade of towering *gajumaru*, a variety of banyan tree indigenous to Okinawa.

Masako Ohnishi in 2011 and shortly after the war

As children played on the vast lawn, the eighty-year-old Ohnishi spoke so quietly that I had to lean close to hear.

"There was what they call the 'ten-ten air raids,'" she said of the first American attack on Naha on October 10, 1944. "They dropped fire bombs, and the city of Naha was burnt. My house was unburnt, so a large group of us escaped."

That house was abandoned, however, when American troops landed on April 1, 1945.

"There was a cave called Hanta about two kilometers from my house. There were a lot of people there," she said of where they lived for several weeks. "It was pitch black, but there was nowhere else to go. There was a baby in the group, and that baby would cry. It was my older sister's child. When she cried, the people around us would say that the B29s will fly over and bomb us because they would hear the baby. They said that we should kill the baby. Do you think we could do that? My family escaped from there, and that was the beginning of the tragedy for my family."

NANSEI SHOTO

There's no use giving you a sightseer's guide to the Nansei Shoto, because after the navy and the air forces have blasted the way for a landing on those islands, they just won't look the same.

This is the first paragraph in *Nansei Shoto,* the military booklet that my father was given, talking about what the marines would find in the Nansei Shoto, the "Southwest Islands" that are the Ryukyus.

In the next paragraph the booklet stated that "the islanders will still be there," as if they would somehow avoid being killed by the 1.76 million rounds of field artillery that would be fired on Okinawa, on top of the 600,018 navy shells. Many of Okinawa's hills were hit by so many explosions that they lost height and changed shape.

There was stunning denial about civilian deaths by the United States. General Lemuel Shepherd believed when he left Okinawa that twenty thousand civilians died in the battle until informed much later that the figure was actually seven times higher, according to Feifer, in a *World Policy Journal* article. American journalist John Lardner, who wrote a battle report for the *New Yorker* in May 1945, described people like the man depicted in the image as "four hundred and fifty thousand somewhat bemused natives," as if they were safely watching a show of war from the sidelines. The story went on about the "commendable restraint" marines took to avoid killing Okinawans. This was true for the infantry. Outside of Kennedy, none of the guys I got to know from Love Company wanted to harm civilians.

The vast majority of the 150,000 civilians were killed by American bombs and shells meant for the soldiers among them. (This later came to be termed "collateral damage.") Other civilians were killed while hiding in caves and often mixed in with Japanese soldiers, incinerated by our flamethrowers; others, a smaller number, leaped from cliffs to commit suicide, believing the Japanese military that Americans would rape the women and kill everyone.

The commanders ordered Love Company into a bad situation.

Ed Hoffman told how he watched a fellow marine plead with people to come out of a cave—that marine was shot dead by the Japanese inside. "You see that, and you stop doing that real fast," Hoffman said. As a result, many caves were burned or blown closed.

Once marines were sent south, it was kill or be killed. What else could they do?

After fleeing the house sixteen members of Ohnishi's extended family went to a tomb east of Naha. They prepared food over a fire inside the low walls at the front of the mausoleum.

"We were there for a few days. My sister and I were cooking dinner when suddenly [US] naval bombs started coming, and the people in the grave next to us were hit by a naval bomb. This person's body flew up into the air and body parts hit my body and went into our pot of food. I can't explain the fear I experienced at that moment."

The family ran inside the safety of the tomb. There was a high-level Japanese officer that she recognized from "when I was in elementary school and I helped dig air-raid shelters for the Japanese army. We expected him to protect us."

Instead, he ordered the family to leave the tomb so that Japanese officers could take refuge in it.

"He ended up swinging his sword around, telling us to, 'Get out of here!' We were forced out."

It was now late May 1945.

She said younger family members took the hand of her grandfather and grandmother and led them away.

"We went farther south, towards Itoman. It rains in Okinawa in May. We continued on, until we found what was rare at the time. It was a building with a roof on it, which was a sugar refinery factory. We went in, and there were many people who were taking shelter there.

"The US had many spy planes. They would circle around. They looked like *tonbo* [dragon flies], so that's what we would call them. So this *tonbo* found out that there were a lot of people in this building, and it signaled the navy ship to attack us. That's when we were bombarded. A mother was breastfeeding her baby right in front of me. A piece of a naval bomb shell hit her in the head and she died instantly. The baby was alive, so I tried to pry the baby out of the mother's arms, but I couldn't do it. The mother protected her baby with her life. It was motherly love. Eventually my cousins were hit by the naval bombs. My sister said, 'Mom, our little brother was hit.' She was hit by a shell herself, and a total of four of my nephews, nieces, and cousins were killed there.

"Even as our family was dying in front of us, we didn't know if the same thing was going to happen to us any second later. My mother thought she had grabbed her grandchildren's hands and ran, but later she realized, 'I had no idea whose hands I was pulling.' That's how panicked we were.

"I left with some lady, but she was immediately hit by a naval bomb shell that went into her stomach. All of her insides exploded—her stomach, intestines—right in front of my face. I got so scared and crawled away when I felt something hit my legs. I looked at my legs, and both were injured."

Ohnishi lifted her pants and showed the scars.

"Many people died there. At the time we didn't bury them nicely. We were only able to cover them with some dirt."

By 1944 war leaders in both Tokyo and Washington knew Japan was going to lose. It had been downhill for Japan ever since the Battle of the Coral Sea and, later, Midway in June 1942. Midway was a decisive victory for the United States. In June 1944 there occurred what Americans called the "Great Marianas Turkey Shoot." This battle of the Marianas Islands resulted in 346 Japanese fighter planes being shot down. The United States only lost 30 planes. This meant the destruction of 75 percent of Japan's naval fighter planes. In addition, American submarines sank two Japanese aircraft carriers. Then Saipan fell. Then Guam.

America desired "total victory," unconditional surrender from Japan—utter revenge for Pearl Harbor.

In the spring of 1945 firebombs meant to burn urban residential neighborhoods comprised 75 percent of the ordnance the United States dropped on mainland Japan. On the night of March 9, 1945, 334 US bombers made an inferno of central Tokyo "with ten times the tonnage of the Luftwaffe bombs that had caused 'the Great Fire of London'" in 1940, wrote Feifer of the two thousand tons of bombs used. This "fiery vortex" consumed a quarter of a million buildings. "People running from the flames . . . who seemed to be escaping burst into balls of fire. Others jumped into canals for salvation and were cooked alive in boiling water," Feifer wrote. An estimated 197,000 people died that night—as many as perished from both atomic bombs that were dropped later that year.

I recall several drunken nights in Guadalajara, Mexico, in February 1985 with one of those B-29 bomber pilots, Jack Goeringer, then sixty-three. He had been a first lieutenant in the 468th Bomber Group. My newspaper sent me to report on the disappearance of two Americans killed by drug warlords. I ran into Jack, and we connected in the way expatriates often do. After the war he became a grape farmer in Fresno, California. I forget if his wife died or if they were separated, but he was then single and retired, in the company of a gorgeous twenty-two-year-old Mexican woman upon whom he doted.

Goeringer told me over copious amounts of whiskey about how he and his crew had to parachute from their crippled B-29 over the Himalayas, and how Chinese sympathizers smuggled them to safety. What stands out is his description of what it was like to bomb Tokyo in the spring and summer of 1945.

"By then, they couldn't shoot at us anymore," Goeringer said. All their defenses were destroyed. "You didn't want to be in the last plane in formation."

"Why?" I asked.

He said they were dropping incendiary bombs, and the heat from burning homes and buildings blowing into the atmosphere was so intense that the turbulence sometimes knocked that last plane out of the sky.

(Even after atomic bombs had been dropped on Hiroshima and Nagasaki, killing around two hundred thousand people, and Japan was trying to surrender, General Henry "Hap" H. Arnold "desperately" wanted as "big a finale as possible" to the war," wrote John W. Dower in *War Without Mercy*. "It was his dream to hit Tokyo with a final 1,000-plane air raid—and on the night of August 14 he succeeded in collecting such a force and sending it against the already devastated capital city. A total of 1,014 aircraft . . . bombed Tokyo without a single loss. President Truman announced Japan's unconditional surrender before all of them had returned to their bases.")

That night with Jack I realized for the first time just how defeated Japan was by the time my father landed on Okinawa. I had in my mind that the Japanese were still going strong. (The soldiers were tough as hell for sure—every man I later talked with who was up against them attested to this fact, that they fought furiously—but as a nation, they had lost. They would have battled with equal vigor had we invaded mainland Japan as planned. Ed Hoffman said, "They told us to expect 80 to 85 percent casualties." He, like my father, was a fan of dropping the atomic bombs because it negated that landing.) Jack laughed sardonically at my naiveté. I suddenly had more understanding of the reason for the young woman at his side. Given what he'd been through, he was going out having as much fun as he could. I never talked with him again. He died in 2009.

The militarists in Tokyo knew it was over. Why did they continue the war? Perhaps it was the *bushido* warrior code. Or perhaps they were merely hoping to save themselves by extending the war so that they could negotiate a surrender when that eventually had to happen so that they would not be tried as war criminals.

The remnants of Ohnishi's family went south the Kunishi and Mezado Ridges were on their immediate left, the East China Sea on their right.

"I was injured in both legs, so I couldn't walk. My father carried me on his back, and we headed south towards the Kiyan Port. If you go that far, the Kiyan Port is a complete cliff. We couldn't go any farther. That's where my father dug a hole in the sand for my mother, my niece, and myself. There was a sandy area right at the cliff, and the three of us were there."

In was now June 5, 1945. Her father and sisters and other relatives dug holes somewhere else, apparently so that they wouldn't all die together if a shell hit them.

"Everyone else split up and hid. They would come back in the evening and say, 'You made it again today. If anyone of us gets attacked by a naval bomb, we won't be able to see each other. Let's do our best to live another day.' Then we would all split up again.

"The Japanese military was short on labor, and they took away two of my older sisters. They were gone for two days. They delivered food and ammunition, but they made it back alive.

"There was nothing to eat. At night my mother would leave and get some sticks of sugar cane or steal a potato from a field nearby. We ate the potato that had dirt on it raw. That's how we survived. There wasn't any water. The one place that had water was being heavily bombed by the Americans, so we couldn't go there. Our family would drink the water from the last time that we washed rice. We would drink it sip by sip. I remember how it tasted, and it was really sour and smelly.

"There was no medication for this injury of mine, so it would just rot. It was summer then, and many people were dying, so *gin hai* [silver flies] would come, and no matter how hard I tried to get rid of them, they would lay eggs and become maggots that ate at my injury. June was just terrible, really terrible.

"When the US military moved forward they would attack very, very far ahead," she said of the bombing and shelling. "On June nineteenth my mother, my niece, and I experienced a terrible time where we couldn't even raise our heads all day. Late in the afternoon my family that would always come didn't show up. They didn't come at night or in the middle of the night.

"My niece, who was six years old at the time, went to where she thought her family might be and found that the area was completely demolished and that nobody would respond when she called their names out. The baby who was in that cave [in Naha] that everybody said to kill ended up dying there."

All that remained of the original sixteen family members were her mother, her niece, and herself.

"On June twentieth there were no air raids or bombings. The Americans were really close."

A US Navy ship was right offshore. Japanese Americans, Nisei, second generation, spoke through loudspeakers to the Okinawans hiding at the top of the cliffs.

"They were born in America and came to fight with the American military. They would call out that Japan has lost the war and to come out. However, at the time we had a Japanese Imperialist education, and we were taught that we were all the children of the Emperor. We believed that Japan would not lose the war, and that if something happened, a *kamikaze* wind would blow and come rescue us.

"At that point the American troops were already behind us speaking in a language I'd never really heard, which is English."

She described their hiding spot as "just a little hole that was covered with some grass. The sky was blue. It was very hot. Suddenly a face came out right near us. His face was red and burnt, and his eyes were blue. It scared me. That was the first time I had ever seen a foreigner. The Americans were the proud winners, so they weren't wearing shirts, and they were sunburnt. A shirtless American soldier had a cross right here," she said, pointing to her neck and the religious symbol he wore there.

"I thought he was a devil because at the time we used to call the enemy country *kichiku beiei*," she said of a Japanese reference to Americans and the British as demons. "That was what we thought of the American military, but they gathered everyone, and they treated my injury, gave us food.

"When we saw that, we realized that we were treated very badly by the Japanese soldiers and that the American military were a people from a country that believed in humanism. I admired that. So for me, even though it was the American military that killed my relatives, I believe there's nothing you can do because it's war. In war, if you don't kill the opponent, the opponent will kill you. I don't resent the US military at all. It wasn't like the American soldiers came out and shot at us. It was the naval bombs that really got us—the B-29s from the sky and the naval bombs that showered us from the ocean. They say that in one square meter, they dropped over ten bombs."

It was *tetsu no bofu*, the violent wind of steel.

"Nowadays, they say the Americans are choosing areas with fewer civilians," she said of the bombing in the wars in Iraq and Afghanistan. "But back then the attack was undiscriminating. They just bombed an unspecified amount of people because that's how it was. My country is bad for being a part of the war as well. I think [the United States and Japan] were both bad. That's why I believe that a country should never go to war."

Ohnishi, who has four children and seven grandchildren, went to the site of the sugar refinery in Itoman two years earlier. It's now a lumber factory. She's also visited the Peace Memorial Park at the bottom of the island, but she's never viewed the black granite monuments engraved with the names of the quarter million people who died on both sides.

"I'm terrified to go there and find the thirteen names of my family there. I don't know how I would react, and it's too painful to go. But I think I should go at least once in this lifetime.

"This is such an important place for a woman, right?" she asked, pointing to her scarred legs. "For sixty years I had to live with something so unattractive. The worst time was when I was in a public co-ed high school. I really wanted to die when I had to show my legs. As long as I'm alive, I have to live with this. That's why I never forgot about the war. I mean, it's my own body, so I have to look at it every time I take a bath or change clothes. That's why it's so hard.

"To be honest, I really don't want to talk about the war. But in Okinawa there are fewer and fewer people that have experienced the war," she said. So she agreed to start talking to school children about it.

"Many students come to Okinawa now for school trips, and they study about the war, and they come to admire the blue sky and the blue ocean. I always tell them to study about the war here, to go into the caves and ask themselves if they understand how important life is. There's only one life for one person, right? They say that life is heavier than the Earth, right? So make sure that you take care of your own life. Even though I don't know how much longer I'm going to live, maybe two or three years, and even though I lost thirteen of my family members, I will cherish my life. When I tell that to these students they send me many letters. I make sure to answer each and every one of them. I want them to cherish food, and family.

"But the war in Okinawa really isn't over yet. There are unexploded bombs. Just recently they said that there are so many unexploded bombs that it would take a hundred years to get rid of them. Every month we have a day set for unexploded bombs to be handled, and they have people within a distance of so many kilometers evacuate. I evacuate when I need to. As long as these unexploded bombs exist, I don't think you can say that the Okinawa war has ended. I'll probably only feel like the war is over when I die."

Mezado Ridge

South of Itoman town a low ridge filled the western skyline. I brought out the US Marine compass my father carried during the war, the one I used to find my allowance as a boy. In the end, I never had to employ in a war the skills I learned with it. Now I used it to plot coordinates on my photocopy of Captain Frank Haigler's battle map to be certain I was in the right place. The compass helped me discover my father's war, though it appears certain that he didn't venture this far south. But other men from Love Company did.

I was looking right at Hill 69, thickly covered with trees.

To be absolutely sure, I went south to the village of Itosu, then dog-legged on small roads back north on the opposite side of the ridge. En route I came to the site where General Simon Bolivar Buckner Jr. was killed on June 18, 1945. He'd come to the front to observe. Most accounts say a Japanese unit saw US military brass and rolled an artillery piece out of a cave entrance to lob one shot that exploded overhead. At 1:15 p.m. shrapnel hit the coral rock, and a stone fragment flew off to strike Buckner fatally in the chest.

As I passed that hill, I thought of four men from Love Company.

Ed Hoffman believed it may not have been a Japanese shell. He was with the First Platoon in front of Buckner's position at that moment, in a sugar cane field directly below the hill. Hoffman said that an American artillery team was firing "air bursts" directly over their heads by mistake. These were shells that exploded in the sky and rained down shrapnel. Someone frantically radioed them to cease fire; miraculously, no one in Love Company was injured. Hoffman wonders if friendly fire killed Buckner and that the military didn't want to acknowledge it.

Jim Laughridge was in the hospital recovering from the bullet wounds when Buckner was brought in. Laughridge told me they went through motions to save him but that "he was dead. The son' bitch had no bidness being that close to the frontline." Alluding to hunting, I noted that if it were a Japanese artillery man responsible, "That dude got himself a fourteen-point buck." Laughridge laughed more deeply than at any other point in our meetings.

Joe Lanciotti left out all the names of the generals in his book. "Because at the end, when it's all over, all you hear is the name of the generals," he said. "They didn't fight the war." Joe didn't want to give them any publicity. In *The Timid Marine* Ralph Krupkowski has a name; Buckner does not. He's just some anonymous general who died.

And for Steve Maharidge, I thought of the day President John F. Kennedy was assassinated. As our television broadcast news into the evening, my father kept shouting at the set, "He's just one guy! What's the big fucking deal?! He's just one guy!" I now know it was the marine in him speaking. I can understand his perspective. Seeing so much death as he did might make someone feel this way. Dad never mentioned Buckner. But I'm sure he felt that he was just one guy.

I didn't stop at the memorial to Buckner.

I was now sure it was Hill 69. I went up a narrow lane that led closest to the escarpment.

I donned tall, white rubber boots. I feared the deadly poisonous *habu* snake that lived in the rocky wilds of the island. The picture on the next page was in the guide my father was given before the landing on Okinawa. Word was that you didn't last long after being struck by one.

I studied the mass of green rising before me. It wasn't like the full-on tropical jungle of Guadalcanal: Technically, Okinawa is subtropical. But it looked like jungle all the same, and I'm compelled to call it that. Sixty-six years earlier it had been more like desert. The hill had been shell-blasted and napalm-burned to bare rock. I plunged into the jungle.

Trees soared to neck-craning heights, stretching for the sunlight that weakly reached the jungle floor. Vines hung like spaghetti from the canopy. Most vines were only pencil thick yet strong as steel, as I discovered when I tried to break through them. In places I had to squeeze between vines; the rough coral rock made going difficult. I looked for *habu,* but there was no seeing them in the litter of leaves and fallen branches. I broke out in a sweat as I gained elevation.

TRIMERESURUS FLAVOVIRIDIS (Japanese, *habu*). Most common and venomous of the poisonous snakes of the Ryūkyū Islands. Widely distributed. Strong head. Double diamond markings on body. Victims many and death rate high.

On top there was a quarter-acre flat. I went to the other side, to a cliff of coral rock. I could see perhaps one hundred meters downhill into the trees. Above and below the scarp were a dozen or so coral rock boulders the size of compact cars—more or less square, as Fenton Grahnert described one of them. In front of me, according to battle accounts, was the direction from where Love Company made the assault on Hill 69. I was looking right at where Grahnert was shot in the face the day before Buckner was killed. One of those dozen squarish boulders was surely where the Japanese grenade thrower was crouched and then the other soldier rose to shoot Grahnert in the face.

Somewhere to the right and downhill, just out of my sight, was where Karl Brothers was blasted with grenade fragments that day.

A cave existed to my left, at the brink of the escarpment. Its opening, about three or four meters below me in a crevasse in the coral rock, was about the size of a giant pickle barrel. It vanished into blackness. This clearly was the main Japanese cave defense for Hill 69. The mouth was surrounded by a whorl of vines.

I clambered down to the hole. It was a great place for *habu*. My boots wouldn't help me now. I clung to vines, then roots as I struggled to find footholds as I descended. I could have been grabbing a snake for all I could see. I felt with my feet as I hung suspended by my arms. I wasn't sure if there was a bottom anywhere close.

My foot hit a narrow ledge. Otherwise, I would have fallen. There were other ledges. I switched on a flashlight I carried and stared into the face of a huge shiny jet-black salamander.

The cave was cool, yet I continued sweating. It appeared to be natural but expanded upon by the Japanese. The floor was littered with jagged rocks, as if fallen from an explosion. I came upon remnants of a shoe—the split-toed kind used by Japanese soldiers, and parts of the cloth top. Then I discovered American grenade fragments. Ahead, ten to fifteen meters distant, I saw daylight through a web of tree roots that grew through the cave's ceiling. I went to that opening.

I then carried the items back and replaced them as they had been. I stayed inside the cave for a long time. I stared at the grenade fragments,

Japanese shoe sole

American grenade fragments

quite possibly thrown by Ed Hoffman, for he was one of the first and few to make the summit. If not him, it was surely thrown by Roy Hollenbeck or someone else in Love Company. The bones from the owner of the shoe were likely carried away in 1952, a year that saw a major attempt to collect and bury the dead. This depiction of that effort was in the war museum at Shuri Heights High School.

Cleaning up the bones.
Courtesy of Shuri Heights High School Museum

I studied the walls. A different kind of metal fragment, flatter than from an American grenade, was blasted into the stone. I suspected it came from a Japanese grenade. Did one of the Japanese soldiers commit suicide?

I emerged and walked south, and I found a way down the cliff face that ranged from seven to fifteen meters in height. I doubled back along the base of the scarp, toward where Grahnert had been hit. It was rough going. Directly below the cave on top I came to several caves whose entrances had been sealed with basketball-sized coral rocks cemented together. The caves must have once connected to the one above. There likely were bones in them. I was told that many bodies were simply sealed where they lay in natural tombs.

In front of a sealed cave were quite a few very old bottles. I would have pronounced them litter had I not witnessed Yoshikuni Yamada placing flowers in a bottle where Tatsuo had died. The bottles told me that all the soldiers who had manned this cave complex did not perish— someone had escaped to remember who was dead inside, and they returned to burn incense and pray. But no one had come in a long, long time; the bottles were dusty and sun-faded. The survivor was either dead or too infirm to climb through the jungle to honor his friend or friends.

Days earlier I'd eaten lunch at the home of Toshiaki Kinjo, who was conscripted into the Imperial Japanese Army at the age of fourteen. He'd fought at Sugar Loaf Hill, and he was on the eastern flank of Love Company here at Mezado Ridge. He recalled that in March 1945 a military instructor gathered students to say, "There is a fleet of fourteen hundred American ships coming towards Okinawa. This might require an honorable death, group suicide." Kinjo used as toilet paper the pamphlets that American planes dropped, urging surrender. He was one of the few survivors from his unit, out of hundreds. He was bitter. He said the suicide orders came from General Hideki Tojo, who the Americans later executed for war crimes. "It really made me angry," Kinjo said of the duplicity of Tojo and other war leaders. "They didn't mind these people dying but tried to survive themselves." As for America, he added, "I don't hold any grudges. There's no point. Japan did terrible things to China in the war. America is better for beating Japan after all Japan did."

I'm sure some Japanese I met harbored resentment that they kept hidden. Only once did I witness the bitterness openly—I was interviewing a Japanese war veteran, and he told me he still hated Americans, though his feelings were not translated to me at the time. He suddenly got up and left and I didn't know why. One night at the Kaca-Fe, a bar in Koza City near Kadena Air Base, I sat and drank beers with Anthony, a US Air Force member who married a Japanese woman. He told me that her grandparents never accepted him; they died disliking him because he was American.

Kinjo's was the voice I thought about while staring at the sealed cave.

I stumbled forward. I stood roughly where I believe Grahnert had been hit, looking up again at the boulders that had concealed the Japanese soldiers.

Weird-sounding birds cried out, with long silences between. The harsh green of the jungle was a blur because of sweat stinging my eyes. I thought of Grahnert and Brothers; Hoffman's friend, Marion Rounds, killed here; the man who had worn the shoe whose sole I held minutes earlier in the cave.

I began the climb back from the murky past, to the present.

Last Evening at the Tomb

I was leaving Okinawa on a morning flight. That final afternoon on the island I traveled the exact route, for the first time, as near as I could repeat it, that the members of Love Company's First Platoon used as they approached the tomb. After crossing the canal I worked south, made a dog-leg turn about where I guessed the flame-throwing tank would have burned the buildings as Joseph Rosplock told me, then arced north.

The swale the company used for cover was impossible to discern. New roads bisected the gradually rising hill, and hundreds of buildings now existed. The shallow gully seemed to have been filled in. My mind raced with thoughts of what I'd witnessed on the island and during the decade of research in America. I grew confused and lost my way.

I struggled to use a pocket Japanese language guide to ask directions—I'd not gotten much beyond *konichiwa* and *arigato* and had no one with me to translate. An older woman offered to take me on foot. I profusely thanked her but said it wasn't necessary. I was constantly amazed by the gentle nature and hospitality of the Okinawans.

Once set on a proper course, I hurried.

I thought about dinner a few nights earlier with Yoshikuni Yamada and his daughter, Natsuko. We'd been talking about posttraumatic stress disorder. Natsuko insisted that her father didn't suffer from PTSD. Maybe Americans did, she said, but he did not.

But is this a fact? Yamada had been going to the site where Tatsuo died since 1954, once and then twice a week. That seemed pretty intense evidence to me, but who am I to define the meaning of PTSD?

Whatever one calls it, Yamada was the opposite of my father. Yamada appeared to want to remember constantly what happened in those months of horror. My father spent a lifetime trying to forget.

I'm not judging either man. I look at myself, a person obsessed with the past and what I could not heal.

I **had by now** come to terms with the fact that my chances of finding Mulligan's relatives were slipping.

A year earlier I'd traveled to Greenville, South Carolina. In the library I discovered that no mention of Mulligan's death appeared in the local newspaper when he was killed in action; other men from more prominent families got stories. (Mulligan, however, was included in a 1947 roundup of the war dead.) At a World War II monument to the fallen outside the county government building, I couldn't locate his name. We say we honor "heroes," but as a society, if they are working class, we really don't seem to care so much—in any era.

Donwood Avenue vanished as surely as any trace of the young man who had once dwelled on that lane. It was not on Google nor any contemporary paper maps. I found where it had existed after poring over a

1940 map of the city. It had been a very short street in West Greenville that created a triangle of land where it connected two large roads.

When I visited I faced a site overgrown with trees and vines of kudzu, the invasive species all over the American South that, coincidentally, was brought here from Japan. There was evidence of the street in the forest—I found fragments of pavement amid which grew robust trees. There were remnants of the foundations of extinct homes. All nearby residents I met were born after the war, save for an octogenarian couple just to the west. They didn't remember Mulligan or Owens, his grandfather, but they said the homes on Donwood were not much more than shacks beneath a towering billboard facing drivers on the two major roads that intersected right in front of Owens's residence. The city directory revealed that Owens moved away in 1958.

I drove to nearby Monaghan Mills, where Mulligan had worked before the war. In the Great Depression the average wage was some forty cents per hour. The plant closed in 2001, killed because of overseas competition. It was now a condo complex called The Lofts.

From obituaries and other records, I learned about his family.

Mulligan's mother, Lois Velma Owens Mulligan, died on July 18, 1940, at the age of thirty-five, from "bilateral renal calculi," or kidney stones. She suffered an infection or urine poisoning, according to the death certificate. I had no luck tracking Herman Walter Mulligan Sr. in any public records. He effectively vanished about 1940. That's when it appears that Herman Jr. moved in with Owens, his grandfather.

Robert Owens died at the age of eighty-four on March 11, 1963, in Red Springs, North Carolina. He'd been senile for ten years, according to death records. He'd moved there where his only other child, Ruth Owens Patterson (Herman's aunt), lived, married to Heywood "H. P." Patterson, a textile mill worker. The couple had relocated to Red Springs from Greenville. H. P. died in 1968. Ruth died in 1998 at the age of ninety, in Mecklenburg, a suburb of Charlotte, North Carolina.

The couple had three sons, Ernest, James, and Willis Patterson. In 1968 there were nine grandchildren according to H. P.'s obituary. There was no obituary for Ruth, so it's unclear how many ultimate descendants exist.

I thought it would be easy to locate them or others on Mulligan's father's side. Not so. Patterson is an extremely common name in the South. I made several hundred fruitless phone calls to Mulligans and Pattersons in key cities in both Carolinas. Amid this, I mailed two hundred and fifty letters to Pattersons without phone numbers in the databases. A few dozen phone calls and e-mails came in response from those who told me they weren't related; all wished me luck in my quest.

I then approached the Joint Prisoners of War, Missing in Action Accounting Command at Hickam Air Force Base in Hawaii, tasked with finding the war missing. Mulligan could be one of some eight hundred unknowns buried in the Punchbowl, the national cemetery in Hawaii, where the dead were transferred from battles all over the Pacific Ocean, each marked by date with the island they died on, Hickam spokesman Lee O. Tucker told me. He warned that records were thin. A problem, he said, was the "Spartan mentality" of the US Marine Corps that was "notoriously skimpy" on documentation. (A National Archives librarian told me that massive amounts of Sixth Division records were never sent for archiving.) Yet unknowns have been exhumed and identified all the time, Tucker said.

The case caught the interest of Hickam historian Andrew "Drew" Speelhoffer. He told me that dental records alone might be enough without DNA.

I'd heard that some guys were buried at sea if they died on hospital ships, but Speelhoffer said that triage was done on the beach. As bad as Mulligan's injury sounded, he was surely dead that day and not taken to a ship. It was likely he was buried as an unknown.

Early in 2011 Speelhoffer wrote an e-mail that said, in part, "A case file has been created for this incident and it has been added to our active case list. I'm looking forward to researching this case further, however, researching unknowns is probably the most time-intensive case that we encounter so please be patient."

I would, later in 2011, receive another e-mail from Speelhoffer that said, "I finally received a cache of unknown files from Washington. These are for unknown remains disinterred from the Sixth Marine Division Cemetery on Okinawa. Now we begin the task of meticulously comparing the circumstances of loss and possibly the dental/biological profiles."

So there was still hope.

Earlier that year when I was on Okinawa, I knew I couldn't count on anything. I wanted to put a name on Mulligan's grave. Lacking that, there was one thing that I could do. I had an idea when I'd watched Yamada at the death site of his friend, Tatsuo.

Before climbing the hill to Mount Jokagu that last day on the island, I visited Kokusai Street in Naha with its many tourist shops, seeking to purchase incense. My pocket Japanese language guide didn't have the word for it, and after much pantomime one helpful clerk told me they were called *kouwa sutikku*. But his shop did not sell it.

After going to many shops I found one with a large rack of incense. I chose vanilla. I thought of Herman Mulligan and the summers when he was a boy. I imagined that he surely must have enjoyed vanilla ice cream cones in the sweltering southern heat. I already had a mandarin orange, a white ceramic cup from the hotel, and a can of green tea. I also had a water bottle and some flowers I'd picked from a bush.

I next bought a lighter at Lawson Station, a convenience store that was oddly named after the milk store of my youth in North Royalton, Ohio—it even had the same sign that was used in Ohio in the 1960s.

It seemed a good idea to follow Okinawa custom. If Yoshikuni Yamada could hear Tatsuo, maybe I could hear Herman Walter Mulligan. It was the closest I was going to get to dealing with the demons surrounding my father and what happened to his friend.

After regaining my bearings, I hurried. It was late in the afternoon.

I ducked behind the office building to the "new" double tomb and the blown-out site next to it.

A man was present. Both crypts were adorned with fresh yellow flowers. They resembled daffodils. The tomb had appeared untended for months until today. I focused on the man standing before me.

"*Konichiwa,*" I said.

"*Konichiwa.*"

The man was in his sixties, perhaps early seventies. He wore clothes of the kind that a white-collar guy puts on to do weekend chores, including work gloves. He was tall for an Okinawan, about the same height as me—five-ten, and he was thin.

I began talking but mostly used pantomime, to point and show the tomb blowing up. My hands waved the air. I said "*BOOM!*"

The man shook his head knowingly.

"This . . . you?" he asked in halting English, holding the note I'd left beneath a stone.

"Yes!" I said.

"You?!"

He pointed to Herman Mulligan in the picture on the note.

"No," I said. "He died here."

I wasn't sure if he thought that Herman was me, or I was his son. Perhaps he thought I was a spirit.

"I speak," he paused, looking for words. "A little English."

Junichi Yamaguchi introduced himself. In broken English he told me "sixty" and "different family before—" and "make sixty—" He pointed to the tombs with fresh daffodils. "Now my family."

His hands waved fast as he struggled to explain more.

"You mean the 1960s?" I asked.

"No, no!" he said, shaking his head. "Long time—"

"Ah, you mean sixty years!"

Junichi nodded affirmatively. It grew clear that his family took over this spot and built the "new" turtleback tombs here right after the war because the family that owned the blown-up tomb prewar was probably dead. It made sense. The minijungle on the right was part of the same tomb complex—everything went up in that volcano of rock.

"Different family had before," Junichi said.

"Ah," I said.

"War long time ago," Junichi said.

"Yes."

"Japan—America—now okay," he said.

He nodded, smiling.

"Yes, now okay," I said.

"No more war," he said. "No more war."

"No more war," I said.

It was a Sunday. There was no sound of traffic, even though we were in the middle of Naha's sprawl. There was just some frog or bird high in the tree towering over the blown-out tomb site next to us. It produced an eerie wail, tropical in sound.

"You, me," I said. "We get along okay."

His head bobbed with enthusiasm.

"No more war," he said.

I nodded with equal enthusiasm. I had just caught him. Junichi's tools were gathered in a pile. He was about to leave. I set down my pack and showed him my incense, the cup, the orange—

"I do Okinawa style," I said. "For Mr. Mulligan—"

"No bones," he said, pointing to the blown tomb next door.

"Maybe his bones out there," I said, pointing to where the rubble would have scattered beneath the office building. Were Herman's remains out there? Or in Hawaii? I couldn't explain the nuance, though I doubted his bones were present. I was certain that it had been Mulligan who Joe Rosplock helped carry to the truck.

"And maybe not," I said. "Maybe no bones. But part of him is here."

Junichi nodded solemnly.

"I pray with you."

"Wow," I said. "You show me right way for Okinawa custom?"

"Yes."

The brush was thick. I began pushing through the philodendrons of the neighboring blown tomb.

"*Habu?*" I asked, pausing, alluding to the deadly snakes.

"Maybe *habu.*"

"I will use stick."

I found a stick and poked and stabbed the thick, leafy litter to the rear of the exploded tomb. I affixed a picture of my father and Herman Mulligan, encased in plastic, to the wall using vines to secure it. I set out the orange, the cup that I filled with tea, the water bottle and flower. To the right were chips in the concrete from the explosion.

This is where the urn of bones would have been located, before the Imperial Japanese Army appropriated the tomb; this is where the munitions had been stacked.

I started to light the incense, but Junichi gently took some sticks and showed me how to ignite them in a bundle of four. Were four sticks a vital combination? I didn't ask. The scent of vanilla filled the air.

Junichi kneeled. I kneeled.

He bowed his head. I bowed.

Prayer scene at the tomb with a
photo of Mulligan and Maharidge

Mulligan had been a Baptist. But I'm not religious. My praying would have sounded hollow. I wasn't sure what to say. I found these words coming out of my mouth:

Herman Walter Mulligan, you died here May 30, 1945. My father, Steve, was very troubled by what happened. He didn't forget you. I want you to know that you were not forgotten.

I said a few more things—something about my father and wishing he could be here. My head reeled. I fell silent.

Junichi seemed in deep prayer. I thought about the life Mulligan did not have. The children he did not raise. The woman or women he did not make love to. The fact that he did not get to go home and sit on his grandfather's porch beneath that billboard in West Greenville, South Carolina, listening to the roar of the cicadas giving way to the crickets on hot southern summer nights—

The frog or bird croaked its spooky cry. I looked up.

Junichi stood.

"Okay," I said.

"Okay," he said.

We walked back into the light. I went to shake his hand. Instead, he threw his arms around me in a strong embrace.

"Thank you," I said.

"Thank you," he replied.

—*Dale Maharidge,*
October 24, 2012,
New York City

AUTHOR'S NOTES

To my surprise, I discovered that the memories of some men in Love Company sharpened as they reached their eighties or neared death; incidents thought forgotten were recalled and grew in detail. It clearly was not manufactured memory; others collaborated what they told me. Men spoke of specific incidents in agreement, even though many of them had not seen each other since the war.

Yet events in this book were recounted to me between fifty-five and sixty-seven years after they occurred, depending on when I interviewed the men. There are inevitable contradictions. I have let them stand, *Rashomon*-like, for the reader to interpret.

I spoke with twenty-nine men, but most of them are not included in this book. A few said they had forgotten details of the war—perhaps this was reticence or that indeed their memory had faded. Others met and talked with me at great length, but I chose not to use their stories strictly as an editorial decision based on the length of this book; everyone couldn't fit.

I feared embellishment. I only include the men whom I trust, Kennedy notwithstanding, in the "Twelve Marines" section. There's one man whose story I did not use. He vividly told about events that records and interviews with other members of Love Company show he was not present to experience. For some reason he felt compelled to lie to others, to me. (Several guys called him a "bullshitter.") He had been in some heavy combat. Why he needed to insert himself into situations he was never in remains a mystery.

Regarding quotes from the story of my family: The short ones from my early life were things my father often repeated and, therefore, I trust my recollection. For other utterances, the searing ones, such as the evening my father screamed in our basement, reliving the Battle of Guam when he wanted the men to shut up around him—I'll never forget those words. There are other things I remember him saying about aspects of the war, but I'm not as certain of the quotes, thus I do not use them. When my father was dying, I took notes, as I often do in life crises.

I purposefully minimized details about my siblings in writing about my childhood. I didn't want to interpret what they experienced growing up. But after reading a typescript of the manuscript, my brother, Darryl, told me that when he was small and had been misbehaving, our father muttered to him as he lay in bed, "I could kill you." Thereafter, Darryl told me, he had night terrors and trouble sleeping the rest of his boyhood. "I thought he might come in and kill me." Given our father's raging outbursts, as a child the threat seemed valid to him. He said he still has difficulty sleeping. He had never before mentioned this to me—it was the first time we'd ever really talked about how we grew up and our father's issues.

With the exception of Kennedy—the rapist and baby killer—all names in this book are real. I changed his name largely in consideration of his family members, who may not know about his crimes. Kennedy remains alive as I write this. He knows who he is, and he must live with himself and the knowledge of his violence in that isolated house in the woods.

I've used old-style spelling in English for places on Okinawa, the way they were known to the participants in the battle. For example, Yontan today is spelled "Yomitan"; the Mezado Ridge is now "Maezato Ridge." The spellings and pronunciations were altered to conform to modern Japanese from that of what was spoken for centuries on Okinawa. Very few old timers on the island still use the original language; one old man I met did not understand Japanese.

Many accounts use 140,000 as the civilian death toll from the Battle of Okinawa. I am using 150,000, the figure cited by George Feifer in his deeply researched *Tennozan*. No one knows for certain the exact number, but I trust Feifer's scholarship. Similarly, there are conflicting numbers of Japanese soldiers killed in the battle. I'm using the estimate of 110,000 from *Okinawa: The Last Battle*, by Roy E. Appleman and others listed in the bibliographical notes section.

This book is not meant to be a comprehensive account of the battles of Guam and Okinawa, the main combat seen by Love Company, or the Pacific War in general. There are other books the reader can turn to learn more, some listed in the bibliographical notes below.

I did not quibble with Masako Ohnishi when I interviewed her, but she was wrong about the United States being more careful about civilian deaths in its modern wars. Throughout the history of the United States as a world power, both military leaders and citizens have ignored the civilian death toll in war. It was true on Okinawa, and it remains true today. It's "convenient" that Americans do this, argues John Tirman, author of *The Deaths of Others: The Fate of Civilians in America's Wars*. In today's wars in Iraq and Afghanistan, Tirman writes of the numbers of civilian dead, "which run into the hundreds of thousands, gain scant attention. . . . We need to adopt reliable ways to measure the destruction our wars cause . . . to break through the collective amnesia that has gripped us. If we do not demand a full accounting of the wages of war, future failures are all the more likely."

Well known is the rampage in Nanking, China, by Japanese troops in 1937. My friend, the late Iris Chang, wrote in *The Rape of Nanking* that male prisoners were used for bayonet practice, in beheading contests, burned alive after being "soaked with gasoline." Tens of thousands of women were raped. Bodies were mutilated. Chang cited sources that estimate more than 260,000 civilians were killed; some place the figure above 350,000. For sure, the 150,000 civilians killed on Okinawa did not have to endure this kind of psychopathic torture. But they ended up just as dead from our aerial bombs, artillery, and naval shells.

So few books on World War II in the Pacific Theater critically analyze how the war was prosecuted. Perhaps this is because the Pacific War was an orphan stepchild in the minds of many at the time—and in later years.

"Admiral Ernest J. King estimated toward the end . . . that 15 percent of the American deployment of men and materiel in World War II had gone to the war against Japan," D. Clayton James wrote in *The Pacific War Revisited*. Everything else was used against Germany and Italy. "The proportion of books and articles on World War II has been similar."

I read dozens of books on the Pacific war. While my research was not utterly exhaustive, anecdotally there was copious critical analysis of General Douglas MacArthur's tactics and very little on those of Admiral Chester W. Nimitz. The publicly quiet Nimitz didn't attract the stones figuratively thrown at the megalomaniacal MacArthur.

Many people hated the general, especially his own troops, William Manchester wrote in *American Caesar*. MacArthur was egotistical, and his self-absorption turned off a lot of people, left, right, and center. Franklin Roosevelt also worried about his running against him for president in 1944. MacArthur was often his own worst enemy.

It's easy to find historians attacking MacArthur as insane, inept, or stupid. Most are quiet on Nimitz, or they heap on praise.

In all of the books that I read on the war, one passage most struck me. It comes from Manchester's *Goodbye Darkness*:

> The longer the casualty lists—the vaster the investment in blood—the greater need to justify the slain . . . thus writers enshrine in memory the Verduns, the Passchendaeles, the Dunkirks, and the Iwo Jimas, while neglecting decisive struggles in which the loss of life was small . . . Hollandia, MacArthur's greatest triumph in that war, is forgotten because the general's genius outfoxed the Japanese and limited his losses to a handful of GIs.

After what I've read, based on his concern for the well-being of ground troops, I come down on the side of favoring MacArthur.

During the war, rare criticism of Nimitz came from Lieutenant General Holland M. "Howlin' Mad" Smith, the highest-ranking marine in the Pacific when the botched navy-controlled battle of Peleliu occurred. "Admiral Nimitz was riding to fame on the shoulders of the marines," Smith said. (Nimitz retaliated by forbidding Smith from being on the deck of the battleship *Missouri* for the Japanese surrender.)

In an equally rare comment following an even rarer article critical of the Okinawa operation in the *Washington Post* on June 4, 1945 (that passed the approval of military censors), Nimitz defiantly told the Associated Press, "Regardless of what casualties were suffered, there was a job to be done and I think it was not bungled and not a fiasco."

Some of the men in Love Company in later years read books on the war and came to understand the Japanese perspective—though wrong, Japan's military leaders had their reasons for waging war. Others realized, such as Bill Fenton, that battle tactics were bad for them as soldiers. George Niland, though no fan of MacArthur, grew animated when he talked about how the US Navy should have just continually bombed the airfields on some islands to render them useless for the Japanese military and not to have ever landed American soldiers on those outposts.

My dislike of Nimitz and his underlings such as Admiral King comes not from hindsight—there were other ways to fight some of the Pacific battles that were known at the time. I won't debate the need for the battle of Guam. But the Battle of Okinawa did not have to happen as it did, and for this, like Joe Lanciotti, I hate the generals and admirals on both sides. The United States couldn't control the fanatical Japanese military leaders. But it didn't have to play into their hands.

Nimitz's folly led to the death of 150,000 Okinawan civilians, 110,000 Japanese soldiers, and over 12,000 US men, including Mulligan. My father walked away with permanent brain damage. My distaste for Nimitz is personal. I have skin in the game. I grew up in a house where the result of his decisions about World War II never ceased.

BIBLIOGRAPHICAL NOTES

INTRODUCTION

page xi   Joe Lanciotti had sent this e-mail in reply to one in which I'd
           asked if he thought he and other Love Company members
           suffered blast concussion.

STARKWEATHER

page 7   History of John Maharidge and St. Theodosius: *St. Theodosious
           Cathedral: The 100th Anniversary Banquet Program Book,*
           October 13, 1996, 11–12.

page 11   Steve Maharidge's employment history: US Marine discharge
           records, March 17, 1946.

GRINDING

page 30   Maharidge family income: Internal Revenue Service tax records
           of Joan and Steve Maharidge.

GUAM

page 67   Former US Senator George Boutwell's warning: John M.
           Blum, Bruce Catton, Edmund S. Morgan, Arthur M.
           Schlesinger Jr., Kenneth M. Stampp, C. Vann Woodward, *The
           National Experience: A History of the United States,* 2nd ed.
           (New York: Hartcourt, Brace, & World, 1968), 533.

page 68   Japanese troops landing on Guam: William Manchester,
           Goodbye Darkness: A Memoir of the Pacific War (Boston: Little,
           Brown and Company, 1979), 280.

page 68   Pedro Artero on Japanese soldiers: Alice Brennan, "At the Tip
           of the Spear: The Cost of the U.S. Military Realignment to
           Guam," Columbia University Graduate School of Journalism,
           master's thesis, 2011.

page 69   Details on William Day: Operation Plan No. 1, 1st Provisional
           Marine Brigade, June 7, 1944. Courtesy of National Archives
           and Records Administration, Washington, DC.

page 69   Fifty-six thousand US soldiers land on Guam: Jeffrey M.
           Moore, *Spies for Nimitz: Joint Military Intelligence in the Pacific
           War* (Annapolis, MD: Naval Institute Press, 2004), 129.

page 69   Japanese exit slammed shut: Bevan G. Cass, ed., *History of the
           Sixth Marine Division* (Washington, DC: Infantry Journal
           Press, 1948), 23.

page 70   Arms and legs flew like snowflakes, twenty-six thousand shells:
           Ibid., 24.

page 70   Evacuate the wounded: Ibid.

page 70   American casualties in the battle of Guam: Moore, *Spies for
           Nimitz*, 116.

page 70   Japanese holdouts and Corporal Shoichi Yokoi: Manchester,
           Goodbye Darkness, 298.

page 71   Japanese home front morale deteriorating; value of prisoners:
           John W. Dower, *War Without Mercy: Race and Power in the
           Pacific War* (New York: Pantheon, 1986), 137.

page 71   Only 5,424 Japanese prisoners: Stephen E. Ambrose and Brian
           Loring Villa, "Racism, the Atomic Bomb, and the
           Transformation of Japanese-American Relations," in *The
           Pacific War Revisited*, edited by Günter Bischof and Robert L.
           Dupont (Baton Rouge: Louisiana State University Press, 1997),
           182.

OKINAWA

page 75   MacArthur summoned to meet with Roosevelt: Douglas
           MacArthur, *Reminiscences: General of the Army* (New York:
           McGraw-Hill, 1964), 196.

page 75   "Corkscrew and blowtorch": George Feifer, *Tennozan: The
           Battle of Okinawa and the Atomic Bomb* (New York: Ticknor
           and Fields, 1992), 415.

page 75   General Douglas MacArthur, "Hit 'em where they ain't":
           Frazier Hunt, *The Untold Story of Douglas MacArthur* (New
           York: The Devin-Adair Company, 1954), 325.

page 75   General Hisaichi Terauchi expected MacArthur to mimic
           Nimitz, "fighting for village after village": William Manchester,
           American Caesar: Douglas MacArthur, 1880–1964 (Boston:
           Little, Brown, 1978), 344.

page 76   Tremendous 400-mile leap: Ibid., 344.

page 76   MacArthur on cutting off the Japanese army in the Borneo-Celebes area: MacArthur, *Reminiscences*, 260.

page 76   MacArthur on meeting with Franklin Roosevelt; not being briefed to bring important staff members: Ibid., 197.

page 77   Days of the frontal attack over: Ibid., 197.

page 77   Bombing with 21,926 US Navy shells on Iwo Jima rearranging the volcanic ash: Manchester, *Goodbye Darkness*, 339.

page 77   Imperial Japanese Army fortifying Okinawa, building tunnels: Feifer, *Tennozan*, 109.

page 78   JICPOA inexplicably transfers photo analysts just before the Battle of Iwo Jima: Moore, *Spies for Nimitz*, 177.

page 78   Japanese tricked American forces; intelligence failure "borders on criminal negligence": Ibid., 217–18.

page 79   Delaying action: Feifer, *Tennozan*, 108.

page 79   General Watanabe tells islanders about imminent death: Ibid., 76–77.

page 79   Okinawa cut off by sea: Ibid., 83.

page 79   Most of Naha left in ashes: Ibid., 90.

page 79   Number of ships for Operation Iceberg: Ibid., 133.

page 79   Three-to-one ratio of superiority needed for attacker: *Spies for Nimitz*, 20–21.

page 79   Not even two-to-one ratio; JICPOA estimates seventy-five thousand Japanese troops: Ibid., 211–12.

COMING BACK FROM THE DEAD: GRAHNERT

page 111   American POWs on Palawan burned to death by Japanese soldiers: Lester I. Tenney, *My Hitch in Hell: The Bataan Death March* (Washington: Brassey's, 2000), 189.

LUCKY STRIKE: PALMASANI

page 121   General Shepherd on the killing of Japanese soldiers: Lemuel C. Shepherd Jr., Benis M. Frank, *Reminiscences of Lemuel Cornick Shepherd, Jr.: Oral History, 1967*, the Marine Corps

project, in the Columbia University Center for Oral History
Collection, 241–42. Used with permission.

page 122   Enemy machine guns on Hill 27: Roy E. Appleman, James M.
Burns, Russell A. Gugeler, and John Stevens, *Okinawa: The
Last Battle* (Washington, DC: The Center of Military History,
1948), 376.

page 125   Physical description of Mulligan: Individual Deceased
Personnel File, Department of the Army, National Personnel
Records Center, St. Louis, Missouri.

THE POET: LANCIOTTI

page 177   "His big left arm stretched outside the poncho": Joseph
Lanciotti, *The Timid Marine: Surrender to Combat Fatigue*
(New York: iUniverse, 2005), 98–99.

page 178   Joe Lanciotti changed the names of his fellow Love Company
members in his book. He used "Dan Kruplowski" as a
pseudonym for Ralph Krupkowski.

page 178   "One must be immersed in the blood": Ibid., xii.

page 178   Sympathize with Eddie Slovik: Ibid.

page 178   Cannon fodder marine: Ibid., 30.

page 179   Hollywood version of war on screen: Ibid., 51.

page 180   Motobu Peninsula and unseen enemy: Ibid., 72–74.

page 180   Coming upon Japanese soldiers with toes on triggers: Ibid., 77.

page 181   Using the cigarette to warn civilians while on guard duty:
Ibid., 79.

page 181   Stopping fellow marines from throwing more phosphorous
grenades into a cave: Ibid., 85–86.

page 182   LaFoo kills wounded civilian: Ibid., 87–88.

page 183   Smell of death: Ibid., 94.

page 183   Obscenely colored flies: Ibid., 91.

page 183   Woman's corpse riddled with maggots: Ibid., 109.

page 183   Writing letter to Krup's family: Ibid., 101–3.

page 184   LaFoo kicking marines pulling Japanese teeth: Ibid., 105–6.

page 184   Regimental commander replaced: Ibid., 110.

page 184   Where Lanciotti died would be a parking lot for a shopping
mall: Ibid., 112.

page 186   Lanciotti walks away from battle: Ibid., 112.

page 186   Realization Lanciotti is "cannon fodder," that he was duped by
            movies: Ibid., 117.

page 187   "Costly Okinawa venture," questions about high casualty rate:
            Hunt, *The Untold Story of Douglas MacArthur*, 387.

page 188   At least 250,000 Japanese soldiers "left to die on the vine":
            Ibid., 389.

page 188   General Arnold denying MacArthur the use of B-29s: Ibid., 338.

page 188   MacArthur strategy paying off "in American boys who came
            home": Ibid., 389.

page 188   Navy-controlled Okinawa battle influencing Truman: Ibid.,
            399.

page 188   Meeting buddy whose leg was amputated: Lanciotti, *The Timid
            Marine*, 118–19.

page 189   No comfort in being among the 26,000 psychiatric cases from
            Okinawa: Ibid., 111, 124.

NOT IN KANSAS ANYMORE, MAY 16, 1945: FENTON

page 193   Marines forced to "cling to their positions . . . That May 16
            was . . . a bitter day": Cass, *History of the Sixth Marine Division*,
            119, 121.

FINDING LIFE: HOFFMAN

page 220   There is no agreement on the percentage of soldiers who
            engaged in combat during World War II. It depends upon how
            one defines combat. The figures I have read range between 5
            and 15 percent. The pertinent fact is that it was a small
            number. George Feifer in *Tennozan*, xiv, wrote, "Of the 11
            million uniformed men in 1945 . . . about 5 percent served in
            infantry combat divisions, of which only about 60 percent were
            in the front lines."

THE LAND OF COURTESY

page 243   Okinawa as a nation of "courtesy," aversion to violence and
            crime: Feifer, *Tennozan*, 61.

page 244   Okinawa opened to outside world, paid tribute to China and
            warlords: Appleman, Burns, Gugeler, and Stevens, *Okinawa*, 9.

page 244   Okinawans looked down upon, couldn't vote: Feifer,
             Tennozan, 72.

page 244   Shimada begs General Ushijima to remain at Shuri: Ibid., 447.

THE TOMB

page 246   Cherry blossoms in bloom as *Yamato* sails: Feifer, *Tennozan*,
             19, 21.

TETSU NO BOFU: OHNISHI

page 278   June the deadliest month for civilians, one hundred thousand
             killed in ten days: Feifer, *Tennozan*, 532.

page 281   Number of shells fired by field artillery and US Navy:
             Appleman, Burns, Gugeler, and Stevens, *Okinawa*, 498, 500.

page 281   General Shepherd believed twenty thousand civilians killed:
             George Feifer, "The Rape of Okinawa," *World Policy Journal*
             17 (October 1, 2000), 33.

page 281   "Bemused natives," denial about civilian deaths: John Lardner,
             "A Reporter on Okinawa," *New Yorker*, May 19, 1945, 32.

page 281   Estimate of 150,000 civilian dead: Feifer, *Tennozan*, 533.

page 283   Japan would lose war, leaders on both sides knew by late 1944:
             Dower, *War Without Mercy*, 293–94.

page 283   "Great Marianas Turkey Shoot": Manchester, *Goodbye
             Darkness*, 267.

page 283   Details of Tokyo firebombing: Feifer, *Tennozan*, 15–16.

page 284   General Arnold's "big a finale as possible": Dower, *War
             Without Mercy*, 301.

LAST EVENING AT THE TOMB

page 297   Lois Velma Owens Mulligan death: "Standard Certificate of
             Death," state of South Carolina, Bureau of Vital Statistics,
             State Board of Health, July 18, 1940.

page 297   Robert Owens: *Greenville News*, obituary, March 13, 1963, 8;
             senility: Certificate of death, state of North Carolina.

page 297   Details of the Patterson family: *Greenville News*, obituary for
             H. P. Patterson, January 16, 1968, 7.

ACKNOWLEDGMENTS

A significant fear is that after twelve years of research, much of it done during times of personal stress amid the deaths of my parents, I will forget to include everyone responsible for helping me on my journey of discovery about my father's war. So up front I offer sincere apologies to anyone I've left out. With that disclaimer, I want to thank the following people and institutions:

First and foremost, the men of Love Company I talked with as well as their spouses and children. Everyone in this book and many others not included were most generous with their time and assistance.

Ed Hoffman was the first veteran I found from Love Company, and over the years he was incredibly helpful, not only providing leads to finding other guys but also for moral support.

Other Love Company members never appeared to tire of my questions, and they gave me unlimited time and friendship. Among them: Karl Brothers, Danny Cernoch, Bill Fenton, Fenton Grahnert, Joe Lanciotti, Charles Lepant, Tom Price, Joe Rosplock. And those who died before I finished: Frank Haigler, Jim Laughridge, George Niland, and Frank Palmasani.

Some of their spouses: Susie Hoffman, Vivian Lanciotti, Nancy Niland, and Vivian Price.

Their children and their spouses: Eric Brothers; Charlene Lepant and Jeffery Hildebrandt; Jim and Carol Lehtonen Grahnert; Wesley Grahnert; Melody Simmons; Lynn Haigler Baker and Gary Baker; Rosanna Palmasani and her brother-in-law, the late Mike Palmasani.

In Cleveland, Glenn Haller at D & D Tool Company.

Regarding my understanding of traumatic brain injury and blast concussion, I am indebted to Dr. Willy Moss and Michael J. King at Lawrence Livermore National Laboratory as well as to Douglas Smith, MD, director of the Center for Brain Injury and Repair at the University of Pennsylvania.

The staff at the Center for Oral History at Columbia University's Butler Library, including Katy Morris and Charis Emily Shafer.

Theresa Fitzgerald, archivist, at the National Archives at St. Louis.

Emily Bazar's emotional support was vital during the deaths of my parents.

Journalists Jan Haag and Jessica Bruder, who were there to lean on as I worked over the years and provided editorial insight as I neared completion.

Two students from Stanford University: Tomoeh Murakami, who gave early assistance, and Makiko Fukui, who proofread Japanese words; Alice Brennan, my student at Columbia, who helped with my understanding of Guam.

Author and journalist Raymond Bonner, for the subtitle, which came out of a conversation while we walked up Broadway in New York City one night.

Among my family members, my uncle, Robert Kopfstein, and my siblings, Darryl Maharidge and Dawn Maden, for filling in my blanks in family history. My aunts, Mary Maharidge and Helen Kozak.

In Japan, the writer Mitsuko Shimomura, who has long guided me about understanding Japanese culture since our Nieman fellowship year at Harvard University.

Journalist Kojiro Yamada, who was with me on Okinawa and provided invaluable assistance, including translating my questions as I worked.

Yutaka Nakamura, at *Shukan Asahi Weekly* news magazine in Tokyo, who had my interviews from Okinawa translated.

The museum staff at Shuri Heights High School provided insight into the war on the island. I came to the island with Sanemasa Yonashiro's training manual in the hope of repatriating it with his family, but I could not find them. I donated the booklet to the high school's museum to the boy soldiers who were conscripted to fight. The school had vol. 2 and it was missing vol. 1—the one I had in my possession. These manuals are extremely rare, and I'm pleased that it is now on display at the museum.

On Okinawa: Yoshikuni Yamada, Natsuko Nozaki, Masako Ohnishi, Toshiaki Kinjo, and Junichi Yamaguchi.

My agent, Jennifer Lyons, of the Jennifer Lyons Literary Agency LLC.

And finally, the people at PublicAffairs. My editor, Clive Priddle, for his passion for this book and his excellent editorial guidance; senior publicist Emily Lavelle, for her early enthusiasm; Perseus Books Group project editor Melissa Veronesi; designer Cindy Young; copy editor Josephine Mariea; Joanna Rothkopf, and others.

Dale Maharidge has been teaching at the Graduate School of Journalism at Columbia University since 2001. Before that he was a visiting professor at Stanford University for ten years and spent fifteen years as a newspaperman. Several of his books are illustrated with the work of photographer Michael S. Williamson. The first book, *Journey to Nowhere: The Saga of the New Underclass* (1985), later inspired Bruce Springsteen to write two songs; it was reissued in 1996 with an introduction by Springsteen. His second book, *And Their Children After Them*, won the Pulitzer Prize for nonfiction in 1990.